WOMEN AND CRIME

Selected Titles in ABC-CLIO's
CONTEMPORARY
WORLD ISSUES
Series

For a complete list of titles in this series, please visit
www.abc-clio.com.

Books in the Contemporary World Issues series address vital issues in today's society, such as genetic engineering, pollution, and biodiversity. Written by professional writers, scholars, and nonacademic experts, these books are authoritative, clearly written, up-to-date, and objective. They provide a good starting point for research by high school and college students, scholars, and general readers as well as by legislators, businesspeople, activists, and others.

Each book, carefully organized and easy to use, contains an overview of the subject, a detailed chronology, biographical sketches, facts and data and/or documents and other primary-source material, a directory of organizations and agencies, annotated lists of print and nonprint resources, and an index.

Readers of books in the Contemporary World Issues series will find the information they need to have a better understanding of the social, political, environmental, and economic issues facing the world today.

WOMEN AND CRIME

A Reference Handbook

Judith A. Warner

**CONTEMPORARY
WORLD ISSUES**

ABC-CLIO

Santa Barbara, California • Denver, Colorado • Oxford, England

Library of Congress Cataloging-in-Publication Data

Warner, Judith Ann, 1950–
    Women and crime : a reference handbook / Judith A. Warner.
        p. cm. — (Contemporary world issues)
    Includes bibliographical references and index.
    ISBN 978–1–59884–423–8 (hardcopy : alk. paper) — ISBN 978–1–59884–424–5 (ebook : alk. paper) 1. Female offenders. 2. Criminal justice, Administration of. 3. Women—Crimes against. I. Title.
    HV6046.W367 2012
    364.3'74—dc23   2012000448

ISBN: 978–1–59884–423–8
EISBN: 978–1–59884–424–5

16 15 14 13 12   1 2 3 4 5

This book is also available on the World Wide Web as an eBook.
Visit www.abc-clio.com for details.

ABC-CLIO, LLC
130 Cremona Drive, P.O. Box 1911
Santa Barbara, California 93116-1911

This book is printed on acid-free paper ∞

Manufactured in the United States of America

Contents

List of Tables

Preface

Women constitute a small and neglected population within our jails and prisons. In this era of emphasis on equality, gender difference does matter in the explanation of how women become criminal offenders. An era of crime control emphasizes incapacitation, the doing of time without rehabilitative measures to keep offenders off the street. This has led to overcrowded prisons that lack physical and mental health facilities to keep women healthy. The inhumanity of incapacitation has led to conditions in which women prisoners with mental illness are not given medicine or counseled, and routine health care is limited. The Eighth Amendment to the Constitution specifies that punishment should not be "cruel or unusual." The packing of women prisoners into underfunded facilities that include prisons-for-profit is meant to protect society, but has allowed the public to turn its back on gendered needs.

The drive to incarcerate women and men has its roots in patriarchal tradition: the management of political, economic, and family life by men. From the period of colonization until the 20th century, women were confined to traditional gender roles and subject to extensive social control. Patriarchal ideology and social structure simultaneously problematized women's sexuality and made them subject to intimate physical and sexual victimization. Women's rise toward equality has not uniformly benefited women of varying social class and race and ethnic background. Women offenders tend to be poor minority women who have yet to benefit from new opportunities as they strive to obtain an education in defunded public schools and deal with family violence and street crime. When women united for a new future, the privileged forged new opportunities and often neglected the diversity within their ranks.

Because men predominate as the vast majority of imprisoned offenders, policies tailored to policing, incarceration, and corrections have focused on men. Women who come to the attention of the criminal justice system have often followed different life trajectories, called pathways, to crime. Crimes of victimization against women, such as child physical and sexual abuse or domestic violence, leave girls and women with few alternatives. The United States, through such legislation as the Violence against Women Act and the Trafficking Victims Protection Act, is only beginning to address the troubled and gendered relationships that negatively shape women's lives. The victimization of women and girls is a major factor in pathways leading to criminal offending.

Although theorists have argued that equality for women would increase the rate and type of crimes that women commit, the criminalization of drug use and the later rise of mandatory minimum sentencing and three-strikes laws greatly increased the imprisonment of women, especially African American and Hispanic women. A major part of the path to crime for women and men is abuse of controlled substances. For girls and women, victimization is associated with drug use. Drugs lead to biological addiction, and the criminal justice system is led by policies that label addiction as an issue of personal choice without considering the biochemical impact of craving or the price of drugs due to criminalization. Women and men with drug convictions are increasingly incapacitated and receive limited, if any, medical treatment, which increases risk for recidivism (reoffending). The illness has not been treated. Similarly, the education, job skills, and counseling needed for a healthier life are withheld. Nevertheless, in the 21st century, the costs of mass incapacitation and crowded prison conditions have begun a swing back to rehabilitation and community corrections alternatives. Drug courts and other community treatment programs are being developed.

The solutions for crime prevention and rehabilitation of women offenders are expensive, but less costly than imprisonment. The social gains from assisting people to lead productive lives include a healthier society. The crime rate has been dropping, year after year, but more women are being sent to prison. Criminologists who do research on women offenders consider that the steps taken to reduce victimization of girls and women and gender sensitive methods for dealing with offenders are major steps toward reducing women's crime and recidivism rates. These are all issues to be explored.

Meanwhile, we cannot assume that women who gained greater educational and occupational opportunity never abused it. From Martha Stewart's insider trading to Leona Helmsley's tax fraud, equality has permitted women to join the ranks of white collar offenders. However, while it has been thought that equality is necessarily equated with a potential for aggression, women's violent crime rate has not increased. Indeed, female-to-male spousal homicide has dropped considerably since the advent of women's shelters for battered women. Apparently, abusive men are more protected, and the rate of male-to-female spousal homicide has *not* dropped.

Women who do deviate from traditional gender roles, like Casey Anthony, declared not guilty of the murder of her daughter, receive sensationalized media coverage. Andrea Yates, Susan Smith, and other mothers who have (allegedly, in some cases) killed their children receive more attention than many male murderers. Indeed, women serial killers are not unknown; but, as with Aileen Wournos, they tend to be sensationalized. What are we to think of women who do not fit the stereotypes or have taken on new roles? Do we understand them? Are their motives gendered, or do they think like men?

Internationally, some countries have experimented with decriminalization of certain prohibited behaviors such as prostitution. For example, in Sweden, only the customer is liable for a criminal conviction. The passage of this law realized a drop in sex trafficking to Sweden. In the United States, states such as California are experimenting with social harm–reduction methods such as decriminalizing marijuana possession. Nevertheless, globally, a massive issue is the gendered victimization of women through female genital mutilation, domestic violence, honor killing, mass rape in wartime, and sex trafficking. As long as sex traffickers deprive women and girls of their rights, the move to decriminalize prostitution and label it sex work will face a massive obstacle.

This volume considers many aspects of an under-researched and often misunderstood subject: women and crime. It covers the legal history of women's limited rights before the 20th century, their patterns of criminal offending, societal response to women offenders, and solutions to women's issues in the criminal justice system. It is not possible to cover all aspects of women and criminal behavior, but an attempt has been made to present information on women's victimization because of its important relationship to the onset of drug-related and other crime and its importance as an international human rights issue. Society has a tendency to place responsibility on the individual while neglecting its own responsibility in providing quality of life.

To the end of understanding the many issues involved in women and crime and proposed solutions, the book is organized as follows: Chapter 1 presents a historical outline of women's status in society and criminal behavior or victimization from Roman civilization to the present. Because of traditional gender expectations, women's criminal activity is connected to prostitution and thievery, while victimization was, historically, often not recognized as such. From the late 1700s onward, women began to ask for rights that, today, they often have on paper only in the developing world. In the latter part of the 20th century, the drive to incapacitate and its impact on women are examined. Chapter 2 looks at information on rates of women's criminal behavior and victimization. Due to a connection between victimization and drug use/criminal activity, the way that women's pathways differ from men is considered. Whether or not incarceration is an effective solution for women is examined in relation to sentencing reform and community corrections alternatives. Chapter 3 gives an overview of women offenders from a global perspective. Women are not overly represented as criminals in transnational crime organizations, but as the case of Mexico indicates, they can become high-level drug traffickers. Women's crime has often been restricted to a more local scale, including prostitution. Efforts to decriminalize prostitution are presented in light of their effectiveness. The strongest point that can be made about female criminality is that it is highly conditioned by economic opportunity and victimization. As in the United States, intimate-partner violence is an issue, but rape and culturally restricted forms of violence such as female genital mutilation and honor killing are largely unchallenged. As a result, international sanctions are being brought to bear, particularly on human trafficking. Chapter 4 presents a historical chronology of major events in women's legal history, their criminal offending and victimization. Chapter 5 provides the biographies of women criminals and contemporary women professionals in the criminal justice system. Chapter 6 presents statistical data on women's offending and victimization as well as examples of legislation impacting women. Chapter 7 provides information on government agencies and nonprofit agencies associated with women in the criminal justice system and human rights advocacy. Chapter 8 presents resources such as books, films, and data on women and crime or victimization and their interrelationships.

My special thanks go to Robin Tutt of ABC-CLIO for the determination and enthusiasm that she brought to this topic. I would also like to thank Brother Bob Warren, an all-around intellectual, for his encouragement.

1

History and Background

Introduction

Why do women commit crimes? For many decades, women were largely invisible as a subject of criminological research. Theorizing and research focused on men, the actual majority of criminals, overlooking gender differences and contributing to a situation in which both women and their rights were neglected. In the 21st century, developed societies provide many rights for women. Women lacked rights for centuries, yet still attempted legal actions related to criminal law, victimization, treatment of women prisoners, and discrimination in the workplace. The status of women is changing, but the historical legacy of traditional gender roles, backed by law, limited women's opportunity and largely restricted criminal behavior to the private realm of the family and public thievery or prostitution. One reason that women were subject to intensive social control was that they were thought to be more evil and dangerous than men. When women committed a violent crime, it vindicated misogyny and could result in harsher punishment than for men. For example, women who killed might be drawn and quartered or burned alive as opposed to hanging. The history of women and crime, relatively unknown and understudied, is one of fascination with women, their sexuality, and evil.

The hidden evidence as to why many women commit crimes is related as much to prior victimization as it is to economic marginality or, in the case of murder, emotional passion or dispassion. Tracing the history of women's rights, one finds that men have exerted extensive social control over women: they had very limited or even no rights. Male domination over women was extensively developed in the laws of Greece, the Roman Empire, and European countries such as England. In this context, women could be raped or physically assaulted without recourse, depending on the willingness of their male family head to intervene. While there are limited historical records of women's victimization, it is understood by women criminologists that child abuse, sexual abuse, rape, and domestic violence often occur in the lives of women offenders and may be a precipitating factor in their crimes, past and present. It is important to understand how a lack of rights (not just women's rights, but human rights) has impacted historical and contemporary women's crime.

Patriarchal Tradition: Greece, Rome, and Judeo-Christian Law

Patriarchy is defined as the domination of society (including women and children) by men. Patriarchal traditions have situated women as the intellectual and moral inferiors of men. From the development of agriculture in the Neolithic through the period of intensive agricultural development, women's economic status declined. In ancient Greek and Roman society, considered the basis of Western tradition, women and children were legally controlled by men: the paterfamilias (male head of the household), husband, or guardian (Rhodes, 1984). A woman had no rights regarding her husband's access to her body, no control over reproduction and the birth of undesired children, and no control over the fate of children her husband ordered to be killed (Nguyen, 2006). In Rome, a wife could not divorce her husband (Lefkowitz and Fant, 1992). Women, children, and slaves could be bought and sold. This social control of women by men was rationalized as due to feminine weakness and the possibility of exploitation. The sexual integrity of women before and after marriage was important because of the need to establish the legitimacy of children. Laws regarding rape were structured to protect the family and its property, not the woman. The impact of sexual violation on a woman was secondary. The social value of a woman's sexual integrity made the rape of a woman a social embarrassment to male members of the family and devalued her permanently.

Slaves and prostitutes were not considered as possible rape victims. In Republican Rome (509–27 BCE), an individual who raped a single or married woman was liable to the death penalty regardless of whether the *paterfamilias* forgave. Circa 49 BCE, the *lex Iulia de vi* considered rape to be forcible intercourse, but only if a freeborn (nonslave) brought the charge (Nguyen, 2006: 88–89). At this time, it was possible for a woman to bring a charge in a Roman court. Nguyen (2006: 89), a legal scholar, considered: "The explicit inclusion of rape in the *lex Iulia de vi* and the fact that it was open to prosecution outside the family denotes rape as criminal violence against the public order which was to be punished, not just by the individual, but by the society as well."

During the Dominate (284–476 CE, Western Empire; 284–565, Eastern Empire) Constantine enacted marriage laws impacting sexual violence (Nguyen, 2006). In 320 CE, he passed a law punishing *raptus*, the abduction of a girl without the agreement of her parents which often included rape. *Raptus* was considered to be theft from the parents and not a matter of the girl's rights or physical violence. A person committing *raptus* could be put to death. Although Constantine was the first Christian emperor, it is not likely that Christian ideas influenced his legislation. It was not until the reign of Justinian (527–565 CE), that the Christian Church's beliefs began to be reflected in law. In 533 CE, Justinian made a public statement that a "woman's virtue was irredeemable once lost" (Nguyen, 2006: 110). One law he enacted was that a woman should not be imprisoned because male guards might abuse her. In 538 CE, the Codex Justinianus defined raptus as the abduction, seduction, or rape of a woman regardless of her social standing and whether she was enslaved.

Roman law substantially shaped the position of women. In England, the legal traditions of the Romans and Normans combined with the canon law of the Catholic Church to shape the common law of England. Blackstone's *Commentaries on the Laws of England* (1765–1769) included the doctrine of coverture, which specified that a woman was under the protection and cover of her husband. A woman's husband controlled her, her person, and her property (Zaher, 2002). Unmarried women and widows could own property, collect rents, and take cases to court (Basch, 1979). Disparate gendered status was reflected in how spousal murder was treated. A man who murdered his wife could be imprisoned or executed. If a woman killed her husband, the crime was considered high treason against her lord, and she could be drawn and quartered and or burnt alive. It was considered that coverture carried out God's word. Genesis 3:16 states: "Your desire shall be for your husband, and he shall rule over you."

The Judeo-Christian tradition represented women in the story of Genesis as introducing evil into the society of man. As Judaism and Christianity developed, textual interpretations that women were lacking in morality were prevalent, although alternative interpretations of the Bible can and are being made today. Ideas about the inferiority or immoral character of women have shaped how society responds to women criminals (Feinman, 1994: 3–4). Greek and Roman mythology and Judeo-Christian tradition have socially constructed women as having dual natures: Madonna or whore. Feinman (1994: 3–4) writes:

> On the one hand, women produced children, which was good and necessary for the survival of the family and community. Exactly how this was done was a mystery, although it was known somehow to relate to menstruation. On the other hand, women inflamed men's passions and prompted them to lose control of themselves. Clearly women were different from men and possessed unique powers that made them both necessary and dangerous.

Medieval English law specifying the "unity of person" of husband and wife, or "coverture," limited women's actions. For example, the appeals allowable to women in court were related to marriage or their status as men's property, as in the case of rape (Cannon, 1999). Women could also appeal criminal cases, such as the murder of a husband. The case of Agnes Colle appealing to Henry le Ternur and Gilbert of Gratham regarding the death of her son illustrates the precarious status of women in court. The two men at first denied that women could make appeals in court. Her court record indicates that women had restricted rights to appeal a death other than that of her husband. The records also indicate that no guilt was established in the case.

The medieval English tavern or inn was a place that both men and women frequented. Nevertheless, the consumption of alcohol and potential for disorderly conduct, as well as the idea that women in taverns would offer sex, tainted a woman's reputation (Hanawalt, 1999). Indeed, women who worked in domestic service in the taverns were at risk of being pimped by the owners for sexual activity. Prostitution of women by outside pimps also occurred.

The roots of traditional gender roles in the American colonies can be found in England. In 17th-century Europe, Mary Dodge (2002: 12) considers that: "A woman's acting out meant that, by definition, the female offender threatened patriarchal authority at the same time that she defied legal and religious codes. Even when she committed the same offense as a man, her actions were often seen as more threatening." In 17th- and 18th-century England, women ranged from 10% to 33% of those charged, while they comprised 20–40% of those in jail or workhouses (Zedner, 1995: 331).

Colonial and Revolutionary America: The 16th Century to 1776

The patriarchal structure of the societies of European colonizers shaped women's limited rights in the new world. The Western legal tradition and British common law has shaped U.S. history. In the English colonies and the United States after independence, women did not have the same status and rights as men. English common law did not classify women and children as property, but upon marriage considered a woman's social and legal identity subsumed under that of her husband (Ulrich, 1991). Physical discipline of wives was accepted. Under English common law, there were English court opinions in the mid-1600s that indicated that while verbal admonishment and confinement was legal, beating was not.

Women in the American colonies were scarce; hence, they were more respected for their contribution than in European societies. A majority of the first colonists were men (Young and Spencer, 2007). Women who came to the new world came to flee poor working conditions or because they were transported as felons: pardoned thieves and prostitutes deported to populate the colonies. Their new status was as indentured servant, and they are considered to have made up about 25% of all transported convicts (Blumenthal, 1973, cited in Young and Spencer, 2007: 65). Their presence was deemed necessary to retain male settlers and laborers (Moller, 1945; Galenson, 1958).

In colonial America, sexual "fornication" was considered an act against God. Ministers considered fornication, adultery, and rape as sins of "uncleanness" (Block, 2006: 51). Many of the victim-blaming ideas about rape existed during this time period, and it was difficult for women to prove rape unless they were considered virtuous and to have resisted. It was commonly believed that "women should regulate men's passions" and were responsible for their own rape (Block, 2006: 50). Sharon Block's (2006) discussion of rape and sexual power in the early United States provides insight into how lack of women's rights enabled men to coerce women to have sex and difficult for them to prove rape. For example, men coerced domestic servants into having sex due to their dependency. When rape became an issue, it was not seen in 20th-century terms as a criminal violation of the individual. Instead, it was viewed as a challenge to the father or husband's right to control the sexual activity of a wife or daughter.

Smith (2003) estimates that women committed about 10% of recorded crime. Women committed homicide against children, servants, and husbands. Theft and sex crime (prostitution) were the most frequent charges. Women were prosecuted for giving birth out of wedlock. From the introduction of imprisonment in the colonies until the 1870s, women and male prisoners were housed in the same buildings.

The Salem Puritan witchcraft trials of 1692 provide an historical case of female-on-female violent crime (Wilson, 2005). Hundreds of women were accused, and ultimately 14 were executed for violent crimes. The trials referred to the *Malleus Maleficareum*, a Church document explaining views on witchcraft and its involvement with the power of Satan. It considered that most witches were women and that women were both more evil than men and easily deceived. Specific crimes connected to witchcraft included male impotence, prevention of conception, abortion, infanticide, and trying to be dominant over the husband. Witches were thought to cause illness and death, particularly of infants, young children, and spouses. The Salem witchcraft episode began when girls had fits in which they felt pricked, choked, or had a seizure. Two of the girls were epileptics, and the other girls may have suffered ergot poisoning or acted through power of suggestion. The Puritans reacted by seeking signs indicating the accused had made a "pact with the devil": confessing, signing the devil's book, attending a witch's Sabbath, taking communion from the devil, or seducing others to take such actions. Nanci Wilson (2005: 20) found that 97% of women brought to trial were accused of maleficum through harming humans, 26% were accused of harming domestic production, and 51% were accused of possessing supernatural powers. Supernatural acts included flying through the air, predicting the future, possessing poppets (rag dolls in the image of an enemy, which could be pricked with pins), and possessing familiars (small animals such as dogs, cats, and birds that the devil sent to assist them). Forty-three percent of the women were accused of unseemly behavior. Wilson explains the situation as an attempt to bring women under social control, including reproductive control, by man—as a way of controlling their "wildness" and keeping the place of men in the Puritan "Great Chain of Being," in which nature, as well as women, were tamed by man.

The idea of "race" gradually developed with the practice of slavery and added a second dimension to the patriarchal social structure. The first Africans were brought as indentured servants to the colonies from 1619 until Maryland legalized slavery in 1640. The institutionalization of slavery varied among the colonies. In 1662, Virginia contravened English common law by legislating that the child of an enslaved woman could not be born free. Maryland sought to control interracial contact by giving women married to black men the status of slaves in 1663 and making such marriage illegal in 1667. Chattel slavery, in which a person is considered legal property, prevailed, particularly in the states that later became aligned as the South. Young and Spencer (2007) indicate that the "peculiar institution" structured raced and gendered practices in the developing criminal justice system.

Colonial punishment included the death penalty and corporal and noncorporal shaming punishments for deviant behavior (Young and Spencer, 2007). The race and gender status of the individual shaped which type of punishment was given. Free whites had higher status than indentured whites and, in turn, free Africans had a higher status than indentured Africans. Gender intersected with these categories, as men had a higher status than women within each race category. Enslaved black men and women lacked status as human beings. Slaves were often punished with a whip by plantation owners or overseers (Keve, 1986). Gendered racism characterized the treatment of enslaved African women and their descendants. When women were whipped, the back was stripped and women were especially demeaned by display of their body. Punishment for infractions ranged from being killed to intimidation with amputation, mutilation, rape, starvation, and separation from the family dubiously in between. Hine and Thompson (1999: 84) indicate that one slave owner placed a pregnant slave in a special hole so that the fetus would not be harmed when he beat her.

It should come as no surprise that enslaved men and women resisted captivity. A limited record of this resistance exists in historical court records. Massachusetts executed Maria, a young enslaved black, for arson-murder in September 1681, and 58 enslaved women were executed prior to 1790 (Baker, 2008: 66). Maria was burned alive for the house fire that caused the accidental death of a baby girl; her two male accomplices were simply banished from the colony (Twombly and Moore, 1967: 245). Male accomplices were more commonly hanged.

Schwartz (1998) indicates that exploitive treatment led slaves to act against their masters. In 1770, Jenny was hanged in chains for the poisoning murder of her master—a death by slow starvation (Morris, 1996: 277). In Virginia, the slave Eve was burned alive for poisoning her master with a glass of milk. Her body was quartered and displayed in public as an example (Schwartz, 1998: 92). For some cases of death by poisoning, the unsafe ways in which food was prepared may have led to false accusation and execution (Streib, 1990).

Emergence of the United States: 1776 through the Antebellum Period

Death was an acceptable punishment in the early criminal justice system. Young and Spence (2007: 68–70) utilized the Espy file (Espy and Smykla, 1987), a thorough listing of executions under civil authority. As of the turn of the 18th century, women accounted for almost one-quarter of executions, but the level dropped to less than 10% at centuries end. "From 1632 to 1861, there were 3,805 executions in the colonies; of these, 271, or 7% of those put to death were women" (Young and Spence, 2007: 68). Among the 7% of women executed, black women made up almost 60%, while white women accounted for about one-third of those receiving the death penalty. Hispanic and Native American women constituted the remainder; a small number of cases did not report race or ethnicity. Women were primarily executed for murder, for poisoning, or for witchcraft (Keve, 1996). Twenty-six white women were executed for witchcraft (Young and Spencer, 2007: 69). These women tended to be older and divorced or widowed (Karlson, 1987; Kurshan, 1996). Other women receiving the death penalty were practicing midwives in competition with male doctors.

Men tended to receive the death penalty for murder, piracy, robbery, and various theft offenses. Other reasons that women were executed include conspiracy or accessory to murder, robbery, arson, housebreaking, concealing birth, adultery, and slave revolts. Kurshan (1996) indicates that two women were punished by burning at the stake for adultery and spousal murder; men were not punished for these crimes. Other evidence for a double standard includes the execution of a woman for adultery and five executions for concealing birth. This pattern indicates patriarchal control of women's sexuality and reproduction inside of marriage. Black women were executed for arson and 12 cases of poisoning: crimes related to resistance against slavery. Burning is thought to account for less than 4% of executions, and all but two of 13 known cases involved enslaved black women (Young and Spencer, 2007: 70).

White and free black women's deviance was punished through public humiliation: wearing a placard identifying the offense, being put in the stocks, sitting in the gallows, the ducking stool, gags, the "branks," fines, and banishment (Young and Spencer, 2007). The dunking stool was a chair set next to water and used to dunk women who had been drunk or disorderly and "scolds." The branks consisted of an iron cage with a spike or iron wheel that was inserted into the mouth on top of the tongue. It was used for quarrelsome or "out of control" women (Dobash, Dobash, and Gutteridge, 1986: 19).

Antebellum-period social control strategies focused on inducing conformity within a social structure that differentiated between white women and free African American women. The Laws of Maryland (1831, chapter 323, cited by Young and Spencer, 2007: 60) established certain laws for free blacks only. They could not own or carry a firelock without a license or attend non-white-only religious meetings. Laws and punishments had been developed by men for men, creating uncertainty as to how to punish women. White middle- and upper-class women followed the "cult of true womanhood": gender role expectations promoting purity, piousness, domesticity, and submissiveness (Welter, 1966, cited in Coe and Young, 2007). Women who conformed to traditional gender expectations had religiously based moral rights and were not subject to great scrutiny in the private sphere of the family. In return, they were legally treated as property, which first belonged to their fathers, and then to their husbands. Women did not have basic rights to vote, list property in their own name, or bring a legal suit to court, and did not have the rights to their own children.

Nonconforming white women risked scorn and severe punishment. Husbands could beat disobedient wives, and the idea of marital rape was nonexistent (Hine and Thompson, 1999). A white woman who violated the criminal code was viewed with moral suspicion, although punishment was based on the law. Adulteresses and women committing infanticide typically received more severe penalties than men, while those who committed theft or fraud received more lenient treatment (Feinman, 1983).

During antebellum slavery, jurisdictions executed more than three times as many enslaved black women than during the colonial period (Baker, 2008: 66). From 1790 to Emancipation, 126 enslaved African American women were executed. These figures are a low estimate of the number of enslaved women killed for infractions. In the antebellum period, 73% of enslaved women were executed for murder, conspiracy to murder, and attempted murder (Ibid.). Enslaved men and women attacked white masters and mistresses, overseers, and children (Jordan, 1968) through available means: shooting, poisoning, hacking to death, clubbing, stabbing, burning, and strangling. For the 109 slave women executions with sufficient background information, 67 murdered a master or family member, and 35 killed unrelated individuals (Streib, 1990). Poisoning and arson were the most frequent means used by slave women to kill their masters or destroy their property (Baker, 2008). Poisoning increased in the antebellum period, and even juvenile female slaves were accused and executed.

Pennsylvania passed a law requiring the gradual abolition of slavery in 1780 (Gross, 2006). The trial of Alice Clifton, accused of murder in 1787, took place as an era of slavery and corporal punishment was being displaced in favor of human freedom and development of a penal system. Clifton, a domestic servant, was accused of killing her newborn illegitimate girl child after concealing her pregnancy. She had sexual relations with a white man, John Shaffer, and told the court that he had asked her to kill the baby in order to curtail scandal. Afterward, he would buy her freedom. The evidence as to the infant's death was mixed. Clifton claimed the baby was stillborn and that she made a cut in her throat to fulfill an agreement with Shaffer. At the close of the trial, the chief justice argued that Alice was "unpitying" and "void of maternal affection" (Gross, 2006: 17). She was found guilty after three hours of deliberation by a jury, but a petition alleged that the trial should be overturned because of the unfavorable remarks of a juror prior to the trial. Her sentence was eventually commuted. Kali N. Gross (2006: 18) writes: "The extremeness of her crime attests to the paradox of resistance; no matter how noble the desire for freedom, actually resisting slavery rendered any adherence to the law or conventional morality impossible."

After the importation of slaves was federally outlawed in 1808, female slaves became even more important as "breeders, not mothers" (Baker, 2008: 71) because the owner had legal control of their children, the emergent workforce (Bridgewater, 2001). At the same time, enslaved women were frequently sexually assaulted and raped by their masters, their masters' sons, and overseers. Sexual assaults on enslaved girls as young as 12 years were frequent. Kolchin (1993: 124) observed that a southern planter considered that white sexual relations with slave women promoted the "absence of Southern prostitution and the purity of white women." The reality is that white and mulatto free women participated in prostitution (Fogel and Engerman, 1964; Genovese, 1974).

Slave women resisted sexual victimization with actions that would now be viewed as self-defense. Baker (2008: 72, citing Higgenbotham, 1996) relates the case of Celia, who was executed by hanging:

> Seventy year old Robert Newsome bought 14 year old Celia and forced sexual relations upon her immediately and repeatedly. One night when Newsome went to Celia's cabin to abuse her, she struck him with a stick and killed him instantly. Celia was pregnant by Newsome for the third time and was very ill when he last approached her. At her trial, the court was concerned only with whether Celia had a right to defend herself against her owner's assault. The trial judge made it clear that Celia did not have that right. To the court, Celia had no sexual rights over her own body because she was Newsome's property and she ought to have submitted to his demands. Celia was guilty of murder and hanged 4 days before Christmas in 1855.

In 1802, Ohio abolished slavery. In the 1820s, slavery was no longer legal in the northern states. From 1831 to 1860, the Underground Railroad helped slaves to escape to freedom. Reformers began movements to abolish slavery and women's rights; these movements were often interconnected. The American Anti-Slavery Society (AASS) was founded in 1833, along with the Philadelphia Female Anti-Slavery Society started by women's activist Lucretia Mott. In 1837, women held an antislavery convention in New York, although women delegates were not allowed to attend an international Anti-Slavery Convention in 1840. This prompted Mott and Elizabeth Cady Stanton to call for a women's rights convention, which was held in Seneca Falls in 1848. Women's rights began to expand state by state. Married Women's Property Acts were passed in Maryland (1839) and New York (1848). Slavery became the main issue. Sojourner Truth began her abolitionist work, and Harriet Tubman repeatedly worked to free slaves. Congress passed a Fugitive Slave Act in 1850, but it was laxly enforced. In 1851, Truth gave her "Ain't I a Woman" speech in Akron, Ohio. Continuing to support southern slavery, the 1857 *Dred Scott* decision of the Supreme Court disallowed African American slaves the right of citizens.

Public sentiment began to change in the decade prior to the Civil War. In 1861, Harriet Jacobs's autobiography *Incidents in the Life of a Slave Girl* was published, detailing the sexual assault and rape she and other women slaves experienced. In 1862, Congress passed the Second Confiscation Act which provided freedom to slaves in Union controlled Confederate territories as well as slaves who ran away from Confederate owners. The Emancipation Proclamation furthered freedom to slaves residing in all states that persisted in rebellion as of January 1, 1963 (Rodriguez, 2007). Ultimately, the Thirteenth Amendment to the Constitution in 1865 abolished slavery. At this point, Elizabeth Cady Stanton, Susan B. Anthony, Frederick Douglass, Lucy Stone, and other men and women began the American Equal Rights Association on behalf of women and African Americans.

From 1800 to 1860, the United States had experienced rapid social change and growth of urbanization (Banks, 2003). Rural-to-urban internal migration, immigration from overseas, and the systematization of a market economy began to change how Americans lived. Unfortunately, the growth of cities is associated with social and economic problems that have especially impacted women due to their lower status relative to men. After the Civil

War, women committed property crimes and prostituted themselves to survive. There were many laws regulating women's sexuality, including public conduct, "lewd behavior," and adultery. Females arrested for sex offenses were regarded as "fallen women" and carried a permanent stigma. Altogether, women made up a small number of all prisoners and were rendered invisible. It was thought that few women committed crimes because of their involvement in the family. Reflecting the influence of the Madonna-whore duality, women prisoners were seen as depraved and unable to reform. The departure of women from their traditional gender roles as wives and mothers was viewed as more serious than male criminality. Virtuous women were regarded as models of morality in the family and given responsibility for socializing values. "Fallen women" were viewed as tempting men rather than giving men the onus of controlling their own behavior. Like felons today, they were regarded as disreputable and had a hard time being hired. As a result, they again looked to crime for survival.

The legal system of slavery had deprived blacks of all human rights, and the transition to freedom carried over the social barriers and established a new race order based substantially on criminalization. Kali N. Gross (2006: 38) writes: "By positioning Blacks in the lowest social rung and by criminalizing blacks through laws and practices that denied their humanity, early laws projected an image of Black women as dishonest and licentious— ultimately disallowing impartial justice for Black female offenders" (Gross, 2006). In 18th-century Philadelphia, a site for migrants looking for opportunity in the North, the criminal charges brought against African American men and women involved property crime, especially theft (Gross, 2006). Blacks, immigrants, and other poverty-level groups were targeted for enforcement in a manner similar to racial profiling today. Blacks were held in such suspicion that possession of almost any property of worth could result in an accusation of larceny. The raced structuring of larceny enforcement resulted in an increase in black men and women's imprisonment disproportionate to their share of the population, In Philadelphia courts, blacks were convicted at a rate 19% greater than that of whites (Gross, 2006: 34). Almost 72% of black women facing criminal charges were convicted by Philadelphia juries (Ibid.). Many worked in domestic service, which provided witnesses for any theft, but was also a source of false accusations if items were misplaced or a wage dispute occurred. Meanwhile, white women received chivalrous treatment (a gendered form of leniency), and were released on bail or had cases dismissed at a much higher rate.

Racial disparity in criminal incarceration went beyond issues of poverty or discrimination and involved the commission of survival crime in the face of social barriers to advancement (Gross, 2006). African American women's work as domestics was low paying and intensive. White and immigrant women were able to find work in industry, while black women felt their work was comparable to slavery. Given proximity and opportunity, they committed larceny, most often petty theft, and in Philadelphia, they became 4% of those in the county prison. To make ends meet, black servants became the majority of offenders. A crime category Gross (2006: 44) called "servant theft" developed. This crime involved dressing as a servant to gain access to middle- and upper-class white homes to burglarize. Certain black women made a decision to use crime, particularly servant theft, as a main source of income. Sixty-nine percent of Black women were first-time offenders, but some women made theft their work (Gross, 2006: 42–43). Kali N. Gross considers this choice to be a response to employment discrimination and quotes a black woman who stated in 1907: "Unless I am willing to engage in a few menial occupations, in which the pay for my services would be very poor, there is no way I can earn an honest living" (*The Independent*, 1907, cited by Gross, 2006: 43). Nevertheless, black women who were career criminals with extensive records were an exception.

The freedom of African Americans reduced the number of executions of black women during Reconstruction. Although African Americans had legally achieved equality, they did not receive the treatment of social equals, and barriers were created by the southern Jim Crow system that greatly restricted their ability to prosper and become socially mobile. By 1886, all southern states had passed black codes (Higgenbotham, 1996). Black codes prevented African Americans from voting, serving on juries, or testifying against whites in court cases. Their labor became devalued, and many men and women were convicted as felons and made to serve as prison labor. Leased work gangs were involved in mining, building the railroads and on prison farms. African Americans came to make up 40–70% of southern penitentiary women prisoners (Baker, 2008: 74). Black women serving as servants and domestic workers for whites were subject to criminal accusation. Their imprisonment was often for commission of property crime, but there were many convictions for violence.

Baker (2008: 74) suggests that execution by public authority was replaced by lynching as a means of social control. African American women remained vulnerable to white sexual assault (White, 1998). Reconstruction collapsed and, by 1890, the system of Jim Crow segregation had been established in the South (Sitkoff, 1981). Execution of black women working as domestic servants and housemaids (Seitz 2005, 41) likely involved acts of resistance to sexual victimization similar to that experienced by enslaved women (Baker, 2008; Rafter, 2004; Seitz, 2005).

At midpoint of the 19th century, public order offenses such as public drunkenness, vagrancy, prostitution, and disorderly conduct marked women's offending (Giordamo, Kerbel, and Dudley, 1981). Separate prisons for women had not yet been developed in most states. As cities grew after 1860, women's arrest and imprisonment increased. In New York and Massachusetts, women prisoners increased by one-third, while males in prison declined by one-half (Banks, 2003). The increased visibility of women committing prostitution and other public order offenses, abortion, and poverty-related larceny-theft crime contributed to increased women's imprisonment. From the mid-to-late 19th century, women swindlers were active perpetrators of fraud (Seagrave, 2007). These crimes included deceptive séances, spirit writing, panhandling, counterfeiting, faking wealth, and pension fraud. After 1860, states gradually began to segregate women from male prisoners, and some states hired women as matrons for custodial supervision of women prisoners (Banks, 2003). As reformers became active, they began to challenge the idea that women criminals were beyond redemption.

Prostitution arrests greatly increased in the 19th and early 20th centuries. Prostitutes were viewed as both symbolic of women's criminality and victims of men's seduction and deception (Hobson, 1987). The social reality was that lack of work and low pay pushed women into prostitution. Prostitutes tended to be young, single women living in poverty. They were susceptible to violence, disease, and alcohol/drugs. Their earnings did not allow then to depart from poverty. Early reformers emphasized venereal disease and immorality in their anti-vice campaigns, but they also worked to bring ideals of rehabilitation to women.

Prostitution was a target of moral reform and attempts to rescue and rehabilitate "weak" women. Stephanie Wahib (2002: 40) takes this position: "The idea that women need to be protected for their own good is grounded in a sexist view of women that perceives women as 'less capable' than their male counterparts. The more a woman deviated from what was considered acceptable female conduct, the more she was seen as lacking in moral character and the weaker she was perceived to be." Mid-1800s evangelical social workers from the middle and upper classes sought to discipline men that they viewed as corrupt seducers of young women. Nonmarital sex was viewed as exploiting women.

The law more closely regulated the behavior of men and did not always clearly define woman-specific criminal behavior. In antebellum St. Louis, prostitution was not illegal. Police used discretion and developed informal procedures for dealing with women offenders (Adler, 2001). The police sought to manage "fallen women" rather than uniformly arrest prostitutes. In middle-class terms, "fallen women" were considered dangerous as they might corrupt young men and turn them into drunkards and criminals. As a crime of morality, prostitution was not a priority for working-class policemen and judges preoccupied with crime in general, but steps were taken to establish boundaries for women's behavior through the use of vagrancy law. The vagrant act covered streetwalkers, procuring, and operating houses of ill repute. In St. Louis, women working in brothels were the subject of raids, although city officials tolerated prostitution. After a night en masse in jail, the women who had a means of support were discharged. These actions were taken to control crimes like robbery in the vicinity of the brothels. The periodic arrests were made to harass brothels if related crime, expansion outside the red-light district, or black patrons were accepted, as the races were segregated.

In the 1870s, St. Louis created a licensing system for brothels (Asher, 2001). Containment was carried out through arresting women at the margins of the trade rather than those most consistently active. The fallen women that police pursued were single and unattached. These women were informal participants in the sex trade and disturbed residential neighborhoods while presenting the specter of introducing vice. Street walkers, women who served beer and did sex work on the side, and promiscuous, drunk, and/or homeless women were all arrested under the vagrancy laws, facing up to six months in a workhouse. Asher (2001) considers that the St. Louis police feared unattached women. This had the latent impact of reducing competition with brothels and allowed madams to offer protection from the police. At the other end of the spectrum, at the end of the 19th century, immigrant women in New York City mobilized against prostitution and sought to reduce exposure of immigrant men to vice opportunities (Johnson, 2006).

When women commit crimes of violence, it is viewed as exceptional in the mass media. Public attention is most easily captured by murder, and the spinster Lizzie Borden, who was acquitted, is a folk crime figure (Asher, Goodheart and Rogers, 2005). In 1892, Andrew Borden, Lizzie's father, and her stepmother, Abby Durfee Gray, were found dead of hatchet blows. Lizzie discovered her father, whose skull was crushed. They had occupied a joint and conflicted household with Lizzie and her sister. Lizzie's discovery of her father's body and a broken and bloodied hatchet found in the cellar linked her to the crime. Nevertheless, fingerprinting was not accepted forensic technology, and definitive evidence from the hatchet was never extracted. No blood was found on Lizzie's clothes and, although she had burned a blue dress in the kitchen stove some days after the crime, she was not proven guilty beyond a reasonable doubt. The case is still the subject of conjecture about whether her illegitimate half brother, the maid, or Lizzie herself, in a delusional state, did it. Lizzie's case was unusual because she came from a wealthy family and became an heiress.

The Western frontier is romanticized as on the edge of lawlessness in countless movies and novels. From 1840 to 1870, 300,000 traveled West, with single men coming as explorers and for adventure. The gold rush drew 80,000 men who created mining camps. Prostitutes followed them and were greatly outnumbered by men. As single women and families entered the West, they brought Eastern attitudes and ostracized prostitutes. The world of the outlaws was male-dominated, although some women kept the company of robbers and cattle rustlers. These women tended to provide support by scouting, fencing stolen property, and the like. Belle Starr, the "Queen of the Bandits," was an exception. She was involved with the purchase of a ranch where outlaws hung out. She had a relationship with the outlaw Cole Younger, and then married another outlaw, Jim Reed. Her second husband was killed by the law in 1874, and she began to ride with a gang and is alleged to have assisted in robberies. In 1880, Belle married Sam Starr, and they were both later imprisoned for horse stealing. Although a model prisoner, she continued to harbor outlaws after her release.

1890s–1930: The Progressive Era

The late 19th and early 20th centuries involved growing efforts by women to improve their status and a progressive movement begun by settlement workers and reformers. At this time, women criminals started to be perceived as misguided rather than evil. Poverty and a compromised family and home life were connected to criminality, and the cause of a woman's fall was often blamed on an evil man (Freedman, 1974). In the 1820s, reformers like Dorothea Dix began to advocate that female wardens should work with female prisoners, who should be housed separately from men. Where there was a lack of public agency response, private institutions were begun, such as the Magdalene Home for "wayward" women, which promoted virtue and offered education, jobs, and religious teaching (Freedman, 1981). The reformer's goal, however, was to establish separate penal institutions for women. As the 19th century progressed, women began to be hired to run separate women's wings or buildings (Pollock, 2002: 24). Women's prison reformers were different from the suffragettes working for women's rights; they were politically neutral and sought to cultivate moral virtue in women (Freedman, 1974). One result of their efforts was the 1870 Prisons Congress that agreed to establish facilities separating women and juveniles from men (Polluck, 2002).

A major focus of the era was to criminalize commercialized vice: sex, drugs, and alcohol (Keire, 2010). Beginning in the 1890s and through World War I, a national debate concerned where to locate and how to regulate urban vice. In the conflict over vice, reformers used varying social order policies: use of licensing, geographic segregation of "red-light districts," and police action through incarceration. In the 1890s, red-light districts were subject to reputational segregation: the confinement of vice to specific city neighborhoods. Known as "tenderloins," these districts actually grew in trade. After 1900, a new generation of professionals succeeded in closing the red-light districts through city-by-city fights until they realized greater success during World War I through the passage of state laws. By 1920, 36 states had passed injunction and abatement laws (Keire, 2010: 95). These laws allowed both public officials and citizens to take action using red light abatement laws against houses of ill repute. Nevertheless, by 1917, this anti-prostitution effort had peaked, and although 85 cities had closed their red-light districts, such municipalities as San Francisco, San Antonio, and New Orleans continued to allow segregated vice despite negative national opinion (Keire, 2010: 97). For participating cities, the closure of the red-light districts made prostitution less profitable for participants and less accessible for consumers. Prostitution scattered to cheap hotels and lodgings or the "white light districts," cafes, dance halls, and other legal entertainment. Some prostitutes left town rather than work outside a brothel's protection and rely on pimps, who could be violent.

World War I generated training camps of servicemen, and both prostitution and drinking became an issue. When Congress issued the Selective Services Act of 1917, it included Section 12, prohibiting the sale of alcohol to soldiers and creating dry zones around camps, and section 13, which authorized the secretary of war to take all steps necessary to remove brothels from around the camps (Keire, 2010: 105). Mara L. Keire (2010) observes that when closure of the districts and banning of brothels did not stop soldiers' sexual activity, progressive reformers began blaming women instead of vice businesses. By ordering soldiers to refrain from paid or private sex, the rules: "made money irrelevant to a woman's reputation as a whore. They referred to women who had non-monetary sexual relations with soldiers as "charity girls and "patriotic prostitutes" (Ibid.). The spread of venereal disease among the soldiers then medicalized the efforts against prostitution. Young girls having sex with soldiers were seen as delinquents in need of reform. Adult women (not the soldiers) were viewed as the carriers of venereal disease. Both military and civilian police could detain women with venereal disease. During the course of the war, the Commission on Training Camp Activities (CTCA) detained 15,520 girls and women in federally funded reformatories and detention houses (Keire, 2010: 109). This figure does not include jailed women or women quarantined in hospitals. Keire (2010) considers that the one-sided focus on women showed disregard for their autonomy. Before, women had brokered meetings with men on equal terms; afterward, men made the arrangements. Keire (2010: 111) notes that male control coincided with a shift in profanity, with women increasingly referred to as "gashes" or other profane terms reducing them in words to their sexual organs. Progressive reform impacted the criminal justice system and impacted the professional role of women and treatment of female criminals. Reaction to adult women's crime focused on prostitution and "social evils" such as white slavery (Chesney-Lind and Pasko, 2004; McDermott and Blackstone, 1994; Rafter, 1990; Schlossman and Wallach, 1978). The women's reformatory movement resulted in the establishment of separate custodial facilities for women (Banks, 2003). It also perpetuated a double standard in which women were more likely to be confined for petty offenses such as being publicly drunk. Women were punished more severely than men for these crimes.

Concerns about prostitution persisted into the new century. In the first decade of the new century, white slavery narratives of sexually violated young women fueled an international scare (Keire, 2001) resulting in the 1910 passage of the Mann Act (prohibiting white slavery but also prohibiting interstate transport of females for "immoral purposes"). Racialized historical accounts of involuntary brothel prostitution are considered exaggerated but provide examples of what would today be referred to as "internal trafficking." Progressive Era reformers utilized white slavery themes to protest municipally tolerated red-light districts. These urban areas included Storyville in New Orleans, New York's Tenderloin, Chicago's Levee, and San Francisco's Barbary Coast. Some red-light districts were created by legal ordinance, while others were tolerated in certain zones.

Prohibition, when the consumption of alcohol was prohibited, prompted a surge in organized criminal activity oriented to "bootlegging," the smuggling and sale of alcohol. Prohibition significantly impacted prostitution. Criminal gangs became more organized in response to competition to sell bootleg liquor and control sales sites (Keire, 2010). In 1920, Polly Adler opened a brothel that sold liquor for privileged clients in New York City (Applegate, 2011). Her bordello was protected by organized crime figures Dutch Schultz and a friend, Lucky Luciano. Her patrons included Mayor Jimmy Walker, literary figure Robert Benchley, and Dutch Schultz. Adler stated: "I could boast a clientele not only from Who's Who and the Social Register, but from Burke's Peerage and the Almanach de Gotha" (Adler, 2006). Low-profile "speakeasies" were tolerated by the police, who resisted enforcing laws that went against urban norms (Keire, 2010).

During the late 19th century, a concern about the rights of minors developed within the Progressive movement. Reformers linked the experience of poverty with the development of delinquency. The Child Saver movement sought to reform youth in trouble and began the juvenile justice system (Platt, 1977). The Child Savers were privileged women who sought discipline in family courts for working class girls' "immorality" and "waywardness" (Chesney-Lind and Pasko, 2004; Schlossman and Wallach, 1978). The middle- and upper-class women who became child savers focused their efforts on girls, particularly immigrants (Chesney-Lind and Pasko, 2004; Messerschmidt, 1987). They were concerned about female victimization and advocated raising the age of consent. They did not want to regulate prostitution, because regulation would decriminalize some forms of it.

The child savers sought to separate girls from boys in houses of refuge—otherwise known as reformatories (Pasko, 2010). The period 1910–1920 saw the creation of 23 reformatories and training schools. From 1850 to 1910, only five reformatories were built each decade (Schlossman and Wallach, 1978). The Progressive Era shaped juvenile justice for girls, who were placed in rural settings, denied contact with men, and taught domestic skills until they were of marriageable age (Chesney-Lind and Pasko, 2004). The child-saving movement is considered to have originated the juvenile justice system and structured it with separate institutions for girls and boys (Chesney-Lind and Pasko, 2004). The courts had defined delinquency as violation of a city ordinance or law by a male or female under the age of 16 (Knupfer, 2001). For girls, however, the charges included "incorrigibility," relationships with persons considered immoral, presence at pool halls or saloons, vagrancy, and use of profanity (Pasko, 2010). The charges involving a girl's sexual behavior and obedience would come to be known as status offenses (Chesney-Lind and Pasko, 2004).

The child savers especially monitored the moral purity of minority and immigrant girls. Family court punishment was harsh and, in Memphis, Tennessee, girls were twice as likely as boys to be committed to training schools (Shelden, 1981). "Immorality" was a catch word for girl's sexual expression. Women reformers would question girls and boys, and even have doctors conduct gynecological exams for virginity (Chesney-Lind and Pasko, 2004: 37). Nevertheless, Mary E. Odem (1995) found the systematic efforts to police girls' morality ineffective, even if they were coerced. The men considered to take away girls' purity received no punishment at all. A double standard existed in evaluating male and female delinquency. From 1904 to 1927, 60–70% of Chicago girls were placed in institutions or on probation for incorrigibility (Knupfer, 2001). Girls were more frequently institutionalized than boys for immorality. Pasko (2010: 1102) writes: "Embedded in these images was a dichotomous image of girls—on one hand, a victim, an errant yet essentially good girl, and on the other, a 'sexualized demon,' a danger not just to herself but to the larger society." All girls who had sexual relations with more than one partner were institutionalized. Juvenile officials noted that 70% of these girls had been sexually victimized in the home, but did not take the implications into account (Knupfer, 2001). The sexual victimization of young girls was viewed as their own choice and delinquent behavior (Pasko, 2010).

The availability of motor cars brought about a dramatic new style of robbery and escape. A "gun moll" was a female companion of a male criminal, often a gangster, who may use firearms. Women complicit with major criminals include Bonnie Parker, the girlfriend of Clyde Barrow; and Evelyn "Billy" Frechette, with John Dillinger.

1930s–1967: The Medical Model and Treatment Era

From the 1930s to 1967, the medical model in criminal justice advocated that an offender was "sick" but could be "cured" (MacNamara, 2006). The medical model of corrections assumed that inmates, men or women, needed the right treatment to be rehabilitated. Therapeutic methods, many still used today, were based on the idea that inmates were psychologically immature. Inmates were viewed as "clients" or "patients" and referred to as "residents" or group members, and individual and group therapy was used. Individual therapy employs a face-to-face relationship, while group therapy relies on insights generated by members of the group. Additional types of therapy used included behavior therapy, drug therapy, aversion therapy, neurosurgery, and sensory deprivation. Because of the faith in rehabilitation, indeterminate sentencing was used, and release was used as a reward for good behavior. Both academic researchers and legal scholars began to attack the legal model for lack of evidence that it worked. Analysis of the treatment era reveals that the medical model was more ideal than reality. Most administrators and guards were trained to regard custody as their chief initiative and were not trained about treatment. Treatment opportunities were inconsistent and not widespread. Although this era is considered to be over, many correctional rehabilitation programs have survived. Nevertheless, an emphasis on individual responsibility and punishment began as U.S. society began to promote crime control.

Although the prohibition of alcohol sales failed, in the 1950s, drug prohibition was accompanied by mandatory minimum sentencing laws for possession, sales, and trafficking. The Boggs Act of 1952 and the Narcotics Control Act of 1956 were the first laws to establish mandatory minimums in criminal sentencing. For example, a woman found to be in possession of marijuana could be sentenced to a minimum term of 2 to 10 years and given a fine of up to $20,000 (*Frontline*, 1998).

Mid-20th-century concerns about juvenile girls still involved incorrigibility (Chesney-Lind and Pasko, 2004). It was thought that the rescue, skills, and protection aims of wayward minor court had placed girls in jeopardy of being over-disciplined. Many girls were brought to court for disobeying their parents or because of a "danger of becoming morally depraved" (Tappan, 1947: 33). Because girls were being charged for sexual behavior that did not involve prostitution, Tappan (1947: 33) was concerned that what happened to girls in family court depended a great deal on the experience and personality of judges.

Odem and Schlossman (1991; cited in Chesney-Lind and Pasko, 2004: 58–59) researched girls' experience in Los Angeles during two years from diverging decades, 1920 and 1950. During this time span, girls were predominately white (73.5% in 1920; 69% in 1950) and working class from families in conflict. In 1920, Odem and Schlossman found that 93% of girls were considered status offenders and, within that group, 65% were charged with sexual immorality. A majority of girls charged with sexual immorality had sex with only one person: a boyfriend. Furthermore, 51% were referred by their parents (Ibid.: 197–198). In turn, the Los Angeles Juvenile Court detained girls prior to their hearings, because of a high rate of venereal disease (gonorrhea, syphilis, and others) among detained girls. Furthermore, only 27% of girls were released on probation. Odem and Schlossman attribute this to forcing treatment, which was painful and protracted. Detained girls did not automatically enter secure facilities. Some were placed in private homes to do domestic service, and others were sent to institutions such as the Convent of the Good Shepard. About one-third of girls were placed in a secure facility.

By 1950, 78% of girls were charged with status offenses, but of a wider variety (Odem and Schlossman, 1991, cited in Chesney-Lind and Pasko, 2004: 60). About one-half were charged with sexual misconduct, typically with a single partner outside of prostitution. Nevertheless, one-third of girls faced emerging status offense charges: school truancy, running away from home, being in public after curfew, and "general unruliness at home." Parallel, referral sources broadened to include school officials and police besides parents. The rate of venereal disease had declined to only 5%, although all girls were subject to gynecological exams. Juvenile justice was clearly functioning to socially control girls exhibiting what was considered "adult" behavior.

1967–1980: The Community-Based Era

The 1960s was marked by prison overcrowding and a degree of continued faith in behavioral change and rehabilitation. This led to the establishment of community correction alternatives. Deinstitutionalization, also referred to as decarceration, was based on the idea that men and women could not be rehabilitated if they were separated from their social environment, a context to which they would eventually be released. Community correction advocates considered prisons to be dehumanizing and claimed that stigma and prison conditions victimized offenders. Decarceration used halfway houses, workplace programs, and open institutions. Although community correction is less and less relied on, halfway houses and work-release programs still exist. In a related effort, most mandatory minimum sentences specified by the Boggs Act of 1952 and the Narcotics Control Act of 1956 were repealed, only to be reinstated in some form in the mid-1980s. At the time, they were considered ineffective and overly harsh.

After World War II, Otto Pollack (1950) reflected patriarchal tradition when he theorized that women were innately deceptive and not to be trusted. In the 1950s, however, women began to resist their traditional role, and the second phase of the women's movement began. In 1968, Richard Nixon ran for the presidency and advocated "law and order." "Get Tough on Crime" began a dramatic increase in the rate of imprisonment of men and women in the United States. Criminologists and the media began to speculate about how women's increased presence in the public sphere would impact the crime rate. The impact of the women's

movement on female offending is disputed. Freda Adler, a criminologist who authored *Sisters in Crime: The Rise of the New Female
Criminal* (1975), proposed the "liberation hypothesis" that
changes in gender socialization and attitudes would generate
major increases in women's crime. Adler (1975, 169) wrote: "In
the future a greater proportion of wealth and power will pass
through feminine hands, and almost all of it will be wielded
responsibly. But it would be an unrealistic reversion to quixotic
chivalry to believe that, for better or worse, women will be any
more honest than men." Converging, Rita Simon (1975) proposed
the "opportunity hypothesis," predicting that increased women's
labor force participation would produce greater female offending.
These ideas produced a negative feminist reaction because they
believed the idea that more women would become offenders
would discredit the women's movement. Pearson (1997, 229)
wrote about the conservative perception that if women had more
freedom, they would "give their baser desires free reign, unfet-
tered by masculine reason, and fall lower into depravity than
any man could." Dodge (2009, 10–11) argues that this view distorts the contribution of these women theorists, particularly
Adler. She maintains that Adler foresaw increased women's
offending due to greater opportunity for women combined with
reduced social control and family supervision. For example,
Dodge demonstrates that the integration of women into the executive class has given them more opportunity to commit white collar crime. Rita Simon (1975), based on FBI Uniform Crime
Reports, predicted that "women should be making a contribution
in white collar, financial crimes commensurate with their representation in society. The fact that female arrests increased for
these offenses and not for all offenses is consistent both with
opportunity theory and the presence of a sizeable woman's movement." Men and women are represented as driven by the same
moral impulses or lack thereof. Gender equality is viewed as providing criminal opportunity.

The 1960s and 1970s era of social reform ushered in concern
about juvenile justice. In 1972, the emphasis on community-
based rehabilitation led Massachusetts to close all of its reform
schools and open group homes (Scull, 1977). At the same time,
institutionalization of girls was scrutinized. Chesney-Lind and
Pasko (2004: 60) note that legal scholars began to see status
offenses as "buffer charges." Vedder and Somerville (1970) found
that there were five major charges: (1) running away from home;

(2) incorrigibility; (3) sexual offenses; (4) probation violation; and (5) truancy. These researchers considered that sexual misconduct was the major reason behind the various charges. A 1970s New Jersey study again found girls being detained for protection (Rogers, 1972). The differential treatment of girls relative to boys led to concern about a double standard. As a result, reform advocates began to argue that the judicial paternalism associated with status offense detention should be ended and replaced by "deinstitutionalization."

In contrast to the trend toward punishment and imprisonment, the Juvenile Justice and Delinquency Prevention (JJDPA) Act of 1974 sought to reduce exposure of juveniles who had not committed criminal acts to delinquents and adult criminal offenders by disallowing placement in secure juvenile detention facilities/training facilities and adult jails. This law prohibited the placement of status offenders in secure facilities. Status offenses are behaviors that are illegal only when an individual has not reached an adult age. Examples of status offenses include failure to attend school, possessing or drinking alcohol, running away from home, and breaking curfew laws. The JJDPA Act also protected dependent, neglected, or abused children from being placed in secure facilities. State cooperation was to be prompted by diversion of federal delinquency prevention funds to deinstitutionalization (Chesney-Lind and Pasko, 2004). As a result of the JJDPA removal of status offenses as a detention charge and efforts to deinstitutionalize girls, the female juvenile detention rate greatly declined (Chesney-Lind and Pasko, 2004).

1980s–Present: The Crime Control Model and Prison Warehousing

In the 1980s, Ronald Reagan began the War on Drugs, which culminated in the passage of the 1986 Anti-Drug Abuse Act. This act established mandatory minimum sentences for drug offenses and became a major driver of mass imprisonment. Previously, most women in prison had property or violent crime convictions. Twelve percent of women prisoners had committed drug offenses. By 2000, 35% of women prisoners were drug offenders (Kruttschnitt and Gartner, 2003, cited in Kruttschnitt, 2010: 33). Drug sentencing changes dramatically impacted African

American women, whose rate of imprisonment to 175 per 100,000 and increased by 50% (Ibid.). A Supreme Court challenge to mandatory sentencing has resulted in a return to judicial discretion. Nevertheless, this trend in women's imprisonment is likely to decline very slowly, as 29 states have passed "truth in sentencing" laws that require mandatory minimums for time served in an overall sentence. For example, 85% of a sentence for a violent offense must be served. Public disappointment with high recidivism rates and media stories about released prisoners who committed violent crimes led to curtailment of prison education and work-release programs. Judges were tired of recidivists and began thinking in terms of 'just desserts" and more punitive sentencing. This, combined with warehousing of prisoners, was intended to protect society (Pizzi, 1986; MacNamara, 1978).

During the 1990s, crime rates began a long period of decline (Conklin, 2003), but women's imprisonment has steadily increased. Individuals aged 15 to 24 years old have a greater likelihood of criminal involvement and their proportion of the population declined. After 1991, there was a shift away from crack usage to marijuana use amongst younger users. John E. Conklin (2003: 195–196) suggests this occurred because of stringent enforcement and penalties for crack possession and sales rather than violence, and risk of overdose or HIV infection. Youth aged 15–24 are more likely to commit crimes to pay for drug usage (Menard, Mihalic, and Huizinga, 2001). Therefore, even a small shift in youth population size is likely to reduce crime. In the same decade, crack-related murders and robberies dropped as dealers shifted to indoor trade from outdoor street sales to avoid police. Indeed, young people responded to mandatory sentencing and incarceration by shifting away from that drug. John E. Conklin (2003: 199) states: "I believe that the rising rate of incarceration was probably the most important reason that crime rates fell after 1991." He indicates that the rate of incarceration was the only factor to increase before crime declined, and that research supports its role in reducing crime rates. This increase has come at great expense in building prisons and giving custodial care to children.

In contrast, juvenile justice legislation continued to follow a more benevolent path. In 1980, the JJPTA Act was amended to prohibit any juvenile from being housed in adult jails (Schwartz, Steketee, and Schneider, 2004). Nevertheless, juvenile justice officials were highly critical of the JJPTA reforms and resisted carrying it out. In 1980, Judge John R. Milligan of the National

Council of Juvenile and Court Judges stated: "The effect of the Juvenile Justice Act as it now exists is to allow a child to ultimately decide for himself whether he will go to school, whether he will live at home, whether he will continue to run, run, run, away from home, or whether he will even obey orders of your court" (U.S. House of Representatives, 1980:136; cited in Chesney-Lind and Sheldon, 2004:176).

The backlash against juvenile girls' reform resulted in a change in the legal definition of a status offender. In a more punitive climate, it became possible to detain any child in violation of a "valid court order" (United States Statutes at Large, 1981). For example, using these criteria, any girl who ran away from a foster home, halfway house, or other court-ordered placement could be detained. Critics challenged reinstatement of the double standard, and the reauthorization of the JJPTA Act in 1992 addressed how many girls were classified as status offenders and the lack of services for them. As a consequence, the reauthorization required an analysis of each state's services for girls and required development of a plan to provide services. In the era of crime control, arrests of girls for status and delinquency offenses have increased at a rate faster than boys (Chesney-Lind and Pasko, 2004). In contrast to Progressive Era and 20th-century trends, detention has become racialized. By 2000, approximately half of girls in detention were African American and 13% were Latino (American Bar Association and National Bar Association, 2001).

By 2007, women comprised 7% of all state and federal prisoners in the United States (Bureau of Justice Statistics, 2008). From 1980 to 2008, women's imprisonment increased from 11 to 69 per 100,000 residents, a sixfold increase. Men's imprisonment increased from 275 to 957 per 100,000, a threefold increase (Kruttschnitt, 2010b). There is a gender gap in both criminal offending and imprisonment, but the mass imprisonment of women raises questions about how the criminal justice system operates. A major cause of increased imprisonment has been the gender neutral policy of determinate sentencing, which sets a mandatory minimum for time served based on the type of crime. Historically, indeterminate sentences gave more leeway to judges. In the 20th century, indeterminate sentencing allowed for assessment of the offender. Sentencing could take into account a woman's role in the offense, prior conviction record, and social background, including whether she was a custodial mother (Kruttschnitt, 2010a). Determinate sentencing ended judicial discretion, and the number of criminal convictions rather than the seriousness or dangerousness of a crime became the major determinant of length of a sentence.

Since 1959, the number of women arrested for drug offenses has steadily increased and driven mass imprisonment trends for women (Bloom and Chesney-Lind, 2007). Again, there is a steep gender gap in offending because men are more frequently arrested for these crimes, which range from possession to sales to trafficking. Regardless of the gender gap in arrests, mandatory sentencing laws for drug violations has greatly increased state and federal imprisonment of women during this historical period of mass incarceration. David Merolla (2008) considers that the War on Drugs made women and girls more vulnerable to arrest regardless of their offending patterns. Both the federally driven intensification of law enforcement efforts and legal penalties and the way that people think about drug use were subject to change. Drug users were socially constructed as criminals and, unlike images of dangerous criminals in the past, relatively "ungendered." Either men or women can be likely targets of drug arrests. In the mass media, women have been represented as more immoral than male drug users. This is partly due to the negative impact of drug use during pregnancy on the unborn fetus and attempts to criminalize it. Drug use is perceived as masculine behavior and violating traditional gender expectations. Merolla (2008) refers to women drug users as "double deviants": they have broken both the law and society's expectations for women. Conspiracy laws, combined with mandatory minimum sentencing laws, have resulted in arrests of women who may know or be romantically involved with drug dealers (Merolla, 2008). The police place pressure on these women to provide information (Lusane, 1991). Women with boyfriends or sons who are drug dealers are at increased risk of arrest. Drug-related crimes are the leading cause of women's imprisonment.

Warehousing of prisoners and mass incapacitation of women has had a disproportionate impact on children and families. By 2000, 65% of women in state prisons and 59% in federal facilities had children under age 18. A majority of women with children were single parents from a lower socioeconomic background. Seventy percent of women in state prison who are mothers had lived on less than $1,000 per month, often relying on welfare and or unemployment insurance for family support (Bureau of Justice Statistics, 2000).

Women have not yet achieved full occupational parity and equality with men. Nevertheless, more women have overcome occupational marginality and are gaining access to the upper managerial sector. Many women have been confined to lower status "pink-collar" positions, and some choose to commit financial fraud or embezzle (Daly, 1989). Contemporary women executives are committing elite crimes at a greater rate (Dodge, 2009). Sandy Haantz (2002) found that, among 1,016 federal offenders imprisoned with white collar crime convictions for embezzlement, forgery, counterfeiting, and fraud, one in four were women. Nevertheless, increased economic opportunity is not the only social factor associated with an increased women's crime rate; changes in the law can prompt increased arrest of men and women.

The use of the death penalty has been limited by state. Only two black women have been executed: Frances Elaine Newton and Wanda Jean Allen (Baker, 2008). Despite the overwhelming anti-crime sentiment of the public, executions are contested. Karla Faye Tucker was executed in 1998 after Governor George W. Bush refused to grant further review of her case by the Texas Board of Pardon and Parole. A controversy had ensued because she became a born-again Christian on death row and a helpmate to women prisoners. Convicted of committing murder with a pick axe, Tucker, on drugs at the time, claimed to experience sexual arousal during the killing. Her case marked the first execution in the United States since 1984 and the first execution of a woman in Texas since the Civil War. International attempts were made to gain her clemency, including by the pope.

Conclusion

Are American women and men among the world population most prone to criminality and/or more deserving of imprisonment or the death penalty? The rate of incarceration in the United States is the highest in the world. This suggests that either Americans are prone to breaking the law or that the penalties for crime are more severe. Looking at the history of reform movements and attacks on vice in the United States, it is clear that there is a prior basis for Americans to implement harsher laws based on attempts to prohibit mind-altering substances from alcohol to drugs and to take a moralistic stance towards prostitution, which is illegal in all areas except certain counties of Nevada. The continuation of the war on drugs and new efforts to end sex trafficking are all connected to the progressive reform tradition and emphasis on morality based in the Judeo-Christian tradition.

References

Adler, Jeffrey S. 2001. "Streetwalkers, Degraded Outcasts, and Good-for-Nothing Huzzies: Women and the Dangerous Class in Antebellum Saint Louis." *Journal of Social History*, 737–755.

Adler, Polly, 2006. *A House Is Not a Home*. Boston: University of Massachusetts Press.

Applegate, Debbie. "Polly Adler." http://www.pollyadler.com

Asher, Robert, Lawrence B. Goodheart, and Alan Rodgers. 2005. *Murder on Trial: 1620–2002*. New York: State University of New York Press.

Baker, David V. 2008. "Black Female Executions in Historical Context." *Criminal Justice Review* 33(1): 64–88.

Basch, Norma. 1979. "Invisible Women: The Legal Fiction of Marital Unity in Nineteenth Century America." *Feminist Studies* 5(2): 346–366.

Blackstone, William. 1765–1769. *Commentaries on the Laws of England*. http://www.lonang.com/exlibris/blackstone/

Bloch, R. H. 2007. "The American Revolution, Wife Beating and the Emergent Value of Privacy." *Early American Studies*, Fall: 223–251.

Block, Sharon. 2006. *Rape and Sexual Power in Early America*. Chapel Hill: University of North Carolina Press.

Bloom, Barbara, and Meda Chesney-Lind. 2007. "Women in Prison: Vengeful Equity." In Roslyn Muraskin (Ed.), *It's a Crime: Women and Justice* (4th ed., 542–563). Upper Saddle River, NJ: Prentice Hall.

Blumenthal, Walter. 1973. *Brides from Bridewell: Female Felons Sent to Colonial America*. Rutland, VT: Charles E. Tuttle.

Bridgewater, P. 2001. "Un/Re/Discovering Slave Breeding in Thirteenth Amendment Jurisprudence." *Washington and Lee Race and Ethnic Ancestry Journal* 7: 11–42.

Cannon, Christopher. "The Rights of Medieval English Women: Crime and the Issue of Representation." In Barbara A. Hanawalt and David Wallace (Eds.), *Medieval Crime and Social Control*. Minneapolis, MN: University of Minnesota Press. Pp. 156-187.

Chesney-Lind, Meda and Lisa Pasko. 2004. *The Female Offender, Girls, Women and Crime*. Second Edition, Thousand Oaks, CA: Sage.

Chesney-Lind, Meda, and Randall G. Sheldon. 2004. *Girls, Delinquency and Juvenile Justice*. Third Edition. Wadsworth: Belmont, CA.

Child Welfare Information Gateway. 2010. Child Abuse and Neglect Fatalities: Statistics and Interventions. http://www.childwelfare.gov/pubs/factsheets/fatality.pdf

Conklin, John E. 2003. *Why Crime Rates Fell*. Boston, MA: Allyn and Bacon.

Daly, Kathleen. 1989. "Gender and Varieties of White Collar Crime." *Criminology* 27: 769–793.

Dobash, R., R. Dobash, and S. Gutteridge. 1986. *The Imprisonment of Women*. New York: Basil Blackwell.

Dodge, Mary. 2002. *"Whores and Thieves of the Worst Kind": A Study of Women, Crime and Prisons, 1835–2000*. DeKalb, IL: Northern Illinois University Press.

Espy, M. W. and John Smykla. 1987. *Executions in the United States: 1608–1991: The Espy File* (machine-readable data file). Ann Arbor, MI: Inter-University Consortium for Political and Social Research.

Feinman, Clarice. 1983. "An Historical Overview of the Treatment of Incarcerated Women: An Overview." *Prison Journal* 12: 26.

Feinman, Clarice. 1994. *Women in the Criminal Justice System*. Westport, CT: Praeger.

Fogel, R., and S. Engerman. 1974. *Time on the Cross: The Economics of American Negro Slavery*. Boston, MA: Little Brown and Company.

Freedman, E. 1981. *Their Sister's Keepers: Women's Prison Reform in America: 1830–1930*. Ann Arbor: University of Michigan Press.

Freedman, E. 1974. "Their Sister's Keepers: A Historical Perspective of Women's Correctional Institutions in the U.S." *Feminist Studies* 2: 77–95.

Frontline. 1998. "Busted: America's War on Marijuana: Historical Timeline." Washington, DC: Public Broadcasting System.

Galenson, David. 1978. "British Servants and the Colonial Indentured System in the Eighteenth Century." *Journal of Southern History* 44: 41–66.

Genovese, E. 1974. *Roll Jordan Roll: The World the Slaves Made*. New York. Basic Books.

Giordamo, P. C., S. Kerby, and S. Dudley. 1981. "The Economics of Female Criminality: An Analysis of Police Blotters, 1890–1975." In L. Bowker (Ed.), *Women and Crime in America*. New York: Macmillan.

Glen, Shirley. 1982. *Belle Starr and Her Times: The Literature, the Facts, and the Legend*. Norman: University of Oklahoma Press.

Greenberg, D. 1974. *Crime and Law Enforcement in the Colony of New York, 1691–1776*. Ithaca, NY: Cornell University Press.

Gross, Kali N. 2006. *Colored Amazons: Crime, Justice and Black Women in the City of Brotherly Love, 1880–1910*. Durham, NC: Duke University Press.

Haantz, Sandy. 2002. Women and White Collar Crime. Washington, DC: National White Collar Crime Center. http://www.nw3c.org/research/site_files.cfm?mode=p

Hannawalt, Barbara A. 1999. "The Host, the Law, and the Ambiguous Space of Medieval London Taverns." In Barbara A. Hanawalt and David Wallace (Eds.), *Medieval Crime and Social Control* (pp. 204–223). Minneapolis, MN: University of Minnesota Press.

Higgenbotham, A. 1996. *Shades of Freedom: Racial Politics and Presumption of the American Legal Process*. New York: Oxford University Press.

Hindus, M. S. 1980. *Prison and Plantation: Crime, Justice and Authority in Massachusetts and South Carolina, 1767–1868*. Chapel Hill: University of North Carolina Press.

Hine, Darlene Clark, and Kathleen Thompson. 1999. *A Shining Thread of Hope: The History of Black Women in America*. New York: Broadway Books.

Hobson, B. M. 1987. *Uneasy Virtue: The Politics of Prostitution and the American Reform Tradition*. New York: Basic Books.

Hull, N. E. H. 1987. *Female Felons: Women and Serious Crime in Colonial Massachusetts*. Urbana: University of Illinois Press.

The Independent. 1907. "What It Means to Be Colored in the Capital of the United States." *The Independent* 62 (3014), January 7. In Gerder Lerner (Ed.). 1992. *Black Women in White America: A Documentary History* (pp. 181–186). New York: Vintage Books Edition.

Johnson, Val. 2006. "The Moral Aspects of Complex Problems: New York City Electoral Campaigns against Vice and the Incorporation of Immigrants 1890–1901." *Journal of American Ethnic History*, 74–106.

Jordan, E. 2000. Crossing the River of Blood between Us: Lynching, Violence, Beauty and the Paradox of Family History." *Journal of Gender, Race and Justice* 3: 545–580.

Karlson, Carol. 1987. *The Devil in the Shape of a Woman*. New York: W. W. Norton.

Keire, Mara L. 2001. "The Vice Trust: A Reinterpretation of the White Slavery Scare in the United States, 1907–1917." *Journal of Social History*, 5–41.

Keire, Mara L. 2010. *For Business and Pleasure: Red Light Districts and the Regulation of Vice in the United States, 1890–1933*. Baltimore, MD: Johns Hopkins University Press.

Keve, Paul. 1996. *The History of Corrections in Virginia*. Charlottesville: University Press of Virginia.

Knupfer, Anne Meis. 2001. "Reform and Resistance: Gender, Delinquency and America's First Juvenile Court."

Kruttschnitt, Candace. 2010a."The Paradox of Women's Imprisonment." *Daedalus* 139(3): 32–42.

Kruttschnitt, Candace. 2010b. "Women's Prisons." In Michael Tonry (Ed.), *Oxford Handbook of Crime and Criminal Justice*. New York: Oxford University Press.

Kruttschnitt, Candace, and Rosemary Gartner. 2003. "Women's Imprisonment." In Michael Tonry (Ed.), *Crime and Justice: A Review of Research* 30: 1–81. Chicago: University of Chicago Press.

Kurshan, Nancy. 1996. "Behind the Walls: The History and Current Reality of Women's Imprisonment." In Elihu Rosenblatt (Ed.), *Criminal Injustice: Confronting the Prison Crisis*. Boston, MA: South End Press.

Lefkowitz, Mary R., and Maureen B. Fant. 1992. *Women's Life in Greece and Rome: A Source Book in Translation* (3rd ed.). Baltimore, MD: Johns Hopkins University Press.

Lusane, C. 1991. *Pipe Dream Blues: Racism and the War on Drugs*. Boston, MA: South End Press.

MacNamara, Donal E. J. 1978. "The Medical Model in Corrections: Requiescat in Pace." In Fred Montanino (Ed.), *Incarceration: The Sociology of Imprisonment*. Beverly Hills, CA: Sage.

McDermott, M. J. and S. J. Blackstone, 1994. "White Slavery Plays of the 1910s: Fear of Victimization and the Social Control of Sexuality." Paper presented at the annual meeting of the American Society of Criminology, Miami, FL.

Menard, Scott, Sharon Mihalic, and David Huizinga. 2001. "Drugs and Crime Revisited." *Justice Quarterly* 18: 269–299.

Messerschmidt, J. 1987. "Feminism, Criminology, and the Rise of the Female Sex Delinquent, 1880–1930." *Contemporary Crises* 11: 243–263.

Moller, Herbert. 1945. "Sex Composition and Correlated Culture Patterns of Colonial America." *William and Mary Quarterly* 2: 113–153.

Morris, T. 1996. *Southern Slavery and the Law: 1619–1860*. Chapel Hill: University of North Carolina Press.

Nguyen, Ngheim L. 2006. "Roman Rape: An Overview of the Roman Rape Laws From the Republican Period to Justinian's Reign." *Michigan Journal of Gender and Law* 13(1): 75–112.

Odem, Mary E. 1995. *Delinquent Daughters: Protecting and Policing Adolescent Female Sexuality in the United States: 1885–1920*. Chapel Hill: University of North Carolina Press.

Odem, Mary E., and S. Schlossman, 1991. "Guardians of Virtue: The Juvenile Court and Female Delinquency in Early 20th Century Los Angeles. *Crime and Delinquency* 37: 186–203.

Pasko, Lisa. 2010. "Damaged Daughters: The History of Girls' Sexuality and the Juvenile Justice System." *Journal of Criminal Law and Criminology* 100(3): 1099–1130.

Pearson, Pamela. 1997. *When She Was Bad*. New York: Penguin Books.

Pizzi, Michael A., Jr. 1986. "The Medical Model and the 100 Years War." *Law Enforcement News*, July 7 (pp. 8, 13).

Platt, Anthony M. 1977. *The Child Savers: The Invention of Delinquency*. Chicago: University of Chicago Press.

Pollack, Otto. 1950. *The Criminality of Women*. New York: A. S. Barnes.

Pollock, Jocelyn M. 2002. *Women, Prison and Crime* (2nd ed.). Belmont, CA: Wadsworth.

Rafter, N. H. 1990. *Partial Justice: Women, Prisons and Social Control*. New Brunswick, NJ: Transaction Books.

Rhodes, H. 1984. *The Athenian Court and the American Court System* (Vol. 2, p. 2). http://www.cis.yale.edu/ynhti/curriculum/units/1984/2/84.02.08.x.html

Rodriguez, Junius P. *Slavery in the United States: A Social, Political, and Historical Encyclopedia*. ABC-CLIO, 2007.

Rogers, K. 1972. " 'For Her Own Protection . . .': Conditions of Incarceration for Female Juvenile Offenders in the State of Connecticut." *Law and Society Review* (Winter): 223–246.

Ronner, Amy D. 1996. "Husband and Wife Are One—Him: *Bennis v. Michigan* as the Resurrection of Coverture." *Michigan Journal of Gender and Law* 4.

Rowe, G. S. 1985. "Women's Crime and Criminal Administration in Pennsylvania, 1763–1790." *Pennsylvania Magazine of History and Biography* 109(3): 335–368.

Schwartz, Ira M., Martha W. Seketee, and Victoria W. Schneider. 2004. "Federal Juvenile Justice Policy and the Incarceration of Girls." In Meda Chesney-Lind and Lisa Pasko (Eds.), *Girls, Women and Crime: Selected Readings* (pp. 115–127). Thousand Oaks, CA: Sage.

Scull, Andrew T. 1977. *Decarceration: Community Treatment and the Deviant—a Radical View*. Englewood Cliffs NJ: Prentice Hall.

Seitz, T. 2005. "The Wounds of Savagery: Negro Primitivism, Gender Parity and the Execution of Rosa Lightner Phillips." *Women and Criminal Justice* 16: 29–64.

Segrave, Kerry. 2007. *Women Swindlers in America, 1860–1920*. Jefferson, NC: McFarland and Co. Publishing.

Shelden, R. 1981. "Sex Discrimination in the Juvenile Justice System: Memphis, Tennessee, 1900–1971. In M. Q. Warren (Ed.), *Comparing Male and Female Offenders*. Beverly Hills, CA: Sage.

Sitkoff, H. 1981. *The Struggle for Black Equality: 1954–1980.* New York: Hill & Wang.

Smith, Beverly A. 2003. "History of Female Crime in the USA." In Nicole Hahn Rafter, *Encyclopedia of Women and Crime* (pp. 73–74). Phoenix, AZ: Oryx Press.

Spindel, D. J. 1989. *Crime and Society in North Carolina, 1663–1776.* Baton Rouge: Louisiana State University Press.

Streib, V. 1990. "Death Penalty for Female Offenders." *University of Cincinnati Law Review* 58: 845–880.

Tappan, P. 1947. *Delinquent Girls in Court.* New York: Columbia University.

Ulrich, L. T. 1991. *Good Wives: Image and Reality in the Lives of Women in Northern New England 1650–1750.* New York: Vintage Books.

Veder, C. V., and D. B. Sommerville. 1970. *The Delinquent Girl.* Springfield, IL: Charles C. Thomas.

Wahib, Stephanie. 2002. " 'For Their Own Good?' Sex Work, Social Control and Social Workers, a Historical Perspective." *Journal of Sociology and Social Welfare* 24(4): 39–57.

Whelter, Barbara. 1966. "The Cult of True Womanhood, 1820–1860." *American Quarterly* 2: 151–174.

White, D. 1998. *Ar'n't I a Woman?: Female Slaves in the Plantation South.* New York: W. W. Norton.

Wilson, Nanci Koser. 2005. "Taming Women and Nature: The Criminal Justice System and the Creation of Crime in Salem Village." In Rosylyn Muraskin, *It's a Crime: Women and Justice* (4th ed., pp. 13–30). Upper Saddle River, NJ: Prentice Hall.

Young, Vernetta D., and Zoe Spencer. 2007. "Multiple Jeopardy: The Impact of Race, Gender, and Slavery on the Punishment of Women in Antebellum America." In Mary Bosworth and Jeanne Flavin (Eds.), *Race, Gender and Punishment: From Colonialism to the War on Terror* (pp. 65–76). New Brunswick, NJ: Rutgers University Press.

Zaher, Claudia. 2002. "When a Woman's Marital Status Determined Her Legal Status: A Research Guide on the Common Law of Coverture." *Law Library Journal* 94(3): 459–486.

Zahn, Margaret. 2003. "Intimate Partner Homicide: An Overview." *NIJ Journal* 250: 2–3. http://www.ncjrs.gov/pdffiles1/jr000250b.pdf

Zedner, Lucia. 1995. "Wayward Sisters: The Prison for Women." In Norval Morris and David J. Rothman (Eds.), *The Oxford History of the Prison.* New York: Oxford University Press.

2

Problems, Controversies, and Solutions

Social Control and Reduced Women's Offending

It was the right thing to do.

> —Andrea Yates, who drowned her five children to save their souls from the devil (Yardley, 2002).

My mother and I were really close. We used to share drugs like lipstick.

> —Karla Faye Tucker, recipient of the death penalty. She was executed in Texas for assisting in the murder of two people—regardless of her reformed behavior (Quinlin, 1992).

I hate lockdown. It's hideous. Bring 'em down a notch, to scare other people. If Martha can be sent to jail, think hard before you sell that stock.

> —Martha Stewart, convicted of insider stock trading (AP Online, 2005).

How can women kill their children, attack strangers, and commit white collar crime? Conservatives believe that committing crime goes against the essential nature of women as nurturers who support their families. Is it a greater crime when women violate their "true nature," or is crime a gender issue? Gender is defined as cultural differences between men and women produced by socialization. This concept is differentiated from biological sex, which refers to physical difference between males and females. Many feminists believe that behavioral differences between men and women are products of culture and location in societal structure. In contrast, essentialists believe that—as Freud put it— "Anatomy is destiny." Essentialists believe that masculine and feminine behavior is innate and not learned. The idea of gender is based on a belief in equality of male and female capability if socialization practice and structural opportunity permit it.

In recent decades, there has been critical public reaction to women who commit homicide, girls who use weapons in fights, female drug users, and other infractions of the law committed by girls and women. They have transgressed traditional gender expectations. Sensational women's crime cases often involve violation of traditional gender expectations of:

- Nurturance
- Obedience
- Chastity
- Monogamy
- Heterosexuality

The roles of Madonna and whore were both defined in relation to subordination to men. A concern with the potentially destructive nature of women's sexuality provided a basis for beliefs that men were superior to women. Thus women were confined to roles serving their husbands and raising children. These ideas about women are currently expressed and debated by advocates for women's equality. Relatively recent social change was initiated by women in the late 19th century, parallel to the development of industrial society. Today's advocates of women's equality often deliberately bypass assertions that one sex is better than the other in favor of arguing equal capability. Nevertheless, when a woman deviates— whether it is a case like that of Andrea Yates killing her five children, or Martha Stewart conducting insider trading—the violation of traditional gender roles (Madonna) and potentially destructive nature of women (whore) influences the sensation these cases cause in the media. Similarly, when a woman carrying a child (Madonna), such as Laci Peterson, is murdered, the stigma fell upon her husband, the adulterous Scott Peterson.

Women are considered to be emotional and embedded in relationships. Until the latter half of the 19th century, women were secondary to their husbands and did not have the legal right to own property. Although now taken for granted, women did not gain the right to vote until 1920. Women's traditional role shaped their patterns of criminal behavior. Historically, there has been a gender gap in women's offending. The fact that women have a much lower crime rate than men is central to understanding the societal reaction to those women who do offend. Women's arrest patterns have not substantially varied from the colonial era to the present but there has been a major increase in incarceration. Minor property offenses, intimate partner violence (IPV) and offenses involving drugs, sex, or morality are the major women's crime categories rather than violent crime. Like men, the majority of women's offending is nonviolent. Criminal offending follows gendered patterns that have been shaped by women's traditional role. Typically, violent crime, burglary, and other more confrontational crimes have been masculinized. Although some changes in women's rate of masculinized crime commission have occurred, a large gender gap remains.

Social control may be formal, such as legal regulations, or informal, as when families discipline or restrict the behavior of children. Both males and females are subject to the law, but women are more likely to conform to it. Women may be more responsive to the effects of informal social control—such as shaming—than men. Alternatively or conjointly, the gendered context for girls and women may limit their exposure to pathways leading to crime. Positive or negative experiences in the family and intimate relationships promote being law abiding or pushed out toward criminal lifeways. Both women's offending and criminal victimization are structured by gender expectations for men and women. As wives and mothers, many women continue to bear an uneven responsibility for household tasks and child rearing. The intensive labor associated with taking care of very young children places constraints on the ability to prepare for and commit many types of active crimes, such as burglary. Many women with children are single parents or compensate for men who work longer hours, including as sole breadwinners. The greater involvement of women in the home structures criminal opportunity and is associated with women's propensity to commit crimes involving intimates rather than strangers.

Women and men commit the same types of crime, but the rate of offending varies by gender and has fluctuated over time. The Uniform Crime Reports (UCR), published by the Federal Bureau of Investigation on an annual basis, reports arrests rather than convictions. The UCR has documented a decline in arrests for many crimes among adults and youth since the 1990s. This decline has occurred at differential rates for men and women, and very small changes in the numbers may inflate the rate at which women's crime commission appears to change, statistical increase and fluctuation occur in relation to a smaller numerical base of women offenders which distorts the importance of statistical trends. Because women have a drastically lower rate of criminal arrest than men, small increases in the number of arrests for a particular crime can seem dramatic. The media contributes to the sensationalism of women's crime patterns by sensationalizing any increase without necessarily explaining the numerical basis for the increase. Many like to read exciting crime news, and it is tempting to make a connection between one particularly horrific crime committed by a woman and statistics that appear to indicate that many women are capable of committing that type of crime.

Violent Offending and Victimization

Eighty percent of violent crimes are committed by men. The disparity in male and female rates of homicide, rape/sexual assault, assault, and robbery is an aspect of what is called the gender gap in crime commission. Attention should focus on how men's disproportionate percentage of violent crime impacts women's victimization. Everyone is familiar with the fact that rape and sexual assault are crimes predominately (but not always) committed by men against women. What is less obvious is the impact of domestic violence victimization upon women and family violence, especially child sexual abuse, upon girls. It is important to examine gendered victimization because of its impact on women and girls' crime and delinquency.

Gendered Patterns of Victimization

Women's victimization involves gendered or sex-specific crime most often committed by men but also occurring in a context of gay/transgender relationships. Violent victimization of women often occurs in intimate relationships rather than encounters with strangers. A major finding of research on women and crime is that they are much more likely than men to have been victimized as children or adults (DeHart, 2008). Types of violent victimization reported in the pathways of girls and women include family violence, rape/sexual assault, and physical and sexual abuse as children. The passage of the 1994 Violence against Women Act has had positive but as yet insufficient impact on domestic violence. In terms of homicide, it appears to have impacted the rate at which men are killed more than male-to-female homicide. Margaret Zahn (2003: 3) pointed out that after 1975: "Intimate partner homicide—the killing of a spouse, ex-spouse, boyfriend or girlfriend—has declined significantly in the past 25 years. But these declines, while truly significant, mask the important fact that women are substantially more likely than men to be murdered by their intimate partner." From 1993 to 2007, IPH of women declined by 35% (Catalano, Smith, Snyder, and Rand, 2009). In 2007, women made up 70% of victims of IPH. Women's IPH rates are four to five times the male rate. Jacqueline Campbell and colleagues (2007: 246) indicate: "The major risk factor for intimate partner homicide, no matter if a female or male partner is killed, is prior domestic violence." IPH is associated with alcohol and drug use as well as firearms availability (Roberts, 2009: 67).

Nonfatal intimate partner violence includes assault, rape, and robbery among current or former spouses, partners, boyfriends, or girlfriends. Women are more likely to be victims of nonfatal intimate partner violence than men (Catalano, 2006). From 2001 to 2006, women experienced nonfatal IPV at a rate of 4.2 per 1,000 aged 12 or over. In 2008, females aged 12 or older experienced 552,000 nonfatal IPV incidents in contrast to 101,000 reported by men (Catalano, Smith, Snyder, and Rand, 2009: 1). The female rate was 4.3 victimizations per 1,000 aged 12 or older and the male rate was 0.8. As is the case with violent crime in general, simple assault is the most common type of IPV (Catalano, 2006). Between 1995 and 2003, both the rate of simple and aggravated assault against women by intimates has declined by two-thirds. Use of alcohol and/or drugs was reported in 42% of incidents. In 2008, females aged 12 or older reported 70,550 (0.5 per 1,000) aggravated assaults and 406,530 (3.1 per 1,000) simple assaults. DeHart (2008) has identified pathways to prison connected to IPV among incarcerated women:

- A partner who abuses the family is implicated in a woman's child abuse.
- An abusive partner coerces a woman to commit crime.
- An abusive partner damages or steals property prompting the woman to commit crime to cover financial loss.
- An abusive partner causes a woman to be evicted, she becomes homeless, connects with criminals, and enters prostitution and or becomes addicted

DeHart (2008: 1366) found cases in which IPV victims were coerced by threat or actual physical assault to commit crimes such as shoplifting, check fraud, prostitution, robbery, or homicide. She considers that the role of victimization in women's crime commission should not be considered an excuse but taken into account. A case example she provides is: "Tanya's boyfriend started wanting to rob banks. She didn't want to, and he beat her up—said she was going to do it or he would kill her. He had a drug habit now. So they ended up robbing banks and that led up to Tanya serving time."

Women can also be intimidated by abusive men into taking a rap: "A 44-year old White woman explained that her husband would hit and slap her. One day he was angry about having to go with her to visit her mother. He had previously lost his driver's license and hit a car on the way. He told the police she had been driving. She was afraid to say it hadn't been her driving, so she got the ticket and had two points taken off her license. This was her first run in with the law" (Ibid.).

Rape/Sexual Assault

Rape is defined as forced sexual intercourse due to either psychological coercion or physical force (Catalano, Smith, Snyder, and Rand, 2009: 5). Sexual assault includes a range of victimization distinct from rape. These attacks involve attempted or completed unwanted sexual contact, including grabbing, fondling, and verbal threats. In 2008, the National Crime Victimization Survey (NCVS) estimated that 182,000 rapes or sexual assaults occurred, 40% against male victims. In 2008, the rate of rape or sexual assault was 1.4 per 1,000 women (Ibid.). Males commit 80% of rapes against females. Although rape is considered a crime committed by strangers, 20% of rapes are committed by an intimate partner. Fifty-seven percent of rapes/sexual assaults were committed by an "offender whom the woman knew." Strangers committed just under one-third (31%) of rapes/sexual assaults. Black women (2.9 per 1,000) are more frequently victims of rape/sexual assault than white women (1.2 per 1,000) or Hispanic women (1.1 per 1,000). Rape and sexual assault is an underreported crime and, in 2008, it is estimated that 47% of these crimes were reported to police. Catalano, Smith, Snyder, and Rand (2009: 6) report: "Based on the NCVS, between 1993 and 2008 the rate of sexual assault against females declined by 70% (from 4.7 to 1.4 per 1,000 females age 12 or older)."

Two types of intimate criminal victimization have predominately gendered male-to-female offending patterns: date rape and stalking. Date rape, also known as acquaintance rape, involves unwanted sexual intercourse, including oral or anal sex or any unwanted sexual contact that is through use of force or threat of force by casual or intimate dating partners. Legally, there is no uniform crime called "date rape," and it is tried under rape statutes. Stalking is a course of conduct aimed at a specific person that would cause a reasonable person to feel fear (Catalano, Smith, Snyder, and Rand, 2009: 6). Over a 12-month period from 2005 to 2006, 3.4 million individuals (14 per 1,000 persons) over age 18 were stalking victims (Ibid.). Females over age 18 (20 per 1,000 persons) are more likely to be stalked than males over age 18 (7 per 1,000). Individuals aged 18–19 and 20–24 are most likely to be stalked. Three out of four victims knew their stalker. Approximately 21% are former intimates and 16.4% a friend, intimate, or neighbor. Sixty-seven percent of female victims were stalked by males. Only 41% of female-stalking victimizations were reported to police. Date rape, stalking, rape/sexual assault, and intimate partner violence are all sources of mental and/or physical trauma reported in the pathways to crime of female inmates.

Ching-Tung Wang and John Holden (2007: 2) conservatively estimate the yearly cost of child abuse and neglect at $103.8 billion in 2007 dollars. Statistics on child abuse and neglect are collected by the National Child Abuse and Neglect Data System (NCANDS). In 2008, 772,000 children were estimated to be victims of abuse and neglect (ACYF, 2010). Approximately 51% were girls. Among child victims, whites were 41.5%, African Americans 16.6%, and Hispanics 20.8 %. Approximately 80% of perpetrators were parents, and 56.2% were women. About 39% were maltreated by the mother acting alone. Other categories of caregiver reported for abuse and neglect include day-care workers (ACYF, 2010: 28). Eighteen percent were maltreated by both the mother and father.

The Child Welfare Information Gateway (2010: 2) states that: "The National Child Abuse and Neglect Data System (NCANDS) reported an estimated 1,740 child fatalities in 2008." Child abuse and neglect fatalities include cases in which injury was a cause or a contributing factor. Children younger than age 4, especially those younger than one year, have the highest rate of fatality. Their small size, dependency on caregivers, and inability to defend themselves are factors in these deaths. Approximately 27% of these fatalities are attributed to the mother acting alone.

In 2008, less than 10% of estimated child abuse victims suffered sexual abuse. Rates of sexual abuse increase with age. About 7% of perpetrators sexually abused a child. About 58% of child sex abusers were friends and neighbors. Other categories of child sex abuser included professionals and "other"—indicating a public connection with the child. Three percent of children who were sexually abused were removed from the home. In general, child maltreatment has been on the decline in American society. The ACYF (2010: 94) reports that: "Sexual abuse has declined 53% from 1992–2007 and physical abuse had declined 52%. Neglect has fluctuated with only a small decline since 1992." Child abuse and neglect, child sexual abuse, and even witnessing family violence are potential triggers to running away and adolescent girls' involvement in delinquency and crime (Chesney-Lind and Pasko, 2004)

What Pathways Lead Girls and Women to Crime?

The pathways-to-crime approach developed from efforts to identify how factors associated with women's entry into crime differed from men. The feminist pathway approach seeks to identify a social context–based sequence over the life course leading to delinquency and/or criminality. Initial qualitative research resulted in biographies and case narratives indicating that victimization and social context impacted women offenders. Kathleen Daly (1992) was the first to suggest a typology of five pathways constructed from a sample of 34 women:

1. *Drug-connected women*: street girls and women who have escaped abuse and violence, been exposed to drug use and addiction and committed survival crimes such as prostitution, theft, and drug dealing.

2. In the drug world, women became users and/or involved in sales through ties to family or spouse/partners.
3. Girls subject to child physical or sexual abuse and neglect developed family and school problems, becoming delinquent in adolescence and chronic adult offenders.
4. Women battered by spouse/partners may exhibit retaliatory violence in the relationship and criminal behavior after escaping to survive.
5. Women economic offenders commit fraud, theft, and embezzlement to deal with poverty or attain social advancement. Women economic offenders lacked histories of abuse, addiction, or violence.

Terrie Moffitt (1993), and Moffitt and her colleagues (2001), expanded the study of pathways to developmental psychology and found that men and women were characterized by two pathways:

1. The *Adolescent Limited (AL)*: After a normal childhood, girls seek delinquent peers to gain freedom and autonomy. Delinquent behavior may recede by the late teens or early adulthood unless "snares" like school dropout, chronic drug use, or teen pregnancy result in diminished life chances and chronic criminal behavior.
2. *Life Course Persistent (LCP)*: Early childhood is marked by problems, disruptive school behavior, failures, and family problems. This is followed by adolescent psychological issues and chronic delinquency leading to a criminal career.

Gender-related life circumstances are associated with girls' and women's pathways into crime. Tim Brennan, Markus Breitenbach, and William Dieterich's (2010) quantitative study of 718 women in California prisons extended pathway typologies. *"Normal women"* entered two pathways characterized by lower risk, lower need, and high capital:

1. *Cluster 1*: drug-involved single parents with supportive families, no history of physical or sexual abuse, no mental health issues, and low scores for antisocial personality and attitudes. These women offenders avoid men who could get them into trouble. Typically they commit drug

and property offenses, averaging 9.7 arrests, with 83% known to have committed crimes while on probation. Often it was their first time in prison.

2. *Cluster 5:* older (average 39 years), not parenting, and drug-involved women. They are similar to Cluster 1 and have extensive education, financial resources, and a strong sense of personal efficacy. Conviction for drug-possession (70%) or drug-sales and property crimes result in their prison terms.

The "normal women" are in contrast to two pathways taken by *"marginalized 'socialized' women offenders."* These women live in poverty and have low human capital, such as education, and low social capital in the community through network ties and organizational access. They have been exposed to drug and anti-social subcultures and do not have mental health issues or antisocial personality characteristics.

Other pathways include:

Pathway 2: "marginalized, addicted and aimless—poor, older and childless women—often homeless" (Ibid., p. 42). Older (average 41 years) single addicts with little education or work experience and a history of drug treatment. Poverty, obtaining housing, and unemployment are constant concerns. They lack life goals and proactive beliefs. They have no history of child physical or sexual abuse and mental health problems. On average, they have been arrested 15 times, have multiple parole and probation revocations and prior jail and prison terms. They appear to be economically motivated offenders who primarily commit drug and property crimes. Forty-two percent had at least one violent felony arrest.

Pathway 3: "Marginalized, Addicted and Stressed- single younger mothers in conflicted relationships" (Ibid., p. 42). Young single parents with little educational or vocational success subject to poverty, and unstable housing situations in high crime areas. They suffer parenting stress and conflicted relations with significant others and experience social isolation and a low sense of personal efficacy. The family of origin participated in drug use and crime. They average 11.8 arrests for nonviolent drug and property crimes.

"Serious, Chronic and violent women offenders" followed two pathways marked by high need and high risk (Brennan, Breitenbach, and Dieterich, 2010: 43). These women show early onset of problems and delinquency, school and employment failure, antisocial personality traits, low self-control, and impulsive behavior. These pathways were identified as:

> *Pathway 6 (7.2%): "Chronic, Serious and Non-Compliant Offenders—Antisocial Personality and Hostility—mental health issues—lifelong abuse—battered—marginalized and Often Homeless"* (Ibid.). These women had a history of child physical and sexual abuse with foster care. Violent intimate victimization followed during adulthood and male partners tended to have criminal histories. These women constantly cycled through jail, probation, prison, and parole. They chiefly commit nonviolent drug and property crime offenses.

> *Pathway 7 (2.8%): "Chronic, Serious, Non-Complaint Offenders—extreme mental health problems and violent hostility—lifelong abuse—marginalized—high parenting stress* (Ibid.)." These women exhibited depression, anxiety, psychosis, and suicidal ideation. Although drug and property crime prevails, violent offenses involving weapons, fights with inmates, and assault that may be connected to domestic violence.

Lifelong Victimization pathways were characterized by exposure and acceptance of a criminal subculture. Parents had criminal and abuse histories, while spouses/partners were antisocial and criminal. The subculture involved drug use and sales among other criminal activity.

> *Pathway 4 (9.5%): Lifelong Victims—stressed, depressed single mothers in abusive relationships* (Ibid.: 44). Experience of extreme childhood sexual abuse links to forming repeat adult relationships with dominating and abusive men. Their families of origin provide little social support. As single mothers, these middle-aged women temporarily bond with men who have criminal records and involve them in crime. Raising children both overwhelms and stresses these women. Their psychological symptoms include depression,

anxiety, and negative reactions to abuse by men, but no mental illness. On average, up to nine arrests, detention, and revocation of parole characterizes these women. In Brennan, Breitenbach, and Dietrich's (2010: 44) sample, 19% committed violent felonies; many had domestic violence convictions, were physically aggressed against and/or hurt someone in the past three years—and reported feeling angry during the most recent crime. Despite the arrest history, 64% were in prison for the first time. "Lifelong Victims" arrests were primarily for drug and property offenses.

Pathway 8 (8.6%) "Older Addicted Women in Abusive Significant Other Relationships." Averaging 40 years in age, single or divorced, and past the parenting stage, these women have been abused in the family of origin and current relationships. Their natal families were criminally involved and substance abusers. The men they bond with involve them in criminal activities and are violent toward them, placing their lives in continual crisis mode. These women had lengthy arrest histories, particularly for drug sales and possession. Seventy-five percent had used drugs or alcohol at the time of crime commission. These women have angry and hostile feelings and are more likely to physically aggress than women in non-lifelong-victimization pathways.

Women's crime commission pathways indicate a need to stop family and partner violence. Research indicates that a history of physical and sexual victimization in childhood has lasting psychological and behavioral outcomes for women. The psychological trauma of victimization is connected to later substance abuse and/or violent crime commission.

What Are Causes and Correlates of Girls' Juvenile Offending?

Girls' offenses occur less often and are typically less serious than boys' delinquency (Zahn et al., 2010). The lesser degree of offenses such as truancy and running away from home may hide problems that the girls have including chronic sexual and physical victimization. Girls fleeing familial victimization may turn to prostitution, survival sex, and drug use. Rockwell's (2008: 105) research on the lives of women street hustlers identified six pathways:

- *All in the Family* group: "individuals with backgrounds and life histories steeped in deviance, for whom crime was just something everyone in their family did"
- *Partners by Trade* group: "women who became involved in crime primarily as a result of their own fast, partying lifestyles to which they had typically run as a result of dysfunctional familial relationships"
- *Show Me the Money* group: "women of more nurturing and privileged backgrounds, who appeared to pursue crime rationally as a means to get the money and things they wanted"
- *Challenged* group: "women with multiple emotional and psychological difficulties who committed crime solely to obtain drugs for self-medicating purposes"
- *Just Another Addiction* group: "women who relished the euphoric feelings they experienced when committing crime and equated their addiction to these as more powerful than any drug"
- *Lives of Loss and Trauma* group: "women who found in crime and criminal cohorts a sense of belonging, meaning, and family that they had been denied or that had been taken from them as a result traumatic losses and events in their lives"

The "all in the family" group were street women who had originated in families enmeshed in street culture and associated illegal behavior: drug use, prostitution, and violence (Rockwell, 2008: 105–108). They had experienced residential instability associated with the imprisonment of family members and were socialized to criminal activity within the family. They viewed themselves as having "lost childhoods" in which they became adult at a very early age. Uniformly, they had experienced childhood sexual abuse or an adolescent rape, and many did not trust men. By way of comparison, the work environments of the "partners by trade" group led them from jobs like waitressing and bartending to waitressing and stripping and subsequent prostitution. These working-class women had poor or nonexistent relationships with biological mothers and had experienced emotional and physical abuse. They lacked career aspirations, started work early, and were self-characterized as "wild" (Rockwell, 2008: 109–112). All began to hang out in bars and on the streets and to party by, on average, 15 years of age. Drinking was followed by drug use. In late adolescence and as adults, these women experienced intimate partner physical and sexual abuse from boyfriends and ex-husbands. Their crime commission involved larceny, forgery, drug possession, and, ultimately, hustling as prostitutes. Each group of women with familial poor treatment became integrated into a violent and criminal environment.

"Show me the money" women were primarily motivated by greed and originated in more nurturing environments (Rockwell, 2008: 113–116). Larceny-theft and drug sales were major means of income to acquire cars, houses, or electronics and to live the club lifestyle. These women did not prostitute and resisted drug addiction although they stole and sold drugs. They were independent and rejected "living off McDonald's wages and Section 8 [federally subsidized housing]" (Ibid.: 116). The opposite proved to be the case for "challenged" women. They grew up in violent homes, and many were circulated to various home settings such as foster care. The challenged did not succeed in school or the criminal life and turned to drug use for relief. Often arrested in relation to mental health issues, their offenses included larceny, prostitution, and jostling (obtaining money for drugs). Their later lives were marked by repeat violent victimization. Men, associates, and family members "who cared for them" introduced them to the drugs they craved. Betty Rockwell (2008: 119–120) presents this case of a challenged woman:

> Viv was introduced to cocaine and then heroin by the father of her now grown children. She continued to use "because of the way it made me feel. I'm a knucklehead. I'm afraid of things, but not when I use. Then I'm a big girl and wanna to be out there." Viv's money for drugs came from prostitution "because I'm too scared to do anything else." Lisa also expressed much fear and she, too, engaged in prostitution for crack—"for the energy inside it gives me." She started smoking through a friend's brother— "that's when Satan jumped all over me," she said.

The women with "just another addiction" had drug use habits that were supported by crime. These women had rejected either childhood or its dependent status very early in life. They identified with being "bad" or "tough" and saw it as necessary in the high-crime neighborhoods they grew up in. Their families had a party lifestyle with drinking or drugs and extensive conflict. They had not taken to schooling and were often expelled for their attitude or fighting. Girls from these street families tended to have been victimized as children and grew up with a capacity for becoming abusers of men and with protective feelings for women. Betty Rockwell (2008: 123) describes cases of a "just another addiction" street woman with aggressive tendencies and a desire to stand up for women:

> Kay, . . . who described herself as a "verbally aggressive" child who manipulated her father over her mother, said she was an abuser of past boyfriends and "detested" women who played "the dumb role," and especially those who "allowed" men to beat them. She seemed to cast herself as a defender of women who sought to empower them as well. Kay claimed that she stabbed one male abuser "on the block," three times, telling him, "if you ever beat her again you're gone."
>
> Janie also claimed to look out for women on the street, especially prostitutes, saying that her street name was "Little Pimp." On the streets for a year and a half, she said that she would sit in the park and watch over the girls, "copping drugs for them" and stepping in it if something turned violent. . . . Althea likewise distrusted men and called herself an abuser of men, and she recalled how she had left her "husband after beating on him" when their son was two days old, after she received "charge bills that weren't mine," which included charges for clothing items she would not have used while pregnant.

Women with "lives of loss and trauma" were highly emotionally damaged, and a significant trauma often proved a turning point in their becoming involved in drugs and crime. Their childhoods were marked by domestic violence, and they had experienced rejection and childhood sexual abuse. Their parents were frequently drug users or alcoholics and abusive. Betty Rockwell (2008: 125) indicates the women described their childhoods as "lonely, depressed, scary, alone, motherless, alone and sad."

Many had a history of running away from home, and they had tried alcohol by age 15, later becoming polydrug users. Women subject to extensive loss and trauma had been repeatedly jailed and placed in rehabilitation and committed a variety of crimes including assault and robbery. The case of Judy, a 37-year-old non-Hispanic white, was related as follows (Rockwell, 2008: 126–127):

> [W]hen asked how many times she had been to jail, [she] responded "Oh my God. At least 25 times." She claimed that her mother, whom she called "Mommy Dearest," was "vain, beautiful and very physically abusive." The woman was "an alcoholic and full blown suicidal," Judy said, and often told her, "I should have aborted you." She was repeatedly molested by her grandfather, who said she'd "be dead before eighteen," and she claimed that her father was in the mafia, naming local operatives who had visited her home. She also said her father was a fence (i.e., someone who sells stolen property), remembering "deliveries of stuff" to the home and refrigerators stuffed with cartons of cigarettes in the garage.
>
> Judy started "avoiding school" by the time she was 12, and when asked what she had wanted to be when she grew up, she got visibly angry and said, "I don't know—What the hell, I had to fight for my life." She left school and home at age 15 to move in with drug associates in the city. Judy said she had used "most every drug out there" and that her drug of choice for the past 13 years was heroin. She said that since she was 16 years old and committed her first larceny, her life had consisted of going "back and forth to jail" and that her offense history included other multiple larcenies, prostitution, assault, and weapons charges.

Gender Gap in Offending

Feminist criminologists consider a major research question to be: Is women's violent crime rate increasing? Women's violent crime commission rates have always been substantially lower than men. Ninety percent of homicides, assault, and robbery arrests are of men, although women, if committing a violent crime, are arrested at greater rates for these specific acts. Women have lower rates of commission of crimes of terrorism, kidnapping, rape, and other forms of sexual assault.

Stereotypes of women encourage the public to view violent women offenders as "bad." Moderate increases in the rate at which women commit assault, robbery, and homicide have been used to support the idea that women's changing gender roles are associated with becoming more masculine or that increased public integration of women promotes criminal opportunity and acts. For homicide, the gender gap in crime commission rates is unchanged (Schwartz, Steffensmeier, and Feldmeyer, 2009). This rate has remained stable during a period of decline in overall crime. Polluck (2002: 20) states: "Female offenders have been a class of people perceived as not wholly feminine, but definitely not masculine either." Instead, women who violate feminine gender roles by committing masculinized crime occupy a liminal or in-between status. Unfortunately, these women have been increasingly propelled into the criminal justice system.

A change in penal philosophy is an alternative explanation for increasing women's arrests for violent crime. Researchers refer to this as the policy change hypothesis. As women's roles change in relation to legal equality in a time of "War on Crime" and "War on Drugs," crime control policies have emphasized increased punishment and gender neutrality: treating women the same as men (Schwartz, Steffensmeier, and Feldmeyer, 2009). Legalistic policing has brought formal police involvement in previously informal matters such as intimate partner violence in the home and minor forms of assault. Victims and witnesses have become more willing to report women. As a result, an increase in arrest is policy driven rather than offender driven. This is demonstrated by government statistics.

The FBI Uniform Crime Reports (UCR) focus on arrests, while the National Crime Victimization Survey (NCVS) takes self-reports from a randomized large sample of the U.S. population. Because the public does not always report crime to the police, and the police do not always file incident reports, the trend is for the NCVS to report higher rates of victimization than the UCR. Since the women's movement and the development of more punitive attitudes toward crime, women's reported rates of violent crime have tended to increase in the UCR and to surpass the NCVS. The UCR reports indicate that an increasing number of women have been arrested for aggravated assault relative to men (Schwartz, Steffensmeier, and Feldmeyer, 2009). In the 1980s, women accounted for 12% of all UCR aggravated assault arrests, but this increased to 20% in the 2000s. The NCVS shows a stable rate of 12% for acts of aggravated assault committed by women in the 1960s through the 2000s. To a lesser extent, women's arrest for robbery has also increased. In the 1980s, both the UCR and the NCVS indicated rates of 8% for women's involvement in robbery. Women became 9% of those arrested for robbery in the 1990s and 10% in the 2000s, while the NCVS rate dropped to 6% in the 1990s and increased to 7% in the 2000s. Historically, rape has been a primarily male-perpetrated crime, and there has been little change in women's arrest rates. The UCR women-perpetrated rape rate has been stable at 1% and the NCVS reports 2–3% over time. Overall, Schwartz, Steffensmeier, and Feldmeyer (2009: 519) conclude that women are more likely to be arrested for assault and, to a lesser degree, robbery than in the past. This reflects crime control policy rather than an actual increase in the rate at which women commit this crime. They state that:

> For the most serious kinds of violent crime including homicide, rape, and robbery, *all* data sources show *female rates have not been rising and there has been very little, if any, change in the gender gap*. Notably, for the most reliably reported offense, homicide, female rates are smaller today than two decades ago and the gender gap has actually widened a bit. Only trends in assault differ by type of data (official versus unofficial data) and across stages in the criminal justice system (arrest to conviction to imprisonment). *Indeed, assault arrest trends are the driving force behind recent concerns about rising levels of female violence.* (Emphasis in original)

Another factor influencing women's arrest rate would be social change in women's roles. It follows that if a majority of women are in the labor force, the social context of crime commission will change. This does not necessarily mean that women have become masculinized, but that their integration into the public sphere changes the criminal opportunity structure for them. Compounding the issue, feminist backlash may impact the exercise of chivalry toward women. Police willing to overlook minor transgressions in the past may act with gender neutral or antifeminist sentiment in the present.

Why Are Certain Crimes More Likely to Be Committed by Men?

Certain common crimes are male specializations. For example, burglary is a highly gender-stratified crime from which most women are mostly excluded as it is connected to street life social networks. Mullins and Wright's (2003) qualitative interview research found that males committed initial burglaries with same-sex older friends, members of the family, or people they met on the street. In contrast, women stated they became involved through their boyfriends. As a women offender stated: "Okay, [on my first burglary] me and my boyfriend, my kid's father, we was together and he was way older than I was anyway. He was into breaking into houses and stuff so it was me, him and his brother." Certain women indicated that their boyfriends coerced them into committing burglary: "Well, it was one like, 'If you love me, you'll do it.' . . . He was saying "If you love me, you do it." . . . So I was really in love with him so that's how it got started" (Mullins and Wright, 2003: 820). Coercion of women into burglary participation could involve threats such as: "I had to go by his rules because I was living with him. He told me that if I wouldn't do it that he would do something to me. I guess drug me up or something" (Ibid.).

It is rare for women to be involved in the gender-segregated world of burglary. The motives for males include supporting a party lifestyle with drug use and paying for status items like jewelry (Mullins and Wright, 2003). One gender difference in motivation was that women would use a part of burglary proceeds to support their children. One women interviewee stated: "I needed money, cause I needed a roof over my head, food to eat and things for my baby . . . cause I needed diapers and I was broke and, you know, my hours had been cut and I didn't have the money to pay rent plus to get the baby what it needed. You know, it's gonna be cold soon, I need winter clothes for my kid, I need clothes" (Mullins and Wright, 2003: 821–822). Unlike this woman, men tended to use burglary money for themselves.

Women often took secondary and subservient roles in burglaries with men (Mullins and Wright, 2003). Females seldom joined in committing the crime and acted as lookouts or drivers and, occasionally, to unlock a door. These were apprentice roles for men but continuing roles for women. Women were seldom partners with men and had that status only in an all-female burglary crew. Mullins and Wright (2003) conclude that sexism reduced women's participation in burglary. Men saw them as weak and emotional and kept them in a secondary role. For women in league with men, severing the relationship was key to desistance from burglary.

Are Female Murderers Always "Mad or Bad"?

Female-precipitated homicide is subject to the most media attention. The idea that women, the "gentler sex," would kill denies the cultural association between the female gender and caring nurturance. Due to gender stereotyping, information about the social context and personality of women committing homicide is considered highly newsworthy. Feminist criminologists have examined the use of the "mad or bad" dichotomy in the explanation of these crimes and public attitudes toward harsh punishment. When a woman kills a child, her actions are often attributed to severe mental health issues—being "mad" or the overuse of discipline. This type of crime is referred to as expressive because the woman is perceived to emotionally act out her anger. Expressive homicide is connected to issues of intimacy, gender role–related stress, and other aspects of the social context. In contrast, instrumental murders are thought to provide a means to an end, such as collecting on life insurance for the deceased.

Neonaticide, the killing of a fetus during the first 24 hours of life, and infanticide, the murder of a baby, are both crimes committed predominantly by women. The statistics, however, seldom provide a separate categorical total for this crime, and public representation is predominantly through exposure to cases with a high media profile.

Typology of Female Homicide Offenders

Frankie Bailey and Donna Hale, criminologist authors of *Blood on Her Hands: Women Who Murder* (2004), have developed a typology for classifying the motivation of females who kill.

Infanticide

Biological and adoptive mothers who take the lives of their children for reasons other than instrumental profit are classified in a variety of ways (Bailey and Hale, 2004: 208). Mothers with

Munchausen by Proxy subject their children to medical procedures and kill them to garner attention. Some mothers kill because they cannot cope with child caretaking, such as crying. Others practice sex-selection killing because they believe the father had rejected the child for this reason, like the case of Paula Sims. Susan Smith and Diane Downs killed their children because they believed they were an obstacle to remarriage. Andrea Yates killed her children because of postpartum psychosis. Postpartum psychosis is a rare mental condition experienced by new mothers, marked by delusions, hallucinations, mood swings, and other psychological symptoms that weaken the woman's connection with reality. Postpartum depression is somewhat more common and less linked to infanticide and child homicide.

Black Widow

A female black widow spider mates and then kills and eats the male spider. Whether a onetime or a serial murderer, human black widows kill for profit (Bailey and Hale, 2004: 208). The prototype of this crime involves a woman who marries a man with assets: bank accounts, stock, property, etc. After killing a husband or boyfriend (who has signed over assets), the women has achieved a measure of financial security. The classic film *Double Indemnity* has this plot, and Jill Coit and Brenda Pavat are contemporary examples.

Fatal Attraction

Women who experience rejection from an intimate acquaintance or spouse/partner may lethally retaliate against the object of their affection or the person they feel has displaced the love object's feelings—such as the wife in the film *Fatal Attraction* (Bailey and Hale, 2004: 208–209). These women offenders believe that they have been used or that they have lost their attractiveness or social position when they lost the man. They are motivated by jealousy, frustration, and a desire for revenge. Famous cases include Jean Harris, Betty Broderick, and the "Long Island Lolita," Amy Fisher.

Team Killers

Excitement and/or obtaining money and valuables can set male and female or female teams on crime sprees (Bailey and Hale, 2004: 209). Such individuals may be psychopaths suffering from antisocial personality disorder and may display sexually sadistic tendencies. Women who have raped and killed young women include Karla Homolka, Myra Hindley, and Carol Bundy.

Caregivers/Nurses/Childcare Providers
Women who work in hospitals, nursing homes, and other caregiving jobs for the young, infirm, or elderly have committed homicide, often multiple times (Bailey and Hale, 2004: 209). The "angel of death" murders are an assertion of power and control, while serial killers may be perversely sexually stimulated by taking the life of another person (Graham and Wood case) or murdering for profit (Dorothea Puente). Activities related to caretaking, such as dealing with difficult patients, understaffed conditions, or simply wanting to stop a baby's crying (Christine Falling) can provoke some women to commit murder.

Femme Fatale
An erotically attractive woman, the "femme fatale" of mystery, convinces a man who is in love or sexually involved with her to kill (Bailey and Hale, 2004: 209). She manipulates the man, exercising power and control to convince him that he is the only one to help her. This type of murderess is the focus of such films as *Double Indemnity*, *The Postman Rings Twice*, and *Body Heat*. Real-life examples include Pamela Smart, Diane Zamora, and Marlene Olive.

Family Ties
Certain women offenders succeed in convincing family relations to commit murder on their behalf (Bailey and Hale, 2004: 209–210). This type of case often involves a mother manipulating her children, often a son. Sisters may encourage brothers to kill a target. In 1991, Toni Cato Riggs talked her brother Michael into murdering her husband, army specialist Anthony Riggs, when he returned from a tour of duty.

Battered Woman/Sexual Assault
This is an unusual category in which the woman can be considered a victim who acted in self-defense against an assailant (Bailey and Hale, 2004: 210). Often the means, such as using a gun on an unarmed man or dousing a bed with gasoline and lighting it, seems disproportionate to consider as a defense. The women who are charged with homicide have a history of experiencing verbal, emotional, sexual, and physical abuse from a spouse/

partner. The dominant character of the male abuser leads them to seek a situation in which the victim is defenseless so that the woman will not be physically overwhelmed and abused or killed. This type of killing was made famous by the film *The Burning Bed*.

Cult/Disciple

Cult members (Moriarty and Freiberger, 2000) and disciples (Dietz, 1986) follow a charismatic leader such as Charles Manson. The "Manson girls" included Lynette "Squeaky" Fromme, Susan Atkins, Leslie van Houten, and Patricia Krenwinkel (Bailey and Hale, 2004: 210). They were involved in the 1969 Tate/La Bianca murders. Lynette "Squeaky" Fromme was not convicted of taking part in the murders but received short jail sentences for trying to prevent Manson family members from testifying. She later attempted to assassinate President Gerald Ford in 1975 and was sentenced to life imprisonment but released on August 14, 2009.

Murder for Profit

Women who kill for financial return may seek to cash in on insurance policies or to obtain their victim's money, valuables, or property (Bailey and Hale, 2004: 211). Eva Coo, Ellen Boehm, and Dana Sue Gray have been convicted of homicides committed for profit.

Venus Flytrap

The Venus flytrap is a plant that lures insects into a leaf with sticky sweet syrup; the leaf then snaps shut on them and permits digestion. Similarly, a woman may bring an individual under their care or entice lovers, friends, or children into a homicidal situation because of physical attractiveness or nurturance (Bailey and Hale, 2004, 211). Examples of women in this category include Velma Barfield, Judias Buenoano, Audrey Marie Hilley, and Virginia McGinnis.

The murder of women by their spouse/partners does not have a clear motivational parallel in any women's homicide category. Meloy and Miller (2009) examined news coverage of the death of Laci Peterson and her unborn child—the reverse, but also sensationalized.

Are Girls Becoming More Violent?

Media constructions of violent girl delinquents make sensational news copy and generate reader interest (Chesney-Lind, 2004).

Research indicates that girl's *arrests* for assault have increased but that victim and self-reported data does *not* show an increase in assaultive behavior (Chesney-Lind, 2002; Steffensmeier, Schwartz, Zhong, and Ackerman, 2005). Schwartz and colleagues (2009) suggest that arrest records produced by the criminal justice system reflect the impact of crime control policies and not just the degree of violent behavior exhibited by girls. Policies that increase police intervention and preventative punishment can increase girl's arrest rate for minor types of violence that they have been historically more likely to commit.

The FBI's Uniform Crime Reports, based on information from more than 10,000 police agencies, is the most reliable source on arrests by sex and age. From 1995 to 2008, according to the FBI, girls' arrest rates for violent offenses fell by 32 percent, including declines of 27 percent for aggravated assault, 43 percent for robbery, and 63 percent for murder. Rates of murder by girls are at their lowest levels in at least 40 years. The National Crime Victimization Survey, a detailed annual survey of more than 40,000 Americans by the Department of Justice's Bureau of Justice Statistics, is considered the most reliable measure of crime because it includes offenses not reported to the police. From 1993 through 2007, the survey reported significant declines in rates of victimization of girls, including all violent crime (down 57 percent), serious and misdemeanor assaults (down 53 percent), robbery (down 83 percent), and sex offenses (down 67 percent). Public health agencies like the National Center for Health Statistics confirm huge declines in murder and violent assaults of girls. For example, as the number of females ages 10 to 19 increased by 3.4 million, murders of girls fell from 598 in 1990 to 376 in 2006. Rates of murders of and by adolescent girls are now at their lowest levels since 1968—48 percent below rates in 1990 and 45 percent lower than in 1975.The Bureau of Justice Statistics' Intimate Partner Violence in the U.S. survey, its annual Indicators of School Crime and Safety, the University of Michigan's Monitoring the Future survey, and the Centers for Disease Control's Youth Risk Behavior Surveillance all measure girls' violent offending and victimization. Virtually without exception, these surveys show major drops in fights and other violence, particularly relationship violence, involving girls over the last 15 to 20 years. These surveys also indicate that girls are no more likely to report being in fights, being threatened or injured with a weapon, or violently victimizing others today than in the first surveys in the 1970s. These striking improvements in girls' personal safety, including from rape and relationship violence, directly contradict recent news reports that girls suffer increasing danger from violence by their female and male peers alike.

There is only one measure that would in any way indicate that girls' violence has risen, and it is both dubious and outdated. FBI reports show assault arrests of girls under age 18 increased from 6,300 in 1981 to a peak of 16,800 in 1995, then dropped sharply, to 13,300 in 2008. So, at best, claims that girls' violence is rising apply to girls of 15 to 25 years ago, not today. Even by this measure, it is not girls who have become more violent faster—it is middle-aged men and women. Among women ages 35 to 54, FBI reports show, felony assault arrests rocketed from 7,100 in 1981 to 28,800 in 2008. Assault arrests among middle-aged men also more than doubled, reaching 100,500 in 2008. In Northampton, Massachusetts, domestic violence calls to police more than tripled in the last four years, to nearly 400 in 2009. Why, then, do we not see frenzied news reports on "Mean Middle-Agers"? What is more, Males and Chesney-Lind (2010) reported that the Department of Justice's Office of Juvenile Justice and Delinquency Prevention concluded that girls' supposed "violent crime increase" in the 1980s and 1990s resulted from new laws and policies mandating arrests for domestic violence and minor youth offenses "that in past years may have been classified as status offenses (e.g., incorrigibility)" but "can now result in an assault arrest." Thus, the Justice Department found, increased numbers of arrests "are not always related to actual increases in crime."

This mythical wave of girls' violence and meanness is, in the end, contradicted by reams of evidence from almost every available and reliable source. Yet news media and myriad experts, seemingly eager to sensationalize every "crisis" among young people, have aroused unwarranted worry in the public and policy arenas. The unfortunate result is more punitive treatment of girls, including arrests and incarceration for lesser offenses like minor assaults that were treated informally in the past, as well as alarmist calls for restrictions on their Internet use.

Fighting

Mylen Cruz was Filipina American, sixteen years old, and in detention for stabbing a boy at her school. [She states:] "I was in the office at my school, and this boy came up to me jus' to fuck with me. He was all 'I'ma get me some of this shit, man.' He touched my butt! He thought we gonna be kickin' it or some shit! We got into a violent fight. I did a violent act. I don't know. I was mad. I couldn't deal with my anger; I couldn't hold it. I'm not a killer, but I would be able to do it. I hoped he wouldn't die, but I didn't want to go home. I wasn't scared to come to juvy." (Schaffner, 2006: 57)

Mylen's physical aggression and sense of self-protection need to be interpreted in light of her social context. Schaffner (2006: 57–58) argues that girls' biographies should be taken into account in "determining their best interests—not as an excuse for physical assault." Mylen lived in a high-crime, inner-city environment. She did not want to go home because her environment was marked by family conflict and disruption that precipitated physical and sexual abuse. The Cruz family was often left homeless, including her little brother (Schaffner, 2006). Her mother was often unable to pay the rent, and they would get evicted. Mylen had been sexually molested by a boyfriend of her mother's and then took up with a guy from the street who abused her. Given this stressful life, Schaffner (2006: 58) considers: "The experience of abuse is gendered. For boys, abuse goes against what they are taught to expect from their position of superiority. Abuse of girls confirms their place in a gendered hierarchy. A distinct process needs to be enacted in order for girls to heal and to regain or achieve a sense of safety and psychological integrity. Thus gender deeply affects how childhood abuse is processed and how recovery occurs."

Prior sexual victimization may be associated with protective aggression. Many girls attending school have been physically and/or sexually abused. They are sexually degraded by neighborhood men, cousins, brothers, friends, and strangers. Their mother's boyfriends, stepfathers, or their own fathers have sexual relations with them. Girls' emotional response to sexual trauma has both unconscious and behavioral impact. Trauma includes intrusive thoughts and memories, losing trust in others, low self-esteem, depression, feelings of hopelessness and angry aggression, and difficulties in beginning intimate relationships. Dissociative behaviors, self-mutilation, using drugs and alcohol to self-medicate, eating disorders, acting violently, or even committing suicide may occur. Sexual abuse is associated with premature sexualization. Girls may seek paternal attention in romantic relationships with adult male predators located on street corners. Pregnancies may result, which result in abortion or unwanted children. A further consequence of this reactive behavior is being detained in a juvenile justice system that does not explore the life histories of girls and formally diagnose them. Schaffner (2006: 72) considers that definitions of community violence should be reconceptualized to include the impact of family violence.

In high-crime neighborhoods, girls try to appear and act feminine while avoiding being raped. Mylen was a sexual abuse victim who may have taken up with an adult man at age 12 to try to leave her conflictive home. Mylen felt negative about school and thought she should not have attended the day the stabbing occurred because: "I knew I was gonna go off on somebody" (Schaffner, 2006: 57). Inner-city schools are not a friendly environment for girls, who report "being hassled by guys" (Schaffner, 2006: 65). Although often unsuccessful, girls attempted to fight back. When they physically aggressed, they were labeled violent offenders by officials who did not "see" or witness the original sexual harassment or who viewed it as inconsequential. Girls in detention had fought back against sexual harassment—with no adult intervening. Yet sexual harassment was not a term used by girls—they used words like "gross" and "hassled." Schaffner (2006: 65) states: "whether it's the criminal version of sexual assault or the civil version of sexual harassment, school is a very violent place for girls." The degree of discipline maintained in inner-city schools does not match the standards of the past. Girls may be subject to verbal abuse and being grabbed and fondled sexually. To protect themselves, some girls carried pocketknives and pepper spray. Continuing, Laurie Schaffner advocates (2006: 67): "Zero tolerance for violence in school, if it is to exist at all, should reflect zero tolerance for the ways that girls experience violence at school —through gender harassment, sexual harassment, homophobia and misogyny." Sexual harassment in school can result in dropout and bootstrapping into the juvenile justice system. Furthermore, Schaffner (2006) found that many girls were in secure detention without committing a criminal offense because they had not attended school. Girls did not attend school because they were suspended for fighting in self-defense against male harassment.

The connection between family violence and physical and sexual abuse is an explanatory factor in girls' physical aggression and subsequent delinquency. Girls in secure detention came from homes in which they had witnessed or experienced being hit, beaten, and knifed or shot (Schaffner, 2006). Needless to say, their mothers were often victims of domestic violence and devalued as women. Schaffner (2006: 80) uses the term "empty families" to refer to unstable living situations in which fathers and stepfathers or boyfriends, mothers or girlfriends, and other relatives erratically disappeared and reappeared at intervals. This instability was due to health issues, family members' own involvement in the criminal justice system through incarceration, overwork or unemployment, divorce, homelessness mental illness, and substance dependency. Absence of family due to reversal of fortune and deaths in the family meant that girls lacked stable protection and guidance. As a result of family instability, some young girls became "parentified": the child did parenting work, taking care of their younger siblings and often their own parents. Another consequence of empty families is that many girls spent most of their childhood in out-of-home placements and then bonded with adult boyfriends in their adolescence (Schaffner, 2006). Backup grandparents, aunts, and other relatives were not there for them. Older men and women they befriended provided assistance with food, transportation, and housing. Often, whether parentified or raised outside their family, these girls suffered a lack of love. Claudia's case (Schaffner, 2006: 120) shows the outcome of empty families:

Claudia: I love to fight! I cracked my tooth in a fight when a guy hit me with a milk crate! I take my anger out when I am triste [sad].

Interviewer: What makes you sad?

Claudia: Well, let's see, uh, I always be fighting with other girls too. My grandmother died when I was twelve and I really miss her. My mom is on welfare, strung all out on dope, so I always stayed over with my gramma. *Mi* papa is not in the picture. I'm always mad at my mom too—she kicked me out one night when it was pouring down rain! I din't have nowhere to go so I just went around under the steps in back [grammatical mistakes in original interview].

The juvenile court system does not involve juries. In cooperation, judges, parents, prosecutors, social workers, and defenders adjudicate girls' cases. As a result, presentation of witnesses and evidence is informal. Psychological evaluation and family investigation may occur. Parents and probation officers may disagree about whether a juvenile is out of control. Certain courts utilize guardians (court-appointed special advocates, or CASAs) to testify about fact in the face of competing interests and interpretations. Juvenile courts may order fathers and mothers to attend parenting class. The subjects covered include adolescence, drug use, socially acceptable styles of punishment/discipline, and juvenile justice court terminology. The public is not allowed access, in order to protect the juvenile's privacy, and is unable to see into any injustice occurring in the system.

Laurie Schaffner (2006) views girls' aggression as a result of living in violent family and community environments. Unfortunately, this violates traditional female gender role expectations. Aggression has been viewed as a male behavior or spoken about neutrally, which implies that it is a male characteristic. The girls' violation of the gender expectation to be nonphysically aggressive led to their "criminalization as violent predators" after earlier criminalization of girls' sexual behavior. Correctional girls view girls who get into physical fights as "acting male." In the case of Claudia (above), a correctional worker stated:

> Claudia thinks she's one of the guys. She's not very lady-like, and that gets her into a lot of trouble. Her first response is to start jumpin' bad [being physically aggressive] but we're working on it. (Ibid.)

Girls are severely formally and informally sanctioned for being aggressive, undertaking physical assaults and using weapons. Their behavior is not understood as commonly related to childhood or adolescent trauma due to hardship, empty families, domestic violence, and child physical or sexual abuse. In general, when experts speak about "youth violence" or "community violence," they are referring to traditional patterns of male aggression. These terms are differentiated from family and domestic violence, child sexual abuse, sexual harassment and other forms of violence that target girls and women as victims. For these girls who fight, witnessing violence in the family and/or community has normalized it for them. They often say that they used it in self-defense. Schaffner (2006: 132–133) believes:

Defining community violence and domestic violence as exclusive can result in glossing over the situations girls face, witness and perpetuate in the natural flow of their everyday lives.... Girls who live in poverty and under-served neighborhoods may be in danger of being victim-ized whether in their apartments or on their way to the store, school, or work. The everyday harshness, anger, fear, and physical abuse, sexual taunting in the street and gendered inequities at home make all violence, in effect, community violence for girls.

The concern about girl-on-girl violence has spread to the problem of school bullying incidents. Every year has top news stories and, in 2010, it was the suicide of 15-year-old South Had-ley High School student Phoebe Prince after she was taunted and physically threatened by six teens, including four girls (Eick-holm and Zezima, 2010). Multiple felony indictments were brought in Massachusetts in relation to adolescent bullying per-ceived to have resulted in Prince's suicide and the harassment of an 11-year-old student from another school. The charges included statutory rape, violation of civil rights including bodily injury, stalking, harassment, and disturbance of a school assembly. As of 2010, 41 states have passed anti-bullying laws of varying severity, and Massachusetts was planning legislation. Bullying in and of itself is not established as a new crime, but existing criminal law will be defined in relation to it.

Males and Chesney-Lind (2010) refer to the South Hadley incident as criminal but present the view that the incident does not validate that there is an "epidemic of mean girls." They state: "But this panic is a hoax. We have examined every major index of crime on which the authorities rely. None show a recent increase in girls' violence; in fact, every reliable measure shows that vio-lence by girls has been plummeting for years. Major offenses like murder and robbery by girls are at their lowest levels in four dec-ades. Fights, weapons possession, assaults and violent injuries by and toward girls have been plunging for at least a decade."

Women's Drug Offending

The chief reason that the number of imprisoned women has increased in the United States is the War on Drugs and related federal and state mandatory minimum sentencing guidelines

(Merolla, 2008). Subtitle B of the Omnibus Anti-Drug Abuse Act of 1986, the Drug Possession Penalty Act, reinstated and or created mandatory minimum federal sentencing for simple possession of drugs. A number of states have enacted three-strikes laws, making a third arrest the key to lengthy prison terms. These laws are preceded in certain states by "habitual offender laws" but were dramatically different in the degree that they did not differentiate between different types of crime, such as violent or nonviolent. From 1993 to 2004, 26 states and the federal government passed three-strikes laws (National Conference of State Legislatures E-Bulletin, 2010). The most sweeping law was "Three Strikes and You're Out," passed by California voters in 1994. The current law establishes that offenders be given three times the prison time for the major offense, 25 years or the term for the offense plus any enhancements; length of prison time being based on the longer duration of the three. As a result, California's prison capacity is greatly exceeded by those incarcerated.

In the 24 states that passed three-strikes laws in the 1990s, many changes have been made, such as eliminating life-without-parole penalties and establishing ranges of penalties. Many women, however, are jailed or imprisoned to incapacitate them. The basic idea of the approach is that if they have broken the law three times, they are not capable of rehabilitation and should simply be kept incarcerated to reduce the crime rate. An entire culture of three-strikes news stories has developed in which a woman or man is given as an example of a nonviolent offender who did not commit costly crimes but is imprisoned for decades for repeat nonviolent offenses. For many women drug users, crimes associated with substance use or obtaining money for an addiction is the reason for a third-strike sentence. This penal approach to drug control is a part of the movement toward incapacitation of criminals to remove them from public life. Traditional rehabilitation such as substance abuse treatment is increasingly unavailable to women in prison, and they may return to public life without a resolution of the problems that led them to use drugs. In order to understand why women drug users recidivate after prison, it is necessary to understand that addiction is a disease that develops with repeated use in biologically susceptible individuals. If a person with a serious illness such as tuberculosis or diabetes has no real access to quality medical care, we would never expect that person to recover. Rather, the illness would progressively worsen. Similarly, if we incarcerate an active addict and do not empower their ability to recover through access to health care, Narcotics Anonymous and or Alcoholics Anonymous, and counseling, the reality is that society has a "dry" addict with all the complications of addiction still active. Forced detoxification through a long prison sentence will not resolve the craving associated with biological addiction or the psychological issues often faced by women, such as prior history of sexual victimization without treatment.

Arguably, women of all race and ethnicities and social class levels are exposed to alcohol and illegal drugs. In 2007, Paris Hilton, celebrity and socialite, was arrested for driving under the influence with a blood alcohol level of 0.08% and pleaded no contest to a reckless driving charge. Her license was suspended and she was placed on probation, violating it by driving not once but twice, and failing to attend a court-ordered alcohol program. In 2008, Hilton had her probation revoked and was given a 45-day jail term. Her case was controversial, as some believed that she was more severely penalized because she was a celebrity. Nevertheless, her imprisonment sent a message about drunk driving through the media. Unfortunately, the punishment was not completely effective; Hilton was subsequently arrested for suspicion of possession of cocaine and, if found in violation of new terms of probation, will need to serve a one-year jail term. Although Paris Hilton was penalized, it is important to recognize that many non-Hispanic White drug offenders are placed on probation to receive substance abuse treatment and bypassing incarceration. If the same programming were applied to minority women, their rate of incarceration would certainly decrease.

Social Strain and Drug-Related Nonviolent Crime

Social strain theory predicts that life stressors will increase probability of women's crime commission. Adult women drug offenders reported being stressed by HIV infection, being addicted, losing custody of a child, or the arrest of their child for murder (Slocum, Simpson, and Smith, 2005). When women experience heightened social strain from various causes, they are more likely to use drugs and commit nonviolent crimes. This link between drug use and nonviolent crime, such as drug dealing, prostitution, and theft, is due to the need to support the habit. Drug use is related to life stressors but also allows coping, although drug use itself can become a stressor. In contrast, negative life events and violent victimization are associated with violent criminal activity. For example, battered women are more likely to resort to violence in response.

A major pathway to drug addiction and related prostitution is child corruption or abuse. Dana D. DeHart (2008: 1376) identified the following drug use pathways in a qualitative study of incarcerated women:

- Guardian pimps to dealers for drugs → prostitution, addiction
- Guardian introduces to drugs → addiction
- Household abuse or household addiction → drugs to numb → addiction
- Household abuse → run away → trade sex → addiction, prostitution
- Statutory rapist as "sugar daddy" → trade sex → prostitution, addiction

Home environment child maltreatment has been viewed as "missocializing," or "corrupting." DeHart (2008: 1365) gives the following example of an incarcerated woman's case history in which drug use and sexual victimization are linked: "Chantelle left home because of the drug use—her mom and dad high all the time, men coming in and out of the house. They'd go straight to Chantelle's room. Chantelle's parents would take money, the keys to a car, whatever. Chantelle laid there and took it. It started as fondling, but then there was also intercourse. It happened more times than she can count—whenever anyone came by with money, every weekend and sometimes during the week."

Child Maltreatment: Sexual Abuse

Female sexual offending has been an underrecognized and researched crime. The traditional gender role script emphasizes that women are nurturing, nonviolent, and nonsexual (Becker, Hall and Stinson, 2001). Various research studies have reported a prevalence of 1–2% female precipitated child sexual abuse (Johansson-Love and Fremouw, 2006: 13). Women commit 20%

of sexual abuse of boys and 5 percent of abuse of girls. Women sex offenders tend to be in their 20s and 30s, and a majority are white (Vandiver, 2006). Victims are relatives and acquaintances—rarely strangers. Women who sexually abuse children and teens may offend alone or act in concert with a male co-perpetrator (Johansson-Love and Fremouw, 2006: 24–25). The preferred gender and typical relationship to victims is not known because of limited research. They may engage in serious forms of sexual abuse such as penetration. Mathews, Matthews, and Speltz (1989) formulated an initial typology of female sex offenders. *"Teacher/lovers"* sought a sexual relationship with a minor based on love or a desire to educate the victim. They saw their behavior as positive and did not understand why it was considered a crime. They had a history of emotional and verbal abuse but did not experience sexual victimization and abuse until later in life, when they developed a preference for adolescent males who were perceived as less threatening. These women act alone. *"Predisposed"* women sex offenders were sexually abused as children, initiated abuse as adults and act alone. Opportunity-based offending in which the sex of available victim did not matter occurred. *"Male-coerced"* women had histories of sexual abuse and abusive relationships with men. Traditional in their gender role expectations, they were passive and persuaded to co-offend by men. A motive was fear of abandonment. They might develop into self-initiating offenders. The *"exploration/exploitation"* category involved young women in baby-sitting situations without prior sexual experience, while *"severely psychologically disturbed"* women had mental health problems. Nathan and Ward (2002) further extended this typology with another category: *"male accompanied: rejected/revengeful."* These women were jealous, enraged, and sought revenge through sexual offending.

Research to develop typologies and offender patterns for women who are sexual offenders has been problematic because of small sample size. Vandiver (2006) contrasted solo and co-offenders. She found that solo offenders were more likely to have female victims, while co-offenders most often acted against male victims. Co-offending women may have been prompted or coerced by an abusive male who is predatory. The woman may be motivated by fear or may be trying to please the male perpetrator. Co-offenders are also more likely to abuse relatives while solo offenders chose unrelated victims. It is possible that male offenders seek out women with children to gain access to victims.

Female sexual offenders are more likely than male sex offenders to have experienced childhood sexual victimization (Johansson-Love and Fremouw, 2006: 24). Mental health issues are common and include depression, anxiety, disassociation, and post-traumatic stress disorder (PTSD). These women are also more likely to abuse alcohol and drugs.

Criminalization of Drug Use by Pregnant Women

Although it seems natural for the acts that are against the law in our society to be criminalized, there is inter-societal variation in what is considered criminal activity. Abortion is legal in the United States because a woman is considered to have the right to control the workings of her own body. In contrast, a fetus, an unborn embryo, is not legally considered to have the status of a person. Despite legal precedence for considering a woman's decisions and life to have priority over carrying a fetus, efforts have been made to criminalize use of illegal drugs during pregnancy, but the verdict is not yet in on the constitutionality of these laws.

Is Sex Work/Prostitution a Victimless Crime?

Globally, many men and women are involved in the sex trade. "Sex work" is considered a neutral term describing a range of activities for payment, which may or not involve intercourse. "Prostitution" is a negative term that characterizes such activities as paying for vaginal sex as immoral. It is cliché, poor scholarship, and offensive to many women to refer to prostitution as the "oldest profession." Although prostitution has a history dating to thousands of years and the earliest agricultural civilizations, the simple subsistence societies preceding more evolved ones lack contemporary research and historical or archaeological evidence for such activities. Indeed, small-scale simple subsistence societies still extent, such as hunters and gatherers, lack such a social form. Prostitution developed in patriarchal (male-dominated) social structures.

Prostitution removes a gendered and intimate behavior, sexual relations, into the social context of the street and/or crime. The social construction of prostitution as a victimless crime, which assumes that all such acts are carried out in independence and freedom, is highly problematic. To understand the varied ways in which advocacy and prohibitionist groups think about the issue, it is necessary to view paying for sexualized activity on a continuum ranging from highly paid independent women working alone to socially coerced women trafficked into prostitution and held as slaves. In between, we find women and girls who are technically "free" citizens but coerced by pimps, in the throes of drug addiction, or engaging in underage "survival sex" as runaways lacking social support. It is a relatively better-off group of women who would characterize themselves as sex workers. Nevertheless, even women who work as escorts risk violence and death (Farley, 2006).

Farley (2006: 103) characterizes prostitution as a "gendered survival strategy characterized by the assumption of unreasonable risks by the person in it." Prostitutes work under varied legal conditions: (1) decriminalized; (2) legal and zoned; and (3) illegal. Legal prostitution is taxed by the nation-state, which provides a framework of regulatory law. Decriminalization removes prostitution from coverage of law. An example of law is the health check. It is important to realize that the health check is for the women, not the consumer—who may have a sexually transmitted disease and communicate it to her (Farley, 2006).

Spatial location also varies between the street, brothels, massage parlors, strip clubs, and escort/hotel or at home. Typically, the more exposed the location, the greater the risk of arrest and danger that the woman will be assaulted. Indeed, both the prostitute's pimps and customers may assert power and control over them in the same manner as spouse/partner violence (Farley, 2006; Hodgson and Stark, 2003). Coercive behaviors that prostitutes face include:

- Verbal and other psychological abuse
- Minimization and denial of abuse
- Economic exploitation
- Social isolation
- Threat of physical violence
- Physical violence
- Sexual assault and torture
- Captivity through physical confinement and/or addiction

Murder is a possible outcome faced by prostitutes (Potterat et al., 2004). Both sexual assault and prostitution itself is psychologically traumatic for women (Farley, 2006). Dissociation is a process of psychological defense in which humans mentally separate themselves from a stressful life situation through avoiding thinking about it. Dissociation is common among prostitutes (Ross et al., 2003) and in people under-going torture. It is considered to facilitate survival. Prostitution is associated with the development of post-traumatic stress disorder (PTSD). PTSD symptoms include:

- Anxiety
- Depression
- Insomnia
- Emotional numbness
- Flashbacks
- Hypervigilence

A research conducted in nine countries found that 68% of prostitutes had post-traumatic stress symptoms (Farley et al., 2003). The inverse of dissociation occurs when clients purchase sex from someone who is objectified and do not relate to them as a person with needs and a personality. A woman prostitute related that: "Every day I was witness to the worst of men. Their carelessness and grand entitlement. The way they can so profoundly disconnect from what it is they're having sex with. . . . There was a system in place that was older and stronger than I could begin to imagine. Who was I? I was just a girl. What was I going to do about it. If I had any power I would make it so that nobody was ever bought or sold or rented." (Tea and McCubbin, 2004).

Family violence is known to contribute to intergenerational intimate partner abuse (Farley et al. 2003). Child abuse and neglect, especially sexual abuse, is evident in the life history of many women prostitutes. Yet prostitution more frequently results in policing of women than men. Outing prominent personalities, such as Elliot Spitzer, former governor of New York is done to hurt personal reputation. Spitzer patronized an "escort service," which charged $5,000 a night. As New York State attorney general, he had brought cases against prostitution and sex trafficking, which made his behavior hypocritical. Admitting to long-term patronage of prostitutes, he claimed that he suffered from a "sex addiction." Many men who engage in illicit sex view themselves as moral and law abiding, making excuses for their behavior.

Prostitution in the United States has involved interstate trafficking of women and children. The Internet has been a major tool for making connections between customers and trafficked women and girls. Craigslist is the world's largest Internet advertising site. Brad Stone (2010), a *New York Times* reporter, stated: "Craigslist, one of the most popular Web sites in the United States, is on track to increase its revenue 22 percent this year, largely from its controversial sex advertisements." These ads, which included escort services, massage, and other solicitations related to prostitution were expected to bring in 36 million (Ibid.). The fees were $10 for the first time an ad was run and $5 thereafter. To generate this degree of profit, a sizable volume was necessary. Since 2008, Chicago had estimated postings of over 200,000 ads. Of great concern was that photos of children available for sexual services were posted on the site. The Coalition Against Trafficking in Women (CATW) and Prostitution Research and Education (PRE) (2010) provided the following case information:

> My first introduction to prostitution was arranged through Craigslist. I answered an ad for online modeling which turned out to be an agency recruiting for "escorts." Escort is a word they use instead of prostitute. First model, then escort and eventually prostitute. After I was eased into prostitution, many of the pimps, massage parlor owners and girls themselves would use Craigslist to post ads for prostitution. They used words like "sensual massage" and "full body massage" to attract johns. I was a prostitute for much of my young life and would say Craigslist is now one of the most effective ways to sell your body on the Internet. It's free and the word is out that if you want to buy sex, you can find it on Craig's List. The sad part is that not everybody knows the dirty secret about Craigslist, so if somebody's little girl wanted to be a legitimate model she could easily by lured into a trap. I fear for the vulnerable, the naive. A young person can easily be lured into prostitution by online pimps like Craig.
> —Nekome, a Bay Area survivor of prostitution, July 2010

Although not the only website with erotic services ads, attention was drawn to Craigslist by the murder of Julia Brisman, aged

26, and the armed robbery and assault of another woman. Both had advertised massage services on Craigslist (Goodnough, 2009). Philip Markoff, aged 23, a second-year student at Boston Medical School, was indicted. Forensic evidence included Internet communications. A unique computer IP address led police to Markoff's apartment.

Illinois sheriff Thomas J. Dart sued Craigslist for running erotic services ads in the Chicago area and asked for $100,000 in policing cost reimbursement (Associated Press, 2009). He said: "Missing children, runaways, abused women and women trafficked in from foreign countries are routinely forced to have sex with strangers because they're being pimped on Craigslist." In October 2009, the Federal Court dismissed the case in favor of Craigslist, stating, "[i]ntermediaries are not culpable for 'aiding and abetting' their customers who misuse their service to commit unlawful acts" (Kunze, 2010). Subsequently, members of the Gambino Mafia crime family were charged with running an interstate sex trafficking ring for prostitution in New York and New Jersey (Weiser, 2010). They used Craigslist to advertise, delivered prostitutes, and kept 50% of their fees. All of the women were under 20, and one was 15 years old—an age for statutory rape charges. Anti-sex trafficking advocates generated controversy over Craigslist sex ads, and mounting law enforcement information from 39 states led to pressure to end adult services ads (Reuters, 2010). During Labor Day weekend, 2010, Craigslist responded by blocking adult services ads with the label "censored" (Miller, 2010a). This was viewed as an effort to invoke public opinion regarding free speech. The federal Communications Decency Act does not make Web sites liable for posted content by users. Seventeen state attorneys had asked for closure of the adult services section along with advocacy organizations protesting sex trafficking and prostitution. The website had sought to comply by manual screening of sex ads and discussion with advocates. By September 15, 2010, Craigslist had closed the section (Miller, 2010b).

The United States is a leading destination for trafficked women and children, and there are interstate cases in which children have been "sold" as sexual slaves. Shaniya Nicole Davis, a five-year-old girl, was alleged by North Carolina police to have been "knowingly provided [by her mother] . . . with the intent that she be held in sexual servitude" (Sax, 2009). Shaniya's mother was arrested because she "permitted an act of prostitution" (Ibid.). Domestic sex trafficking is different from other sex crimes against children because it is a financial transaction. It can involve drugs, providing money, or canceling a debt. Robin Sax (2009) indicates that "We need to get the word out that human trafficking for sex is a problem not just in Thailand or Cambodia but right here at home." Although women's and girls' advocates are organizing to further combat trafficking, legal action is still formative. New York passed the Safe Harbor for Exploited Youth Act in 2008, which requires that prostituted minors be treated as victims rather than criminals. It remains for other states to take further action.

What Is the Impact of Increasing Women's Imprisonment?

Tough-on-crime policies have led to an era of mass incarceration. Major issues for women prisoners include a prior history of physical and sexual abuse, drug dependency or abuse, and mental health problems. The prison system has moved away from the objectives of rehabilitation and treatment toward simple incapacitation and "hard time." As the United States dramatically reduced the social safety net for families of marginal income, investment in prisons that function like storage facilities greatly increased. Social observers argue that it is more expensive to confine people for major portions of their lives than to treat them.

Since the War on Drugs, women's imprisonment rates have steadily climbed (Belknap, Bloom, and Chesney-Lynd, 2007; Chesney-Lynd, 2004). In 1981, 26% of women served time for drug-related offenses. By the end of the 1990s, the Bureau of Justice (1999) reported that this had increased to 1 in 3 women and the increase has continued. When the prisoner population of local jails is added to the state and federal total, 1 in every 134 U.S. residents was in custody at midyear, 2009 (Bureau of Justice Statistics, 2010: 2). This rate of imprisonment reflects racial disparity. Black non-Hispanic males were incarcerated at six times the rate of non-Hispanic white males, 4,749 per 100,000 U.S. residents as compared to 708 per 100,000. Hispanic males were imprisoned at a rate of 1,822 per 100,000 U.S. residents. This racial disparity is paralleled in the rate of women's incarceration: 1 in 300 African American females was imprisoned, as were 1 of every 704 Hispanic females. In 2009, white women were a majority of those imprisoned: 92,100. In addition, 64,800 incarcerated women are black and 32,300 are Hispanic.

Two-thirds of women in state prison committed nonviolent offenses. In 2006, 28.9% of imprisoned women committed property crimes and 27.5% committed drug-related offenses (Bureau of Justice Statistics, 2008). Women's advocates use these figures to argue that women should be placed in correctional alternatives. Because of mandatory minimum sentencing and the War on Drugs, drug offenses and economic crimes related to support of drug use and/or family are considered to drive women's imprisonment trends. In 1997, 62.4% of women state prisoners reported drug use in the month before their offense, dropping slightly to 59.3% in 2004 (Mumola and Karberg, 2006: 3). Approximately 37% of women in federal prisons reported drug use in the prior month in 1997, increasing to 47.6% in 2004. A new trend tells us that over the past 15 years, methamphetamine use has increased in the United States. In 2004, female inmates in state (17%) or federal prison (15%) were more likely than male prisoners (10%) to report using methamphetamines in the month prior to committing an offense. Meth arrests are impacting on racial trends in imprisonment as white inmates (29%) are more likely than black (1%) or Hispanic (5%) inmates to report meth use.

Sixty percent of women state inmates and 43% of federally imprisoned women were classified as meeting DSM-IV criteria (American Psychiatric Association, 1994) for drug abuse or dependence (Mumola and Karberg, 2006: 7). Inmates who are dependent on or abuse drugs are more likely to report having three or more prior prison sentences. This category of prisoner is more likely to report a personal history of parental substance abuse, physical or sexual victimization, parental incarceration, unemployment, and homelessness.

Increasing incarceration of women is occurring despite a decline in crime commission that began in the 1990s and continued to the present. In 2009 at midyear, women were 6.7% of all U.S. prisoners (Bureau of Justice Statistics, 2010). In 2009, about 1 of every 198 U.S. residents was held in state or federal prison with a sentence of one year or more (Bureau of Justice Statistics, 2010: 2). The overall rate was 524 imprisoned per 100,000 Americans. Men were 14 times more likely to be imprisoned than women. There were 958 males imprisoned per 100,000 and 68 women imprisoned per 100,000 U.S. residents (Ibid.). This reflects the gender gap in criminal offending. Increasingly, race and social class intersect with gender to predict the social characteristics of incarcerated women. Racial-ethnic women (African American,

Native American), lower socioeconomic status, and single women are more likely to be arrested and sentenced and to serve time in jails or prison.

Mental Health

In 2005, over half of all inmates in state or federal prisons and jails met criteria for classification with a mental health problem (James and Glaze, 2006: 4). Women prisoners had even higher rates: state prison (71.3%), federal prison (61.2%), and local jails (75.4%). Twenty-three percent of women in state prisons or local jails, as compared to only 8% of male prisoners, stated that they had been diagnosed by a mental health professional. Nine percent had stayed overnight for mental health treatment. Women inmates used medication (39% of state inmates; 30% of jail inmates) at more than twice the rate of men (16% of state inmates; 12% of jail inmates). Thirty-two percent of women in state prison and 23% in jail had received therapy.

Co-Occurring Disorders

When an individual is diagnosed with both a mental disorder and substance dependence or abuse, they are considered to have a co-occurring disorder. This is also called "dual diagnosis." The National Survey on Drug Use and Health (2004) reported that in 2002, nearly two million women had co-occurring disorders. Most frequent mental disorders that were dually diagnosed were post-traumatic stress disorder (PTSD), depression, anxiety, and eating disorders. Given this high incidence of dual diagnosis among women in the general population, it is of great interest that Doris J. James and Lauren E. Glaze (2006: 10) found: "Three quarters of female inmates in state prisons who had a mental health problem met criteria for substance dependence or abuse." Approximately 42% reported a problem with alcohol and 65.5% had a drug-related issue. The relationships between female inmates' mental health problems and other indicators were as follows:

- Current or past violent offenses (40%)
- Used cocaine or crack in the month before arrest (34%)
- Used methamphetamines in month before arrest (17%)
- Homeless in the year before arrest (17%)
- Three or more prior sentences to probation or incarceration (36%)

- Past physical or sexual abuse (68%)
- Parental abuse of alcohol or drugs (47%)
- Physical or verbal assault charge since admission (17%)
- Injured in a fight since admission (10.3%)

Depression

Women offenders report depression at a higher rate (Thompson, 2008). Contact with the criminal justice system (arrest, incarceration, probation, parole) is a cause of depression. Depressed women are more likely to commit the crime of assault. Individuals who self-medicate for depression are less likely to commit crimes than those who do not. Both drug and depression treatments, including use of antidepressants, appear to increase women's offending with the exception of among older individuals (Thompson, 2008). Contact with the criminal justice system is associated with women's illegal drug use. Melissa Thompson (2008) suggests that a "one-size-fits-all" approach to treatment does not help men or women and that gender-responsive treatment is needed. Clemens Bartollas (Von Wormer and Bartollas, 2010: 100) states: "Mental disorders are biological in their origins, genetically and constitutionally." Serious mental illnesses are thought to be caused by abnormality of brain chemistry and increasingly treatable with newly developed pharmaceutical drugs.

Funds for the wave of imprisonment have largely gone to building and staffing prisons, not taking care of the prisoners. Comfortable with the idea of incapacitating criminals, the public has lost sight of the conditions women prisoners face. Rates of communicable diseases such as HIV/AIDS, tuberculosis, and viral hepatitis C (HCV) infection are much higher among women in prison (Springer, 2010: 13). Nijhawan, Salloway, Nunn, Poshkus, and Clarke (2010) found that 40% of women prisoners surveyed in a 70% survey of an inmate population reported that they tested positive for viral hepatitis C—a rate 20% higher than the nonprison population.

Women are 7% of the U.S. prison population and have a higher prevalence of HIV and sexually transmitted diseases (STDs) than male prisoners (Altice, Marinovich, Khoshnood, Springer, and Selwyn, 2005; Springer, 2010). The Centers for Disease Control (2006) reported that heterosexual contact is the most common means of HIV transmission to women. Many of the women who are imprisoned for drug-related crimes and prostitution have engaged in risky behavior such as sharing needles and unprotected sexual intercourse, which exposed them to HIV and STDs. Prisoners have high rates of gonorrhea, syphilis, and *Chlamydia* infection. Cervical cancer, which can result from exposure to human papilloma virus (HPV), occurs more frequently in imprisoned women (Proca, Rofagha, and Keyhani-Rofagha, 2006). Research indicates that women in prison are undertested with Pap smears and that, among those who receive the test, 40% are abnormal, six times the rate of the general population (Nijhawan, Salloway, Nunn, Poshkus, and Clarke, 2010). Springer (2010: 13) states: "Routine preventive age-appropriate cancer screening should be offered to all inmates in order to detect and treat cancers earlier to prevent unnecessary deaths."

Failure to carry out custodial medical treatment for women in prison and post-release creates the risk of spread of disease to communities. Upon release, prisoners often do not continue their antiretroviral prescriptions and develop higher HIV-1 viral concentrations in their bodies and are more infectious in contact with non-infected individuals. When women again share needles or engage in sex without protection, they are more likely to transmit blood-borne disease such as HIV and viral hepatitis C (Baillargeon, Giordano, Rich, et al., 2009; Springer, 2010; Springer, Pesanti, Hodges, Macura, Doros, and Altice, 2004; Stephenson, Wohl, Golin, Tien, Stewart, and Kaplan, 2005). Springer (2010: 13) believes: "All correctional facilities should offer mandatory HIV testing as recommended by the CDC in 2006 and counseling to prevent future acquisition and transfer of STDs within the community. Given the revolving door of prison, better linkages to care for diagnosed medical and psychiatric conditions need to be developed to prevent the loss of any potential benefit acquired during the incarceration period." In this era of for-profit and fiscally restricted federal and state prisons, women's health care is an issue only for practitioners and activists. The score of what is needed would greatly increase the cost of women's imprisonment. Sandra A. Springer, MD, of the Yale Aids Program indicates that:

> [U]pon incarceration, important screening and prevention services should be offered universally to all prisoners, including immediate STD screening, including HIV and HCV testing; vaccination against hepatitis A and B; cervical cancer screening with Pap smears; breast cancer screening with mammograms; and offering not only treatment of nicotine dependency but also pharmacotherapies

for drug and alcohol abuse and dependency. Such all encompassing preventive testing and treatment programs in correctional settings linked with continuity of care clinics in upon release would likely not only decrease the morbidity and mortality of disease among released prisoners but also potentially decrease transmission of STDs and other communicable diseases to noninfected persons within the community.

A major issue in women's prison treatment is the shackling of women immediately before and during birth. Shackling refers to the use of restraints that can include placing a chain around a woman's waist and cuffing her hands to it or chaining an ankle to a hospital bed. Two factors make shackling a dangerous practice: (1) a woman needs freedom of movement to position herself in labor; and (2) complications may make it necessary to rapidly move the woman, and time spent in unshackling her creates a delay. Amnesty International (1999) first brought national attention to this issue and provided the story of how "Maria Jones" gave birth as a Cook County, Illinois, inmate:

> The doctor came and said that yes, this baby is coming right now, and started to prepare the bed for delivery. Because I was shackled to the bed, they couldn't remove the lower part of the bed for the delivery, and they couldn't put my feet in the stirrups. My feet were still shackled together, and I couldn't get my legs apart. The doctor called for the officer, but the officer had gone down the hall. No one else could unlock the shackles, and my baby was coming but I couldn't open my legs . . . Finally the officer came and unlocked the shackles from my ankles. My baby was born then. I stayed in the delivery room with my baby for a little while, but then the officer put the leg shackles and handcuffs back on me and I was taken out of the delivery room.

In 2008, the Federal Bureau of Prisons changed its policy of shackling women during birth except in extreme circumstances (ACLU, 2008). By 2010, seven states had passed laws discouraging the practice of shackling of pregnant women during birth: California, Colorado, Illinois, New Mexico, New York, Pennsylvania, Texas, and Vermont. The American Medical Association voted to ban the shackling of pregnant woman prisoners. Walker (2010) reported: "The resolution refers to the practice as 'barbaric' and 'medically hazardous' and calls for the AMA to support language that no restraints of any kind should be used on an inmate who is in labor, delivering her baby, or during recuperation unless there is a 'compelling' reason to believe she poses serious harm to herself or others, is a flight risk, and 'cannot be reasonable constrained by other means.'" In 2011, Hawaii and Rhode Island legally banned pregnant women's shackling during birth (ACLU, 2011). Other states are receiving requests for legislation from activists, including feminist lawyers. This issue demonstrates that proactive change can occur for women prisoners.

How Does Women's Imprisonment Affect Children?

Ninety percent of men entering prison indicate their children reside with the mother. Only 28% of women report that their children reside with the father. Fifty-three percent live with a grandparent or other relative, and 10% are placed in foster care (Mumola, 2000). Candace Kruttschnitt (2010: 35) found that instability results from shifting children among relatives and foster homes. She reports that a woman prisoner stated: "My daughter is having problems because I am not home with her, you know? And sometimes they treat her good where she lives, and sometimes they don't, you know? She lives with my cousin. . . . they start messing with her and that makes her sad" (Ibid.).

Parental incarceration increases the risk of school failure, delinquency, and drug abuse by children (Ibid.). Kruttschnitt (2010) suggests that losing access to a mother is harder on children because they are often primary caretakers. Furthermore, state prisons are often located at a distance and may lose contact with children except by phone or mail. Few prisons provide programs for mothers to bond with children after giving birth to children or a means for women to raise infant or preschool children.

After the passage of the 1996 Welfare Reform Act, Aid to Families with Dependent Children (AFDC) became Temporary Assistance to Needy Families (TANF). Forty-two states modified their welfare laws to exclude women with drug felonies (Kruttschnitt, 2010). Because drug-addicted women often recidivate after imprisonment, 20% of mothers with children in state prison reported lacking housing before their most recent term.

Clearly, a decline in eligibility for such federal safety net benefits contributes to women's recidivism and, through the impact on their children, community social problems—including crime, unemployment and delinquency.

Did Women's Equality Decrease the Gender Ratio of Crime?

At the turn of the 20th century, a biological explanation of criminality by Cesare Lombroso and W. Ferrero (1895) introduced the idea that women criminals were masculinized. He believed that female offenders were atavistic throwbacks to an earlier stage of evolution. Biologically, he believed they displayed masculine characteristics such as increased body hair and considered that they lacked maternal instinct. Lombroso's view of 19th-century women was openly sexist as he saw them as weak and passive. Although Lombroso's ideas are dated, vestiges influence the Liberation hypothesis, which predicts an increase in women's offending.

The Liberation hypothesis proposed by Freda Adler (1975) predicted that the women's movement would increase women's educational and employment opportunities and impact on their crime rate. Entrance into the previously male-dominated workplace would encourage women to develop male traits: aggressiveness, assertiveness, and risk-taking. Naffine (1996) criticized Adler for assuming that male traits were the societal standard for women to be compared to and measured by. By seeking to become like men, female traits were devalued, and women were marginalized as a gendered group (Cain, 1990). Yet, predictions that the women's movement might equalize women's offending do not explain continuity in women's significantly lower likelihood of arrest and crime commission patterns.

A major question addressed by researchers is: how much has women's economic status changed, and how does that impact their crime rate? The "economic marginalization thesis" predicts that women's offending will increase when their economic well-being decreases (Heimer, 2000). In short, poverty is a predictor of crime. In the United States, women are more likely to live in poverty than men, which is conceptualized as the "feminization of poverty" (Heimer, Wittrock and Unal, 2006, 121). Mother-only or female heads of households with children, the relative high school graduation rates of women and men, the proportion of women relative to men working in the service sector, and the relative unemployment rates of men and women are all predictors of economic marginalization of women and criminal propensity. In sum, to the degree that women experience increased economic hardship relative to men, their rate of offending will increase.

Heimer, Wittrock, and Unal (2006) found that both violent and property crime rates fluctuate in relation to women's degree of economic marginalization relative to men. They indicate that women's violent offending rates are associated with certain measures of poverty. Women's rate of aggravated assault fluctuates in relation to level of unemployment, although the rate at which women graduate from high school moderates this factor. Robbery increases when women-headed household families are an increasing proportion of population. Similarly, burglary and larceny increase when women's unemployment rates increase, reducing the gender gap in rates of arrest. Heimer and colleagues indicate that the most important factor predicting an increase in women's violent or property offending is an increase in the ratio of female to male unemployment.

It is important to ask how much the changing economic status of women has impacted their crime rate. As women have entered the labor market, they have constantly earned less than men although the gender gap in earnings has fluctuated. Over time, women are selecting to attend college and earning degrees at a faster rate than men, which pushes their earnings upward relative to less educated men. The "equal opportunity theory" (Simon, 1975), a variant of the "Liberation hypothesis," predicts that women's crime would *not* increase in all categories, but only in those where they realized *more* opportunity. Simon and Ahn-Redding (2005) believe that women's changing participation in the labor force has given them greater opportunity to commit fraud, embezzlement, and forgery. For example, women comprised 36% of the labor force in 1963 and 60% in 2001. Simon and Ahn-Redding point out that the types of jobs women hold also significantly changed. In 1969, 11.7% of college educated women worked in professional positions; this increased to 60% by 2000. Similarly, in 1969, 13.8% of college educated women worked in managerial and administrative jobs, as opposed to 18% in 2000. The emergence of women into public life has increased opportunity to commit crimes involving large sums of money. Women find a criminal niche in commission of property crime and, increasingly, white collar crime.

Women's opportunity and equality is not necessarily a predictor of women's violent offending. Vicki Jensen (2001) hypothesized that social and economic equality for women would be associated with reduced female homicide-commission rates. In the case of acquaintance homicide, because it is connected to stress, she thought that low gender equality would predict the women's rate. She found that gender equality in income was associated with reduced women's homicide rates. Economic equality, however, did not predict women's rate of intimate partner homicide. Jensen's log linear multiple regression analysis showed that the percentage of families in poverty, a measure of economic deprivation, predicts both men and women's increased homicide offending. Most women's homicide offending occurs in the context of the home: spouse/partners, children, and family members. Jensen found that the higher the rate of poverty in a city, the greater the rate of women's intimate partner homicide. Family instability, as measured by the rate of divorce and separation, increased the rate of offending for men and women, but men were more strongly impacted. The percentage of divorced and separated was associated with increased acquaintance homicides by women but not men. The best predictor of women's homicide rate was actually men's intimate partner homicide rate. Jensen theorized that low gender equality reduces opportunity and resources for women to leave abusive partners, increasing the probability of women's intimate partner homicide. The obverse, as Jensen (2001: 99) states: "economic opportunity, not relative status as shown in employment and income equality, is more important in decreasing women's intimate partner killing rates." A higher women's employment rate was also associated with a lower intimate partner homicide rate, indicating that women's ability to leave abusive relationships may be a protective factor.

Women are competing for advanced labor market positions, which present criminal opportunity. Definitions of white collar crime tend to emphasize that individuals are of higher socioeconomic status and a respectable occupation (Dodge, 2009: 14). By 2010, women were more represented in managerial/administrative and professional positions but continue to hold minor positions in the status hierarchy (Dodge, 2009: 51). This permits another test of the equal opportunity hypothesis if women become more integrated into this corporate structure. At present, case studies provide information on gendered corporate and professional deviance. For example, the following women have been convicted of various offenses: Martha Stewart (insider stock trading), Leona Helmsley (federal tax evasion), Diana Brooke (price fixing), and Bess Myerson (political corruption). Many women were also tied to corruption in the Enron corporate scandal. Until a greater degree of gender equality is realized, men will continue to dominate elite deviance.

Solutions

Mandatory Minimum Sentencing Reform

When women and men are imprisoned, the length of time is expected to be commensurate with the seriousness of the crime. The U.S. Mandatory Minimum Sentencing Guidelines passed in 1986 specified lengthy sentences for drug possession with "intent to distribute." This has been a major factor in increased imprisonment of women and African Americans in the United States (Merolla, 2008). In particular, the length of sentences for crack cocaine, as opposed to cocaine, has created a racial disparity in imprisonment that many consider to be unjustified. Crack cocaine, a dilute form of the drug, is cheaper, and users are often from poverty and minority backgrounds, particularly inner-city African American women and men. The penalty for crack cocaine use was established at 100 times that of cocaine, a more expensive drug with middle- and upper-class white users. In 2005, the U.S. Supreme Court ruled that the guidelines could not be mandatory, yet many judges still apply them. In 2007, initial reductions were made in the crack cocaine mandatory minimums and 16,433 federal prisoners were released (U.S. Sentencing Commission, 2011a: 1–8). The commission undertook a research study that compared the crack cocaine offenders given an early release with a control group of similarly offenders who had served their full terms with only credit for early release used to attenuate the longer sentences. They found that 30.4% of the group released by the 2007 amendment recidivated, while 32.6% of the control group were rearrested or had parole revoked for a criminal act. Sentence shortening did not increase criminal potential for two-thirds of the crack cocaine offenders. The most common causes for rearrest in the crack cocaine amendment group were drug possession (21.8%); drug distribution (13.7%); assault and battery (13.7%) and driving under the influence (9.6%). In the comparison group, rearrest patterns were for drug possession (20.7%); driving under the influence (12.4%); assault and battery (10.7%) and drug distribution (9.9%). The U.S. Sentencing Commission (2011: 11) considered:

> The offenders in the two groups [early release versus full crack cocaine time served] re-offended at similar rates and in similar ways. Among those who re-offended, the ratio of new arrests to revocations of new crimes, and timing of recidivism are all comparable. While two factors are related to greater recidivism- higher criminal history category [greater number of prior offenses] and younger age—this relationship is found within each group in comparable numbers. In summary, the analysis shows no statistically significant difference in the recidivism rate of the two groups, despite the early release of one group pursuant to the retroactive application of the 2007 Crack Cocaine Amendment.

In 2010, the Fair Sentencing Act again increased the volume of crack cocaine that would result in a mandatory minimum sentence (Savage, 2011). There is still a disparity of 18–1, but this represents a considerable reduction. Under the older mandatory minimum, an individual arrested for possession of 75 grams of crack cocaine faced 10 years to life in prison. The new minimum is 5 to 20 years, still a very substantial time to keep a person imprisoned. In June 2011, the U.S. Sentencing Commission (2011b) voted to retroactively apply the new guidelines for sentence reduction on November 1, 2011. This will result in further release of women from prison, particularly African Americans. Sentencing reform provides a major solution to overcrowding and lack of capacity in the nation's jails and prisons. Because incarcerated women are primarily drug offenders, each federal change, if effected at state and local levels, would reduce women's imprisonment in an era in which the crime rate has been dropping. For those who support punishment, it still occurs—but not to a degree as to disrupt the offender's entire life and possibility for rehabilitation.

What Are the Alternatives to Incarceration?

The U.S. Supreme Court, in the case *Brown v. Plata*, No. 09-1233, ruled 5–4 that California prison conditions violate the ban on "cruel and unusual punishment" of the Eighth Amendment to the Constitution (Liptak, 2011). The state of California was ordered to reduce the number of prisoners by over 30,000 to 11,000, still 135.7% of capacity, by 2013. According to majority opinion writer Justice Anthony M. Kennedy, the California prison system's standard of care was so low that it did not provide sufficient medical and mental health care and caused "needless suffering and death." California is able to build new prison space, transfer prisoners out of state, or use county facilities. One measure that California will undertake is to provide new mental health facilities at the California Institution for Women (California Department of Corrections and Rehabilitation, 2011). Under realignment, California governor Brown indicated that prisoners would not be given early release, but that nonviolent offenders might be moved to county facilities. Another initiative will be to establish evidence-based probation programs for women and men. The punitive legal measures undertaken over four decades have institutionalized a major segment of population, and the pendulum is swinging back toward rehabilitation as the situation is critiqued.

Kelly Turner, a 42-year-old thief sentenced to 25 years to life under California's three-strikes law is believed to be the first women ever released under that law (Kaplan, 2011). She had served 13 years' imprisonment for her third offense, writing a bad check for $146.16. The California law specified that the first two offenses must be violent or serious crimes, but the third offense could be any felony. Individuals have been given maximum terms for crimes such as attempting to break into a soup kitchen for food and shoplifting low-priced items.

Gender-Sensitive Strategies

The pathways that lead women to crime are increasingly recognized as both different from men and associated with physical and mental health consequences. Criminologists and criminal justice research professionals advocate that incarcerated women and those under corrections observation need gender-appropriate treatment. Unfortunately, the increase in women's imprisonment has not been matched by an increase in services that recognize their physical and gendered psychological differences, the relationship between victimization and criminal behavior, or their central position in the family for children. The National

Institute of Corrections (Bloom, Owen, and Covington, 2005) has made the following recommendations for gender-responsiveness:

- Acknowledge that gender makes a difference
- Create an environment based on safety, respect, and dignity
- Develop policies, practices, and programs that are relational and promote healthy connections for children, family, significant others, and the community
- Address substance abuse, trauma, and mental health issues through comprehensive, integrated, and culturally relevant services and appropriate supervision
- Provide women with opportunities to improve their socioeconomic conditions
- Establish a system of community supervision and reentry with comprehensive, collaborative services

The crime control policies of the late 20th century were meant to deter crime by harsh punishment and incapacitation: simply keeping people out of the streets and in prison. Because of lack of sufficient treatment resources in jails and prisons to treat inmates for neurochemical addiction, public debate and research has swung back to consideration of community alternatives to incarceration, with either criminal justice involvement through a public health approach or a system of drug courts. When considering public health, the lack of social underpinnings for prisoner reentry should be understood. Many newly released prisoners are homeless and lack health insurance (Springer and Altice, 2007). The vast majority of states revoke Medicaid or Medicare, and released inmates have to reapply to receive health payment assistance (Morrissey, Dalton, Steadman, Cuddeback, Haynes, and Cuellar, 2006; Morrissey, Steadman, Dalton, Cuellar, Stiles, and Cuddeback, 2006). Springer (2010) indicates that insurance reenrollment may take as long as three months. Thus, released inmates miss medical appointments, screening, and treatment of chronic illness and addiction. It is in the public interest to improve the socioeconomic basis of reentry, partly in the case of the most common risk factor for women's imprisonment: drug use.

Public health is impacted by injection drug use because it is a risk factor for contracting HIV or viral hepatitis C and a common reason for women's imprisonment (Springer, 2010). From 30% to 80% of inmates have a substance abuse or dependency history

(Ibid.: 14; see also Mumola and Karberg, 2006). Upon community release, 85% of opioid-dependent former inmates will relapse before a year is up, regardless of sentence length (Mumola and Karberg, 2006). This occurs despite the fact that methodone and buprenorphine, which are opioid agonist treatments, have some success in preventing relapse to opioid use and reduction of recidivism internationally (Springer, 2010: 14). Few federal and state prisons provide opioid agonist treatment. Similarly, women prisoners who are alcoholics or alcohol abusers seldom receive pharmacological treatment such as the number-one-FDA-approved naltrexone for alcohol relapse prevention. Springer considers that: "Future studies, therefore, should evaluate whether treatment of opioid dependency and alcohol dependency within incarcerated settings within the United States and upon release can prevent relapse to drug and alcohol use and concomitantly reduce HIV and other STD risk-taking behaviors."

President Obama has advocated the use of drug courts as a part of the National Drug Control Strategy (Office of National Drug Control Policy, 2011). First established in 1989, drug courts provide an alternative to incarceration for nonviolent drug offenders. They are special courts that interlink the judiciary, community corrections agencies, substance abuse treatment providers, and community resources. The access to treatment and recovery services is viewed as preventing further criminal activity and reducing the substantial costs associated with imprisonment. There are over 2,500 drug courts in the United States, and the number is growing. The philosophy of therapeutic jurisprudence and individual responsibility has come to characterize drug courts (Miller, 2009). Many drug court judges emphasize the disease model of addiction. Miller (2009: 447) suggests:

> In its therapeutic jurisprudence form, the disease model suggests that the addict has a pathological character for which she is not responsible but which is amenable to treatment. This approach reconstitutes the "therapeutic" not as medicinal but as physical regulation or discipline imposed by an expert in various forms of surveillance and constraint: the judge. The court gains its authority as better able to engage in discipline and surveillance necessary to treat the offender's addictive disease than the other experts, in large part because the court is able to engage in discipline and those other experts are not.

Judicial discipline demands responsibility in a manner
that medical or social work professionals cannot.

Although embraced by many conservatives and liberals, the
emphasis on individual responsibility, backed by incarceration,
is thought to insufficiently address the social problems of impov-
erished racial and ethnic groups connected to drug use (Miller,
2009). The issue is that many drug court studies, which do provide general results (Drug Policy Alliance, 2011), do not closely
examine the varying pathways to drug use of girls and women.
There is a need to expand research on the impact of drug courts
on women of varying social class and race ethnicity. In one study,
researchers have used a quasi-experimental design to compare
nonviolent, predominately white women drug offenders who
were moderate- to high-risk drug users (N=91) with probationers
(n=80). Over two years, the women sent to drug court had a significantly lower rate of recidivism than the probationers (Schafer,
Hartman, and Listwan, 2009). Would this result be the same for
minority women in a much larger sample? Advocates of decriminalization of drugs have criticized drug courts. The Drug Policy
Alliance (2011: 3) states: "Most drug courts have done a poor
job of addressing participant's health needs according to health
principles, and have not significantly reduced participant's
chances of incarceration. They have also absorbed scarce resources that could have been better spent to treat and supervise
those *with more serious offenses* [emphasis added] or to bolster
demonstrated health approaches, such as community-based
treatment." The verdict on the usefulness of drug courts for
women is not yet in.

Against Women's Violent and Sexual Victimization

Women and girls' victimization is a risk factor for crime and
delinquency that can be prevented through educational practice
and legal change. The 1994 Violence against Women Act (VAWA)
and its renewals have made intimate partner violence a crime and
supported funding for women's shelters and other helping activities. This legislation is associated with a reduction in female-to-
male intimate partner homicide. Despite this progress, many
lower-socioeconomic-status minority women, especially African
Americans, are in state and federal prisons or jails serving time

without access to services. These women often have the following interrelated characteristics related to victimization:

- Survival of sexual or physical abuse as children
- Substance abuse problems
- Multiple physical and mental health problems (Bloom, Owen, and Covington, 2005)

The nation's prisons and jails are not equipped to deal with victimized women's problems and often fail to end an intergenerational cycle of crime connected to women's poverty and victimization. The criminal justice system operates on a control model, but treatment is based on behavioral change (Bloom, Owen, and Covington, 2005). Substance abuse, trauma, and mental health treatment will require integration of therapeutic services into imprisonment, transition to the community, and supervision.

References

Adler, Freda. 1975. *Sisters in Crime: The Rise of the New Female Criminal.* New York, NY: McGraw-Hill.

Administration on Children, Youth and Families. 2010. *Child Maltreatment 2008.* http://www.acf.hhs.gov/programs/cb/pubs/cm08/cm08.pdf

Altice F. L., A. Marinovich, K. Khoshnood, K. M. Blankenship, S. A. Springer, P, and A. Selwyn. 2005. "Correlates of HIV Infection among Incarcerated Women: Implications for Improving Detection of HIV Infection." *Journal of Urban Health* 82: 312–326.

American Bar Association and National Bar Association. 2001. *Justice by Gender: The Lack of Appropriate Prevention, Diversion and Treatment Alternatives for Girls in the Justice System.* Washington, DC: Author.

American Civil Liberties Union. 2008. "Bureau of Prisons Revises Policy of Shackling Pregnant Inmates." Washington, DC: American Civil Liberties Union. http://www.aclu.org/2008/10/20/bureau-of-prisons-revises-policy-on-shackling-of-pregnant-inmates

American Civil Liberties Union. 2011. "Hawaii Lawmakers Ban Practice of Routinely Shackling Pregnant Inmates." Washington, DC: American Civil Liberties Union. http://www.aclu.org/prisoners-rights/hawaii-lawmakers-ban-practice-routinely-shackling-pregnant-inmates

American Psychiatric Association. 2004. *Diagnostic and Statistical Manual of Mental Disorders. Fourth Edition (DSM-IV).*

Amnesty International. 1999. " 'Not Part of My Sentence': Violations of the Human Rights of Women in Custody." Washington, DC: Author. http://www.amnestyusa.org/node/57783?page=show

AP Online. 2005. "Martha Stewart Calls Lockdown Hideous." July 5. http://www.highbeam.com/doc/1P1-110747995.html

Associated Press. 2009. "Illinois: Sheriff Sues Craigslist." *New York Times*, March 5.

Bailey, Frankie Y. and Donna C. Hale. 2004. *Blood on Her Hands: Women Who Murder*. Belmont, CA: Wadsworth.

Baillargeon J. T., P. Giordano, J. D. Rich, et al. 2009. "Accessing Antiretroviral Therapy Following Release from Prison." *Journal of the American Medical Association* 301: 848–857.

Becker, J. V., S. R. Hall, and J. D. Stinson. (2001). "Female Sexual Offenders: Clinical, Legal and Policy Issues." *Journal of Forensic Psychology Practice* 1(3), 29–50.

Bloom, Barbara, Barbara Owen, and Stephanie Covington. 2005. "A Summary of Research, Practice, and Guiding Principles for Women Offenders." Washington, DC: National Institute of Corrections. http://static.nicic.gov/Library/020418.pdf

Brennan, Tim, Markus Breitenbach, and William Dieterich. 2010. Unraveling Women's Pathways to Serious Crime: New Findings and Links to Prior Feminist Pathways." *Perspectives: The Journal of the American Probation and Parole Association* 4(2): 35–46. American Probation and Parole Association. http://www.northpointeinc.com/pdf/Spring %202010_Cover_Article.pdf

Brown, Stephen, Becca Cardoff, and Amy Fettig. 2011. "Rhode Island Stands Up for Pregnant Women in Prison." Washington, DC: American Civil Liberties Union. http://www.aclu.org/blog/prisoners-rights -reproductive-freedom-womens-rights/rhode-island-stands-pregnant -women-prison

Bureau of Justice Statistics. 2000. *Incarcerated Parents and Their Children*. Washington, DC: U.S. Department of Justice.

Bureau of Justice Statistics. 2009. *Prison Inmates at Midyear 2008— Statistical Tables*. Washington, DC: U.S. Department of Justice.

Bureau of Justice Statistics. 2010. *Prison Inmates at Midyear 2009-Statistical Tables*. Washington, DC: U.S. Department of Justice. http://bjs.ojp.usdoj .gov/content/pub/pdf/pim09st.pdf

Butcher, Kristen F., and Robert J. LaLonde. 2006. "Female Offenders Use of Social Welfare Programs before and after Jail and Prison: Does Prison Cause Welfare Dependency?" Working paper series 07.18. Chicago, IL: Harris School, University of Chicago.

Cain, M. 1990. "Towards Transgression: New Directions in Feminist Criminology. *International Journal of the Sociology of Law* 18: 1–18.

California Department of Corrections and Rehabilitation. 2011. "State Responds to Three Judge Court Order Requiring a Reduction in Prison Overcrowding." *CDCR Today,* June 7. Sacramento, CA: Author. http://cdcrtoday.blogspot.com/2011/06/state-responds-to-three-judge-courts.html

Campbell, Jacqueline C., Nancy Glass, Phyllis W. Sharps, Kathryn Laughon, and Tina Bloom. 2007. "Intimate Partner Homicide: Review and Implications in Research and Policy." *Trauma, Violence and Abuse* 8(3): 246–269.

Catalano, Shannan. 2006. *Intimate Partner Violence in the United States.* Washington, DC: Bureau of Justice Statistics. http://bjsdata.ojp.usdoj.gov/content/pub/pdf/ipvus.pdf

Catalano, Shannan, Erica Smith, Howard Snyder, and Erica Rand. 2009. "Female Victims of Violence." Washington, DC: Bureau of Justice Statistics. http://bjs.ojp.usdoj.gov/content/pub/pdf/fvv.pdf

Centers for Disease Control and Prevention. 2008. "HIV Prevalence Estimates—United States." *Morbidity and Mortality Weekly Report* 57: 1073–1076.

Chesney-Lind, Meda. 2002. "Criminalizing Victimization: The Unintended Consequences of Pro-Arrest Politics for Girls and Women." *Criminology and Public Policy* 2: 81–90.

Chesney-Lind, Meda. 2004. "Girls and Violence: Is the Gender Gap Closing? *VAWNET Applied Research Forum.* http://new.vawnet.org/Assoc_Files_VAWnet/AR_GirlsViolence.pdf

Chesney-Lind, Meda, and Lisa Pasko. 2004. *The Female Offender, Girls, Women and Crime* (2nd ed.). Thousand Oaks, CA: Sage.

Coalition Against Trafficking in Women and Prostitution Research Education. 2010. "Craiglist Protest Fact Sheet." http://www.prostitutionresearch.com/pdfs/Craigslist-Facts-7-8-10.pdf

Daly, Kathleen. 1992. "Women's Pathways to Felony Court: Feminist Theories of Lawbreaking and Problems of Representation." *Review of Law and Women's Studies* 2: 11–52.

DeHart, Diana. 2008. "Pathways to Prison: Impact of Victimization in the Lives of Incarcerated Women." *Violence against Women* 14(12): 1362–1381.

Diaz-Cotto, Juanita. 2007. "Latina Imprisonment and the War on Drugs." In Mary Bosworth and Jeanne Flavin (Eds.), *Race, Gender and Punishment: From Colonialism to the War on Terror* (pp. 184–199). New Brunswick, NJ: Rutgers University Press.

Dietz, P. 1986. "Mass, Serial and Sensational Homicides." *Bulletin of the New York Academy of Medicine* 62: 477–491.

Dodge, Mary. 2009. *Women and White Collar Crime*. Upper Saddle River, NJ: Prentice-Hall.

Eckholm, Eric, and Katie Zezima. 2010. "6 Teenagers Are Charged After Classmate's Suicide." *New York Times*, March 29. http://www.nytimes .com/2010/03/30/us/30bully.html?_r=1

Farley, Melissa. 2006. "Prostitution, Trafficking and Cultural Amnesia: What We Must Not Know in Order to Keep the Business of Sexual Exploitation Running Smoothly." *Yale Journal of Law and Feminism* 18: 101–136.

Farley, Melissa, Ann Cotton, Jacqueline Lynne, Sybille Zumbeck, Frida Spiwak, Maria E. Reyes, Dinorah Alvarez, and Ufuk Sezgin. 2003. "Prostitution and Trafficking in Nine Countries: An Update on Violence and Post-Traumatic Stress Disorder." In Melissa Farley (Ed.), *Prostitution, Trafficking and Traumatic Stress* (pp. 33–74). New York, NY: Routledge.

Ferraro, Kathleen J. 2006. *Neither Angels nor Demons: Women, Crime and Victimization*. Lebanon, NH: Northeastern University Press.

Goodnough, Abby. 2009. 'Medical Student Is Indicted in Craigslist Killing." *New York Times*, June 21. http://www.nytimes.com/2009/06/22/us/22indict.html

Heimer, Karen. 2000. "Changes in the Gender Gap in Crime and Women's Economic Marginalization." In Gary LaFree (Ed.), *Criminal Justice 2000*, vol. 1, *The Nature of Crime and Continuity and Change* (pp. 427–483). Washington, DC: National Institute of Justice.

Heimer, Karen, Stacey Wittrock, and Halime Unal. 2006. "The Crimes of Poverty: Economic Marginalization and the Gender Gap in Crime." In Karen Heimer and Candace Kruttschnitt (Eds.), *Gender and Crime: Patterns in Victimization and Offending*. New York, NY: New York University Press.

James, Doris J., and Lauren E. Glaze. 2006. "Mental Health Problems of Prison and Jail Inmates." Washington, DC: Bureau of Justice Statistics. http://bjs.ojp.usdoj.gov/content/pub/pdf/mhppji.pdf

Jensen, Vickie. 2001. *Why Women Kill: Homicide and Gender Equality*. Boulder, CO: Lynn Reiner.

Johansson-Love, Jill, and William Fremouw. 2005. "A Critique of the Female Sexual Perpetrator Research." *Aggression and Violent Behavior* 11: 12–26.

Kaplan, Tracey. 2011. "Three Strikes Change Possible." California Correctional Peace Officers Association, July 4. http://www.ccpoa.org/news/three_strikes_changes_possible/

Kruttschnitt, Candace. 2010."The Paradox of Women's Imprisonment." *Daedalus* 139(3): 32–42.

Liptak, Adam. 2011. "Justices 5–4, Tell California to Cut Prisoner Population." *New York Times*, May 23. http://www.nytimes.com/2011/05/24/us/24scotus.html

Lombroso, Cesare, and W. Ferrero. 1895. *The Female Offender*. London, UK: T. Fisher Unwin.

Males, Mike, and Meda Chesney-Lind. 2010. "Op-Ed: The Myth of Mean Girls." *New York Times*, April 1. http://www.nytimes.com/2010/04/02/opinion/02males.html

Mathews, R., J. K. Matthews, and K. Speltz. (1989). *Female Sexual Offenders: An Exploratory Study*. Orwell, VT: Safer Society Press.

Meloy, Michelle L., and Susan L. Miller. 2009. "Words That Wound: Print Media's Presentation of Gendered Violence." In Drew Humphries (Ed.), *Women, Violence and the Media: Readings in Feminist Criminology* (pp. 29–56). Boston, MA: Northeastern University Press.

Merolla, David. 2008. "The War on Drugs and the Gender Gap in Arrests: A Critical Perspective." *Critical Criminology* 34: 255–270.

Miller, Claire Cain. 2010a. "Some See a Ploy as Craigslist Blocks Sex Ads." *New York Times*, September 5. http://www.nytimes.com/2010/09/06/technology/06craigslist.html?scp=2&sq=Craigslist+and+Sex+Trafficking+&st=nyt

Miller, Claire Cain. 2010b. "Craigslist Says It Has Shut Its Section for Sex Ads." *New York Times*, September 15. http://www.nytimes.com/2010/09/16/business/16craigslist.html?scp=1&sq=Craigslist+and+Sex+Trafficking+&st=nyt

Miller, Eric J. 2009. "Drugs, Courts and the New Penology." *Stanford Law and Policy Review* 20(2): 417–461.

Moffitt, Terrie E. 1993. "Adolescent-Limited and Life-Course-Persistent Antisocial Behavior: A Developmental Taxonomy." *Psychological Review* 100(4): 674–701.

Moffitt, Terrie E., A. Caspi, M. Rutter, and P. A. Silva. 2001. *Sex Differences in Antisocial Behavior*. Cambridge, UK: Cambridge University Press.

Moriarty, L., and K. Freiberger. 2000. "Classifying Female Serial Killers: An Application of Prominent Typologies." In R. Muraskin (Ed.), *It's a Crime: Women and Justice* (2nd ed.). Upper Saddle River, NJ: Prentice Hall.

Morrissey J. P., K. M. Dalton, H. J. Steadman, G. S. Cuddeback, D. Haynes, and A. Cuellar. 2006. "Assessing Gaps between Policy and Practice in Medicaid Enrollment of Jail Detainees with Severe Mental Illness." *Psychiatric Services* 57: 803–808.

Morrissey J. P., H. J. Steadman, K. M. Dalton, A. Cuellar, P. Stiles, and G. S. Cuddeback. 2006. "Medicaid Enrollment and Mental Health Service

Use Following Release of Jail Detainees with Severe Mental Illness." *Psychiatric Services* 57: 809–815.

Mullins, Christopher W., and Richard Wright. 2003. "Gender, Social Networks and Residential Burglary." *Criminology* 41(3): 818–839.

Mumola, Christopher. 2000. "Incarcerated Parents and Their Children." Washington, DC: Bureau of Justice Statistics. http://bjs.ojp.usdoj.gov/content/pub/pdf/iptc.pdf

Mumola, Christopher J., and Jennifer C. Karberg. 2006. "Drug Use and Dependence, State and Federal Prisoners, 2004." Washington, DC: Bureau of Justice Statistics. http://bjsdata.ojp.usdoj.gov/content/pub/pdf/dudsfp04.pdf

Naffine, N. 1996. *Feminism and Criminology.* Philadelphia, PA: Temple University Press.

National Council of State Legislatures. 2010: E-Bulletin: Three Strikes Laws: Past and Present. Washington, DC: National Council of State Legislatures. http://www.ncsl.org/default.aspx?tabid=21422

National Institute on Alcohol and Alcohol Abuse. 2004. "Alcohol's Damaging Effects on the Brain." *Alcohol Alert* 63. http://pubs.niaaa.nih.gov/publications/aa63/aa63.htm

National Institute on Alcohol Abuse and Alcoholism. n.d. *Alcohol: A Woman's Health Issue.* Washington, DC: Author. http://pubs.niaaa.nih.gov/publications/brochurewomen/Woman_English.pdf

National Institute on Drug Abuse (NIDA). 2008. Methamphetamine. http://www.nida.nih.gov/Infofacts/methamphetamine.html

National Survey on Drug Use and Health. 2004. Women with Co-Occurring Serious Mental Illness and a Substance Abuse Disorder. Washington, DC: Substance Abuse and Mental Health Services Administration (SAMHSA). http://oas.samhsa.gov/2k4/femDual/femDual.pdf

Nijhawan, A. E., R. Salloway, A. S. Nunn, M. Poshkus, and J. G. Clarke. 2010. "Preventive Health Care for Underserved Women: Results of a Prison Survey." *Journal of Women's Health Care* 19: 17–22.

Office of National Drug Control Policy. 2011. "President Obama: Drug Courts are Smart Investments." *Of SubstanceBlog.* Washington, DC: Office of National Drug Control Policy. http://ofsubstance.gov/blogs/pushing_back/archive/2011/05/16/51883.aspx

Potterat, John J., et al. 2004. "Mortality in a Long-Term Open Cohort of Prostitute Women." *American Journal of Epidemiology* 778.

Proca, D. M., S. Rofagha, and S. Keyhani-Rofagha. 2006. "High Grade Squamous Intraepithelial Lesion in Inmates from Ohio: Cervical Screening and Biopsy Follow-up." *Cytojournal* 3: 15.

Quinlin, Anna. 1992. "Public and Private: A Murder, A Mother, A Mystery." *New York Times*, September 20. http://www.nytimes.com/1992/09/20/opinion/public-private-a-murder-a-mother-a-mystery.html

Roberts, Daryl. 2009. "Intimate Partner Homicide: Relation to Alcohol and Firearms." *Journal of Contemporary Criminal Justice* 25(1): 67–88.

Rockell, Barbara A. (2008). *Women Street Hustlers: Who They Are and How They Survive*. Washington, DC: American Psychological Association.

Ross, Colin A., Melissa Farley, and Harry L. Schwartz. 2003. "Disassociation in Women Undergoing Prostitution." In Melissa Farley (Ed.), *Prostitution, Trafficking and Traumatic Stress* (pp. 199–212). New York, NY: Routledge.

Reuters. 2010. "Craigslist Is Subpoenaed over Sex Ads." *New York Times*, May 3. http://www.nytimes.com/2010/05/04/technology/04craigslist.html?ref=craigslist

Savage, Charlie. 2011. "Retroactive Reductions Sought in Crack Penalties." *New York Times*, June 1. http://www.nytimes.com/2011/06/02/us/02cocaine.html

Sax, Robin. 2009. "Shaniya Davis: A Case of Domestic Human Trafficking." Women and Crime Ink, December 2. http://womenincrimeink.blogspot.com/2009/12/shaniya-davis-case-of-domestic-human.html.

Schaffner, Laurie. 2006. *Girls in Trouble with the Law*. New Brunswick, NJ: Rutgers University Press.

Schwartz, Jennifer, Darrell J. Steffensmeier, and Ben Feldmeyer. 2009. "Assessing Trends in Women's Violence via Data Triangulation: Arrests, Convictions, Incarcerations and Victim Reports." *Social Problems* 56(3): 494–525.

Shaffer, Deborah Koetzle, Jennifer L. Hartman, and Shelley Johnson Listwan. 2009. "Drug Abusing Women in the Community: The Impact of Drug Court Involvement on Recidivism." *Journal of Drug Issues* 39 (Fall): 803–827.

Sherman, C. 2007. "Impact of Drugs on Neurotransmission." National Institute of Drug Abuse (NIDA). *NIDA Notes* 21(4): 1–4.

Simon, Rita J. 1975. *Women and Crime*. Lexington, MA: Lexington Books.

Simon, Rita J., and Heather Ahn-Redding. 2005. *The Crimes Women Commit: The Punishments They Receive* (3rd ed.). New York, NY: Lexington Books.

Slocum, Lee Ann, Sally S. Simpson and Douglas A. Smith. 2005. "Strained Lives and Crime: Examining Extra-Individual Variation in Strain and Offending in a Sample of Incarcerated Women." *Criminology* 43(4): 1067–1110.

Springer, S. A. 2010. "Improving Health Care for Incarcerated Women." *Journal of Women's Health* 19(1): 13–14.

Springer S. A., and F. Altice. 2007. "Improving the Care for HIV-infected Prisoners: An Integrated Prison-Release Health Model." In: R. Greifinger (Ed.), *Public Health Behind Bars: From Prisons to Communities*. New York, NY: Springer Science.

Springer, S. A., E. Pesanti, J. Hodges, T. Macura, G. Doros, and F. L. Altice. 2004. "Effectiveness of Antiretroviral Therapy among HIV-Infected Prisoners: Reincarceration and the Lack of Sustained Benefit after Release to the Community." *Clinical and Infectious Diseases* 38: 1754–1760.

Stark, Christine, and Carol Hodgson. 2003. "Sister Oppressions: A Comparison of Wife Battering and Prostitution." In Melissa Farley (Ed.), *Prostitution, Trafficking and Traumatic Stress* (pp. 17–32). New York, NY: Routledge.

Steffensmeier, Darrell, and Dana Haynie. 2000. "Gender, Structural Disadvantage and Women's Crime." *Criminology* 38(2): 403–438.

Steffensmeier, Darrell, Jennifer Schwartz, Hua Zhong, and Jeffrey Ackerman. 2005. "An Assessment of Recent Trends in Girls' Violence Using Diverse Longitudinal Sources: Is the Gender Gap Closing?" *Criminology* 43: 355–405.

Stephenson B. L., D. A. Wohl, C. E. Golin, H. C. Tien, P. Stewart, and A. H. Kaplan. 2005. "Effect of Release from Prison and Re-Incarceration on the Viral Loads of HIV-Infected Individuals. *Public Health Reports* 120: 84–88.

Thompson, Melissa. 2008. *"Gender, Mental Illness and Crime."* Washington, DC: U.S. Department of Justice.

U.S. Sentencing Commission. 2011a. *Recidivism among Offenders with Sentence Modifications Pursuant to Retroactive Application of 2007 Crack Cocaine Amendment*. Washington, DC: Author. http://www.ussc.gov/Research/Research_Projects/Miscellaneous/20110527_Recidivism _2007_Crack_Cocaine_Amendment.pdf

U.S. Sentencing Commission. 2011b. "U.S. Sentencing Commission Votes Unanimously to Apply Fair Sentencing Act of 2010 Amendment to the Federal Sentencing Guidelines Retroactively." Washington, DC: Author. http://www.ussc.gov/Legislative_and_Public_Affairs/Newsroom/ Press_Releases/20110630_Press_Release.pdf

Van Diver, Donna M. 2006. "Female Sex Offenders: A Comparison of Solo Offenders and Co-Offenders." *Violence and Victims* 21(3): 339–353.

Walker, Emily. 2010. "AMA House of Delegates Backs Ban on Shacking in Labor." ABC News, June 19. http://abcnews.go.com/Health/ MindMoodNews/shackling-female-inmates-labor-banned-ama/story ?id=10934689

Wang, Ching-Tung, and John Holden. 2007. *Total Estimated Cost of Child Abuse and Neglect in the United States*. Chicago, IL: Prevent Child Abuse America.

Weiser, Benjamin. 2010. "Charges Called New Low for Gambinos." *New York Times*, April 20. http://www.nytimes.com/2010/04/21/nyregion/21extort.html

Yardley, Jim. 2002. "Trial Opens in Case of Drowned Children." *New York Times*, February 19. http://www.nytimes.com/2002/02/19/us/trial-opens-in-case-of-drowned-children.html?ref=andreayates

Zahn, Margaret A., Robert Agnew, Diana Fishbein, Sharl Miller, Donna Marle-Winn, Gayle Dakoff, Candace Kruttschnitt, Peggy Giordano, Denise C. Gottfredson, Allison A. Payne, Barry C. Field, and Meda Chesney-Lind (Girls Study Group). 2010. *Causes and Correlates of Girls' Delinquency*. Washington, DC: U.S. Department of Justice, Office of Juvenile Justice and Delinquency Prevention. http://girlsstudygroup.rti.org/docs/GSG_Causes_and_Correlates_Bulletin.pdf

Zickler, P. 2004. "Long Term Abstinence Brings Partial Recovery from Methamphetamine." *NIDA Notes* 19(4): 1.

3

The Globalization of Women's Crime and Victimization

Women are subject to social harm because of their membership in a relatively less powerful social group (Cain and Howe, 2009). Edwin Sutherland (1949, 31) specified that conceptualization of social harm requires "legal description of an act as socially harmful" and legal provision of a penalty." Cain and Howe (2008: 3–4) indicate that harm is "an act which, if generalized, is contrary to the common welfare of society and which has been legally defined as such by the use of harm language." Members of the sex worker's rights movement have contested the legality of prostitution, and the United States' policy of criminalization is in contrast to that of many international destinations. Other gendered policies subject to variation include the age of consent and the right to abortion.

As globalization increases the means, degree, and frequency of economic contact between societies, the transborder context of social harm has expanded. Globalization has led to the development of transnational criminal organizations. Although women have not traditionally held positions of rank in global crime, the international trafficking of drugs, humans, and body parts had increased their visibility as criminal organizers and victims. Social harms impacting women include sex trafficking, risks of undocumented entry, and violence against women, which is a U.S.-Mexico-border and international-asylum issue.

Transnational Drug Trafficking and Women Offenders

Drug trafficking between the United States and Mexico impacts American women arrested for drug-related offenses and nonciti- zen women who transport drugs: couriers or drug mules, and increasingly, Mexican women involved in the trade. Historical background begins in the 1960s, when the U.S. law-enforcement campaign against domestic and international drug trafficking was a first step toward the war on drugs of the 1980s (Andreas and Nadelmann, 2006: 128–131). The U.S. official policy narra- tives have emphasized the importance of prohibition of drug use rather than alternative harm-reduction approaches including drug treatment. Since the 1980s, the U.S.-Mexico border has emerged as the major site of drug trafficking into the United States and comprises a national security threat (Payan, 2006: 28). It threatens the Mexican government due to high levels of vio- lence and associated corruption. Mexican drug-trafficking organ- izations grow and transport marijuana and heroin and manufacture methamphetamines. Of the cocaine entering the United States from South America, 90% is trafficked by the Mexi- can cartels over the southwestern border (U.S. Department of Justice National Drug Intelligence Center, 2006). The smuggling of drug money and arms south is also equally significant.

The successful enforcement effort against the Columbian Cali and Medellin cartels led to the emergence of Mexican drug- trafficking organizations (DTOs), which took over the trade (Payan, 2006: 28). Previously, Columbians trafficked cocaine through Florida. Mexican smugglers made ties with Columbian traffickers and relocated the problem to the southwestern border. The Mexican government has a history of tolerating DTOs (Beittel, 2009: 7–8). In the 1980s and 1990s, it pursued a policy of accommodation in which government officials and police accepted bribes while appeasing the United States by making some arrests and running a crop-eradication program. Narco- terrorism is defined as the use of terrorism to increase profits from drug trafficking or the taking of profits from drug trafficking to fund terrorism (Casteel, 2003). In the case of Mexico, drug organ- izations have used executioners, gangs, and paramilitary groups to intimidate the public and government officials, and Mexico has experienced extensive violence (Beittel, 2009: 5–6; Cook, 2007: 6–9). Police chiefs, prosecutors, elected government representatives, journalists, and civilians of all ages have been killed (Beittel, 2009: 10–12). The violence is considered terroristic because of the torture that marks some of the threats used to intimidate, killings, and their extent. DTOs are torturing and maiming victims and decapitating the corpses (Bunker, Campbell, and Bunker, 2010: 146–148). Torture is practiced for intimidation and extortion and can include beatings, breaking bones, knife lacerations, starvation, and sexual abuse. More extreme torture methods include acid, fire, water, electricity, and suffocation. Maiming in connection with murders can involve decapitation; placing bodies in car trunks, drums, or acid baths; taping the eyes and mouth shut; and quartering of the body.

Since 2007, the Mexican government estimates that 22,700 people have been killed in drug-related violence (Castillo, 2010). In 2009, 9,635 people were murdered, more than triple the total of 2,837 in 2007. Since, 2006, 4,324 of these deaths occurred in Ciudad Juarez, a Mexican border city. In the first four months of 2010, 3,365 died. This 2010 total includes the deaths of a pregnant U.S. Consulate employee and her husband, and another husband of a U.S. Consulate employee (Lacey and Thompson, 2010). DTOs made threats against U.S. diplomats stationed on the U.S.-Mexico border prior to the incidents. Previously, the State Department decided that consulate workers could evacuate their families across the border for protection in the United States. Mexican president Felipe Calderón (2006–present) considers Mexico's drug-related violence a threat to the nation (Beittel, 2009: 3).

In Mexico, narco-trafficking has increased criminal opportunity for women (Campbell, 2009). Women have moved up through their relationships with men at the top of DTO hierarchies. Howard Campbell, an anthropologist at the University of Texas–El Paso, indicates that Mexico has a history of female "drug lords." These women include the Arellano-Felix sisters of the Tijuana Cartel, "Lola La Chata" and "La Ma Baker" in Mexico City, Sandra Avila of Sinaloa and "La Nacha" in Juarez. Campbell's interviews with "Zulema," a powerful woman drug dealer, reveal that she worked her way up smuggling drugs, and when confronted over a drug-smuggling deal involving cartel trickery (cocaine substituted for alcohol), she impressed the men and was invited to join their crime organization. Zulema did rise in the organization to develop her own drug-smuggling ring through partnership with male lovers. Through relationships with powerful related men, the Arellano-Felix sisters came to be reputed as drug lords. Regarding her gendered self-representation Campbell (2009: 248) writes: "As a trafficker, Zulema operated in a largely male environment and she adopted the macho ethical behavioral and verbal style of that milieu." As a tough-minded "macha," Zulema violated traditional gender roles for Mexican women, but her gender identity neither simply mimics male *narcotraficante* models nor fits neat images of politically conscious feminist heroines. Nevertheless, other women who have become drug lords do not necessarily adopt a masculine style, although they achieve considerable self-agency.

Given the expansion of violence associated with narco-trafficking, one can well ask if women can authorize or commit terroristic acts. According to Howard Campbell (2009: 250), the answer is yes. He states: " 'La Güera' ('The Blond'), a high-level Juárez trafficker, is responsible for several quite public drug executions." He continues: "For these high-level female traffickers, drug smuggling, though an unstable, dangerous pursuit allowed them a pleasurable lifestyle and relative autonomy from men." Things are different for women at the middle level of drug organizations in Mexico; they display more traditional gender role behavior in their occupations as go-betweens, operators of legitimate businesses funded by drug money, and money launderers. Despite being at the middle level, these women are at high risk of violent injury and death. Some of these women have functioned as *sicarios* (hit men) as well. Because of movies like *Maria Full of Grace* and news stories about "drug mules" or couriers, women are associated with this role. This is at the bottom of the organizational hierarchy and involves a high level of risk. Mexican women, especially single mothers, try to earn money by smuggling loads across the U.S.-Mexico border.

Narco-traffickers have engaged in corrupt practices, bribing law enforcement and government. Mexican women police officers have been known to accept bribes and even assist drug transport through the border to the United States. Recommendations for changing policy to deal with the Mexican drug crisis include reducing the demand for drugs among developed nations while increasing the costs of doing business for organized crime. Mexico has a crisis of public security due to homicide, kidnappings, robbery, and piracy.

Criminalization of Prostitution

Prostitution encompasses social practices found in both the developed and the developing world. Criminalization refers to the classification of behavior as unlawful and subject to penalties. Internationally, social policies regulating prostitution range from legalization to criminalization. Twenty-eight countries are known to permit legalized prostitution, including Argentina, Austria, Belgium, Brazil, Canada, Costa Rica, Denmark, England, Estonia, Ethiopia, France, Germany, Greece, Guatemala, Iceland, Israel, Italy, Kyrgyzstan, Latvia, Mexico, Netherlands, New Zealand, Norway, Peru, Senegal, Singapore, Switzerland, and Turkey. Among these countries, brothel keeping is legal in Belgium, Costa Rica, Germany, Greece, Guatemala, Netherlands, New Zealand, Peru, Singapore, Switzerland, and Turkey. Brothels are illegal in Argentina, Austria, Brazil, Canada, Denmark, England, Ethiopia, France, Iceland, Israel, Italy, Kyrgyzstan, Latvia, Mexico, Norway, and Senegal. Prostitution and brothel keeping has limited legality in Australia and Spain. Prostitution is prohibited through forms of criminalization in Angola, China, Cuba, Egypt, India, Iran, Japan, Kenya, Liberia, Philippines, Romania, Rwanda, Saudi Arabia, South Africa, South Korea, Sweden, Taiwan, Thailand, Uganda, United Arab Emirates and the United States (with the exception of 11 counties in Nevada). Countries prohibiting prostitution regard it as immoral in any context but reserve harsher penalties for coerced prostitution such as sexual exploitation of children or trafficked women and children.

In the United States, prostitution is criminalized in all states with the exception of certain counties in Nevada. The American mass media sexualizes African American men and women, objectifying them as prostitutes and pimps. African American youth from lower socioeconomic strata, including the working class, face meager job prospects. Girls enter sex work with the relative protection of citizenship and may not be subject to the degree of exploitation of women trafficked for prostitution. Adolescent runaways may engage in "survival sex," prostitution to meet costs of necessities. This pathway to delinquent behavior is connected to exploitation by pimps and addiction, which situates them in the life. Young women with children or elderly parents may desperately need money and engage in prostitution (Sack, 2001). What may be regarded as immoral behavior is connected to economic need.

Kevin Sack (2001) found one outcome is that needy young African American women in the rural South have trouble persuading men to use condoms and the rate of HIV/AIDS has increased. Many found out they were HIV positive when pregnant. These young women felt that they had little control over their lives and that God figured in whether or not they contracted AIDS (Collins, 2006).

Partial Decriminalization and Legalization of Prostitution in Europe

The radical feminist Andrea Dworkin (1988) proposed that prostitution should be decriminalized for women and that those who pay for sex or otherwise manage prostitutes, such as pimps, should continue to be guilty of a crime and targeted by police. In Sweden, a law was passed that criminalized the behavior of those paying for or managing payment of sexual services (customers, pimps, and traffickers) but decriminalized those providing the service (Farley, 2006). The Swedish law states "in the majority of cases ... [the woman in prostitution] is a weaker partner who is exploited" and provided social service funding to: "motivate prostitutes to seek help to leave their way of life" (Farley, 2006: 131). This approach situates prostitution as a form of violence against women that is associated with sexual inequality.

Emergent evidence indicates that demand for prostitutes has declined in Sweden, reduced the number of active prostitutes, and discouraged sex traffickers. Prior to passage of the law, 2,500 to 3,000 prostitutes, including 650 streetwalkers, were estimated in Sweden (Waltman, 2010: 23). Swedish police indicated that reports of street prostitution declined by 80% through 2001 and then redeveloped at a greatly reduced level. By 2008, research sources indicate this decreased to 350 women on the street and 300 women advertising on the Internet. Furthermore, Sweden's National Criminal Investigation's Wiretapping Department indicates that sex traffickers and pimps have scaled down their enterprises to 3–4 women indoor operations that rely on secrecy and move quite frequently (Ibid.).

Global Lockdown of Women

Julia Sudbury (2005) refers to "global lockdown," a trend in which economically marginalized women and men are increasingly imprisoned. Adam Liptak (2008) in the *New York Times* reports: "The United States has less than 5 percent of the world's population. But it has one-quarter of the world's prisoners." This news about the impact of U.S. "get tough on crime" policy is not sensationalized. Roy Walmsley (2008: 1) of the International Center for Prison Studies at Kings College, London, indicates: "More than 9.8 million are held in penal institutions throughout the world, mostly as pre-trial detainees (remand prisoners) or as sentenced prisoners. Almost half of these are in the United States (2.29 m), Russia (0.89 m) or China (1.57 m. sentenced prisoners)." The United States rate of 756 per 100,000 residents in 2008 was the highest in the world. Imprisonment is a not just a woman's issue or a racial issue, it is a human rights issue with particular implications for women.

Worldwide, over 500,000 women are held as pretrial detainees or convicted prisoners (International Center for Prison Studies, 2010). Women comprise 2% to 21.6% of prisoners in 200 countries providing incarceration statistics. The United States reported 8.8% imprisoned females in 2009 (Ibid.). Hong Kong (China) reports 19.6% women incarcerated; the Russian Federation, 8.1%; and Thailand, 14.2% (Ibid.). Continental statistics indicate that the Americas and Asia have a higher median level of female imprisonment (5.3% and 5.4%) than Europe and Oceania (4.4% and 4.3%), or Africa (2.65%), the lowest (Walmsley, 2006).

Global women's imprisonment is viewed by feminist criminologists as a form of backlash against women. Meda Chesney-Lind (2006) calls this trend "vengeful equity." Global capitalism and neoconservative politics are seen as promoting "equal treatment" of women when their status and needs are different. Increasing worldwide imprisonment of women in Europe and Australasia is related to international economic trends and the influence of American policy (Sudbury, 2002). Neoliberal globalization is associated with the spread of a "prison-industrial complex" linking national governments, politicians, and for-profit prison corporations. Because of the international impact of the U.S.-led drive to criminalize drug use, women's incarceration in developed countries for drug-related offenses has climbed. Parallel to the United States, black women are a disproportionate number of the imprisoned. This is partly due to the use of minority women as couriers in drug trafficking and related to reduced economic circumstances.

The United States has been internationally criticized for having the highest rate of incarceration in the world. Human rights organization Amnesty International criticized U.S. prisons as not meeting international humane treatment standards (Amnesty International, 2010). The PEW Center on the States (2008: 3) reported in 2007 that "for the first time, more than one in one hundred adults is now confined in an American jail or prison." Racial status and gender are major factors structuring imprisonment: "Men still are roughly 10 times more likely to be in jail or prison, but the female population is burgeoning at a far brisker pace. For black women in their mid- to late-30s, the incarceration rate also has hit the 1-in-100 mark" (Ibid.).

In a time when feminist advocates and criminologists are urging gender-responsive programming in the United States (Bloom, Owen, and Covington, 2005), an international mandate for better treatment of women prisoners has been set by the United Nations. The UN Rules for the Treatment of Women Prisoners and Non-Custodial Rules for Women Offenders (2010: 1), known as the "Bangkok rules," was developed with Thailand as a lead nation Its general principle specifies that "the distinctive needs of women prisoners" be taken into account in implementing the standard minimum rules for prisoners. Providing for these needs to achieve gender equality will not be viewed as discriminatory. Other areas targeted for minimum standards include:

- Admission procedures for women and children
- Registration of children confined with women
- Accommodation of female hygiene needs
- Medical screening of women and children on entry
- Gender-specific health care services
- Mental health care
- HIV prevention, treatment, care, and support
- Substance abuse treatment programs
- Suicide and self-harm prevention
- Preventative health care services
- Safety and security
- Dignity in personnel searches to be conducted by women staff
- Pregnant women, women with infants, and breast-feeding women are not to be subject to close confinement or disciplinary segregation

- Restraints are not to be used on women giving birth
- Inspection after a woman's report of abuse
- Facilitate contact with the outside world
- Institutional training for women's reentry support
- Prohibition of sexual harassment and discrimination

Globally and in the United States, women's custodial care often does not meet the minimum standards for the treatment of women prisoners. Taking the United Nations' minimum rules for treatment of women prisoners at face value, we find that the United States has taken the lead in criminalization of drugs and human trafficking (Andreas and Nadelmann, 2006), but is very lacking in meeting many minimum prison standards for both men and women.

International Women's Victimization

Human Trafficking and Slavery

Modern slavery—be it bonded labor, involuntary servitude, or sexual slavery—is a crime and cannot be tolerated in any culture, community, or country . . . [It] is an affront to our values and our commitment to human rights."

—Hillary Rodham Clinton, secretary of state (U.S. State Department, 2010)

Human trafficking is undertaken to bring undocumented individuals into a country for unpaid labor. Human trafficking is differentiated from human smuggling because it involves force or deception, fraud, or coercion (Aronowitz, 2009). Human smuggling involves the consent of the smuggled person and cooperation with the smuggler. A trafficked person may or may not cooperate depending on the use of deception. Human traffickers use individuals for forced labor and exploitation. Because of the use of force and deception, persons trafficked are viewed as victims, while individuals who volunteer to be smuggled are not. A smuggled person is violating immigration law while, if discovered, a trafficking victim may receive legal help. Once trafficked, the victim is enslaved and confined with minimal movement. Their documents are also confiscated and they are further coerced by being told that if immigration officials find them, they will be deported. In contrast, a smuggled individual is free to move about and change jobs. Trafficking may not even involve the actual physical movement of the victim, while smuggling always involves crossing a border (Aronowitz, 2009). There has been a major change in how trafficking is legally defined. Trafficking can occur within a country when a person is under 18 years of age. This change in the law is due to recognition of child sex trafficking. This involves taking a minor captive, whether a citizen or noncitizen, and forcing them to work as prostitutes or in other sex enterprises or to labor.

Obi I. Ebbe (2010: 41–42) provided the details of a New York City immigration court sex-trafficking case involving a Nigerian woman:

> In Nigeria, "Pat," a 21 year old female, was fraudulently recruited by her mother's close friend "Grace" to work in the latter's hair salon in Milan, Italy. Below is part of Pat's paraphrased testimony before the United States Immigration Court in New York City.
>
> Between July and August 1999, Grace visited Pat's parents four times in very gorgeous attire. Grace then asked Pat what she was doing for a living. Pat replied that she was experienced in hair care, but she had no job. Grace offered to take Pat to Milan, Italy, to work in the former's hair care salon. She told Pat that she had spoken to her parents and they had agreed. Grace also told Pat how great life would be in Milan and how she could make a lot of money and help her poor parents.
>
> When Grace and Pat arrived, Grace approached a man who seemed to be waiting for her. Grace introduced the man to Pat as her husband "Christopher." On the next day, Grace disappeared, leaving Christopher and Pat in [an] apartment. At night, Christopher raped Pat several times after beating her for resisting. He told her that he had paid 50,000,000 Lira (equivalent to $25,000) to bring her to Italy, that she had to prostitute herself in the street until he recovered his money. He added that he would be in the street to protect her.
>
> When [Pat] refused to be a prostitute, Christopher beat her so badly that she nearly died. At long last, Pat agreed to become a prostitute for Christopher. Christopher started taking her to the street at night, where

Christopher collected money from men and Pat had to have sex with the men in their cars. Pat testified that after she had had sex three times, on three different occasions with one of the men, while Christopher was out of earshot, she told him how she had been brought to Italy and wanted to run away, that Christopher was raping her every day and night no matter how tired she was, and that Christopher had seized her passport. The man told Pat that anywhere she ran to in Italy that Christopher would find her and might kill her. But he told Pat that he was going to find a Christian organization (a nongovernmental organization [NGO]) that would help her leave Italy.

On the night of the planned escape, Christopher and Pat went to the same location. Pat's "escape man" had arranged for another man to lure Christopher's attention away from him and Pat when they entered his car to have sex. When the escape man and Pat entered the former's car and pretended to be having sex, the decoy presented himself to Christopher as the next man to have sex with Pat and then led him to a corner. Then the escape man drove away with Pat through a different direction to the NGO's designated rendezvous. That night, Pat was taken to the airport and flown to the United States.

The case of Pat, who was granted asylum in the United States in the late 1990s, reveals linkages to coerced prostitution and violence against women. Girls and young women on their own with limited means of support who establish relationships with males, especially those who engage in drug use, may find that the "protective" bond leads to their sexual exploitation. Physical assault and rape are characteristic of men who use violence to break women and train them into prostitution. The moral condemnation of prostitution has led to much confusion in definition of who is a victim or a willing individual engaging in "sex work." Due to coercion and violence, it is hard for many social scientists to accede to the argument that prostitution should be treated as sex work. Similarly, because some girls and women may voluntarily engage in prostitution, it is difficult to view citizens or noncitizens coerced into prostitution as the victims that they are. Walking a fine line, if it were not for economic need, how many women would enter prostitution?

Internationally, it is estimated that 800,000 persons become trafficking victims each year. In the United States, it is estimated that 14,500 to 17,500 individuals are trafficked every year. Fifty percent of those trafficked are children. Human traffickers exploit adults and children in prostitution (46%), domestic servitude (27%), agriculture (10%), factories (5%), and other forms of work (12%). The majority of international trafficking victims brought to the United States originate from East Asia and the Pacific. In 2000, the United Nations organized countries to create and sign the Protocol to Prevent, Suppress and Punish Trafficking in Persons, Especially Women and Children. The United States responded to the Palermo Protocol by establishing its own legislation: The Trafficking Victim's Protection Act of 2000. The United States is attempting the difficult work of confirming human-trafficking cases. The Trafficking of Victims Reauthorization Act of 2005 required creation of a Human Trafficking Reporting System (HTRS) to track incidents of suspected trafficking. HTRS incidents are defined as: "Any investigation into a claim of human trafficking or any investigation of other crimes in which elements of potential human trafficking were identified (Kyckelhahn, Beck, and Cohen, 2009: 2). In fiscal year 2007–2008, 1,229 incidents were reported. Approximately 83% of incidents concerned sex trafficking: 48.5% were suspected forced prostitution and 31.8% involved child sex trafficking. Another 12% of cases involved labor trafficking. Fifty-nine percent of alleged sex trafficking cases involved adults and 38% child victims. Less than 10% of all incidents were confirmed; another 10% were pending validation, and 58% lacked information on whether or not the cases were substantiated.

Gender is a significant factor in trafficking victimization. Ninety-two percent of alleged victims of traffickers are women and girls (Kyckelhahn, Beck, and Cohen, 2009: 7–8). Due to proximity to the U.S.-Mexico border, 40% of victims are Hispanic. Whites (22.6%), blacks (20.7%) and Asians (13.2%) were also reported in victim incidents. Approximately 27% of victims were age 18 or younger. Approximately 55% are U.S. citizens, 6% are legal immigrants, and 38% are unauthorized immigrants. The characteristics of the smaller number of confirmed victims follow these trends, with the exception that 61.7% of confirmed victims are Hispanic and 64.4% were unauthorized entrants. Lack of legal immigration status compromises the situation of trafficking victims and their overseers exploit this.

Trends in case reporting have changed since fiscal year 2008. Banks and Kyckelhahn (2011: 1), Bureau of Justice statisticians, indicate that 2,515 suspected cases of human trafficking were opened by federally funded human trafficking task forces between 2008 and 2010. Eighty-two percent of cases involved sex trafficking including 1,200 alleged adult sex trafficking cases and over 1,000 reports of child prostitution or sexual exploitation. Three hundred and eighty-nine incidents were confirmed as trafficking, and 527 victims and 488 suspects were identified. One hundred and forty-four arrests ensued. Thirty percent of human trafficking reports were confirmed, 38% were not confirmed, and the remaining cases are still open. Indicating that the problem is primarily home-grown, 83% of confirmed sex trafficking incidents involved U.S. citizen victims. In contrast, 67% of labor trafficking cases involved undocumented individuals and noncitizens who entered the United States legally. Given the extent of concern about human trafficking, the number of identified women victims is low. Limited confirmation of cases and incompleteness of information given to law enforcement in trafficking cases suggests that the extent of the problem is still being mapped out and defined as internal or international. The classification of enslaved U.S. citizens, adults or children, as trafficking victims complicates understanding of human trafficking. U.S. citizens are more likely to be enslaved in the sex industries than in labor trafficking, which is dominated by foreign nationals. U.S. citizens are often runaways and homeless preteens and teens (U.S. State Department, 2010: 338). Noncitizens were more likely to be found in labor trafficking, contradictory to public expectation developed during the past two decades, which associate the importation of foreign women with sex work. Concern exists that foreign nationals who have entered under work or student visas may be trafficked, although they have a protected status as documented entrants. Foreign victims are primarily from Thailand, Mexico, Philippines, Haiti, Guatemala, and the Dominican Republic.

Internationally, women and girls are considered the primary trafficking victims and, reciprocally, men predominate among suspects. Approximately 78% of trafficking suspects were male (Kyckelhahn, Beck, and Cohen, 2009: 6). Women, often previous victims, are known to enter recruitment to lure new victims (Aronowitz, 2009). Among suspects, blacks were a majority (36.1%), followed by Hispanics (30.6%), Asians (16.2%), and whites (13%)

(Kyckelhahn, Beck, and Cohen, 2009: 6). Approximately 56% of suspects were U.S. citizens, and 21.4% were unauthorized entrants. Almost 11% were documented aliens and 7.1% were permanent residents. It would appear that certain U.S. immigrant communities may have both smuggling and trafficking connections. However, problems in obtaining incident reports may indicate that unauthorized entrants are more vulnerable to prosecution than citizens. Among suspects who have proceeded to trial, sentencing data was reported for 45 individuals (Kyckelhahn, Beck, and Cohen, 2009: 10). Of these, 64% were sentences to prison or jail for one year or more, while the remainder received probation, time served, or less than one year in jail.

The process of human trafficking involves three stages, which may include additional crimes committed against the victim (Aronowitz, 2009). The first stage, recruitment, may involve false promises to gain cooperation or kidnapping. Traffickers also use forged documents, in itself a criminal act. The second stage is transportation and entry. During this process, trafficking victims may be subject to assault, rape, forced prostitution, and false imprisonment. Additional trafficking-related offenses committed at that stage include corruption of government officials and violation of immigration laws. The third stage is exploitation of the victim. Traffickers employ unlawful coercion, the threat of extortion, theft of documents, and false imprisonment. Violence, including aggravated assault, sexual assault, and murder can occur. Many victims are forced to work in prostitution. Government officials may take bribes to look the other way. When adult women and girls or even boys are forced to prostitute themselves, it is important to recognize that they have not consented—it is rape. They are not being paid for sex; the trafficking organization receives the money. The proceeds from enslaved workers are then subject to money laundering—a way to "clean" and process funds into legitimate enterprises—and tax evasion. Again, corruption of police and other government officials may be involved. Internationally, the U.S. State Department maintains a ranking system that classifies countries according to whether they are taking sufficient action to control and then end human trafficking. It is organized into three tiers:

> *Tier 1*: Countries whose governments fully comply with the Trafficking Victims Protection Acts (TVPA) minimum standards.

Tier 1 Developed Nations: Australia, Austria, Belgium, Canada, Denmark, Finland, France, Germany, Ireland, Italy, Luxembourg, the Netherlands, New Zealand, Norway, South Korea, Spain, Sweden, Taiwan, and the United Kingdom.

Tier 1 nations known to have trafficking of women to developed nations in the European Union: Bosnia-Herzegovina, Croatia, Czech Republic, Georgia, Lithuania, Poland, and Slovenia.

Tier 1 Developing Nations: Columbia, Mauritius, and Nigeria.

Tier 2: Countries whose governments do not fully comply with the TVPA's minimum standards, but are making significant efforts to bring themselves into compliance with those standards, AND: a) the absolute number of victims of severe forms of trafficking is very significant or is significantly increasing; b) there is a failure to provide evidence of increasing efforts to combat severe forms of trafficking in persons from the previous year; or, c) the determination that a country is making significant efforts to bring themselves into compliance with minimum standards was based on commitments by the country to take additional future steps over the next year

Tier 2 Developed Nations: Israel, Japan, Portugal, and Switzerland

Tier 2 Developing Nations (majority of nations): Eastern European and nations within the former Soviet Union ranked Tier 2 include: Albania, Belarus, Bulgaria, Estonia, Hungary, Kazakhstan, Kosovo, Kyrgyz Republic, Latvia, Moldova, Romania, Russia, Serbia and the Slovak Republic, Tajikistan, Turkmenistan, Ukraine, and Uzbekistan.

Tier 3: Countries whose governments do not fully comply with the minimum standards and are not making significant efforts to do so. (U.S. State Department, 2010)

Tier 3 Developing Nations: Burma, Cuba, the Democratic Republic of the Congo, the Dominican Republic, Eritrea, Iran, Kuwait, Mauritania, North Korea, Saudi Arabia, Sudan, and Zimbabwe.

Examination of the tiers reveals that the developed nations, which are receiving nations for traffickers, tend to have responded to the issue. Developing nations tend to be placed in Tier 2 except for some Eastern European nations cooperating with the European Union to end trafficking. The Tier 3 list reveals a parallel, with a limited number of developing countries that are perceived as less cooperative, if at all, with the world's developed democracies. The United States ranked itself as Tier 1 (U.S. Department of State, 2010), while Mexico and Central American nations were ranked Tier 2. Examining the progress of the United States reveals many issues in preventing human trafficking, including effective training for law enforcement.

Bresler (2005) estimates the global profits from human trafficking and forced labor at $31.6 billion. Forty-nine percent of this amount is thought to be generated in developed economies. Another 30.6% is realized in the Asia-Pacific region, and Latin America/Caribbean (4.1%), sub-Saharan Africa (5%), and the Middle East/North Africa (4.7%) accounts for the remainder. In Great Britain, it is estimated that 18,000 trafficked females, including girls as young as 14 are working in brothels, massage parlors, and suburban residences (Milmo and Morris, 2008). The joint police Operation Pentameter resulted in the release of 153 women and 13 girls. Organized gangs are believed to cooperate on the internet to increase earnings. Technology used ranges from mobile phones to e-mail.

Trafficking Victims Protection Act (TVPA)

The U.S. Congress enacted the Victims of Trafficking and Violence Protection Act (VTVPA) to bolster the Thirteenth Amendment to the Constitution, which outlawed slavery. The VTVPA defines the two "severe forms of trafficking" as "sex trafficking in which a commercial sex act is induced by force, fraud, or coercion, or in which the person induced to perform such an act has not attained 18 years of age"; and "the recruitment, harboring, transportation, provision or obtaining of a person for labor or services, through the use of force, fraud or coercion for the purpose of subjection to involuntary servitude, peonage, debt bondage or slavery" (U.S. Department of State, 2010: 8–9). Forms of exploitation of trafficking victims include forced prostitution or labor, slavery, and/or removal of body organs. Preceding this law, the Protocol to Prevent, Suppress and Punish Trafficking in Persons, Especially Women and Children, an international law, was passed in 2001, making antitrafficking a principle of international law (United Nations, 2010). Both immigration and organized crime laws are broken when human traffickers bring a victim to the United States illegally.

The Protocol to Prevent, Suppress and Punish Trafficking in Persons, Especially Women and Children is an international legal agreement that requires its signatory countries to take action to prevent trafficking, prosecute traffickers, and provide victim protection. In the United States, the Victims of Trafficking and Violence Protection Act (VTVPA) requires international cooperation with sending countries to identify human traffickers. Law-enforcement task forces include the FBI (Federal Bureau of Investigation) and Immigration and Customs Enforcement (ICE) agents, which work with international police to acquire intelligence on human-trafficking rings. The U.S. government seeks to educate women abroad about trafficking and to provide funding to create economic opportunities in developing countries. In the United States, VTVPA, in conjunction with the Peonage Abolition Act of 1867, which made it a crime to force labor of any man, woman, or child as a slave, provides for prosecution and sentencing of human traffickers. The new law makes it a crime to deceive or threaten harm to coerce work regardless of whether it is sex work or any other kind of labor. Traffickers and knowing customers can receive up to 20 years' imprisonment for forcing adult labor. In the case of child labor, or if an adult victim dies, is kidnapped, or endures severe sexual abuse, the sentence expands to life imprisonment. This act also specifies that any U.S. citizen traveling to another country for sex tourism can be imprisoned for up to 30 years.

The VTVPA authorizes two types of immigration relief for trafficking victims: Continued Presence (CP), and T visas. "Continued presence" is a temporary status issued by law enforcement that allows a victim of severe trafficking to stay in the United States during an investigation. A "T visa" gives nonimmigrant status to victims of severe forms of trafficking who are at or near a port of entry because of trafficking, have helped with investigation or prosecution of trafficking, or are under 18 years of age and who would suffer extreme hardship if deported. They may stay in the United States up to four years, and the stay may be extended of it is needed for an antitrafficking investigation. After three years, holders of T visas can apply for an adjustment to permanent resident status.

The U.S. Office of the Attorney General (2010: 19–20) provides statistics on human trafficking. In fiscal year 2009, 380 victims were identified. Since 2001, 2,076 trafficked persons have been assisted. Fifty-three percent of FY 2009 adult victims were female. Among victims, 15% were identified as trafficked for sex, and another 8% were trafficked for both labor and sex. Sixty-six percent of minor victims were female and 38% were sex trafficked, with an additional 6% trafficked for both sex and labor. Certification and eligibility letters were sent to individuals in 29 states, the District of Columbia, and Saipan, a U.S. territory. Major countries of origin for all trafficking victims, sex and/or labor related were Thailand (26%), Mexico (13%), the Philippines (11%); Haiti (6%), India (6%), Guatemala (5%) and the Dominican Republic (6%). The U.S. district attorney's office indicates that psychological and/or physical trauma, victim concerns about their safety, and language barriers prevent identification of victims.

Police in sending countries may accept bribes or even participate in human-trafficking organizations. Involved police are called "corrupt guardians" (Farr, 2005). Bribery can ensure that false identification and travel documents are accepted, and U.S. inspectors have been known to take money to allow fraudulent entry. Alarmingly, corrupt guardians may help to enforce enslavement if they recapture and turn over victims or take bribes protect business using forced labor. They may also warn traffickers of investigations and raids (Farr, 2005).

Attempts to combat human trafficking are considered to be integrated with international border security measures. Nevertheless, it is difficult to determine whether an individual is being trafficked at the point of unauthorized entrance. Individuals who consent to being smuggled often do not realize they are being trafficked for sex or forced labor until after they have successfully made unauthorized entry (Kleeman, 2009: 419). If trafficking victims are apprehended at an international border, police complacency may result in the victim being treated as a criminal alien and deported. Fraudulent documents and payment to traffickers for border crossing make victims appear to be willing accomplices. Consent to being smuggled makes law enforcement reluctant to assign a status as a victim. The details of a trafficking crime are likely to go unknown because criminal aliens are denied due process and access to a lawyer, Sex trafficking and forced sex-labor victims are less likely to be helped by police because prostitution and sex work is criminalized. Police view victims as criminals, although victims were forced to act against their will. Police inaction creates a forgotten victim population and perpetuates their mistreatment. Human traffickers act with impunity because of law-enforcement inaction. Although efforts are being made to broaden police knowledge of this crime, many officers continue to need training in how to conduct trafficking investigations.

The U.S. VTVPA provides for protection of victims of human trafficking found in the United States. Victims are to be placed in shelters with security and given psychological, medical, legal, and job assistance. They are to be provided with temporary visas for their testimony against traffickers and will ultimately qualify for permanent resident visas. The United States has faced issues in carrying out this law because of problems in prosecuting cases in which the individual gave consent. They may have consented to the use of fraudulent documents and unauthorized entry. The VTVPA requires proof of harm and that work was forced or coerced. It is hard to prosecute cases of travel across international borders or instances in which individuals agreed to work in the sex industry. The victim has to prove victimization. Individuals are evaluated in a process called certification by the Department of Health and Human Services to determine if severe treatment due to trafficking occurred before receiving a temporary visa. This means that individuals who have difficulty proving their case may be deported and be subject to retaliation in the home country.

Violence against Women and International Advocacy

Violence against women is an international issue pursued by feminist advocates. Internationally, women's social and economic status has not shown the degree of increase of the developed countries, including the United States and the European Union. When women are considered not equal to men and devalued, violence against women and girls may be sanctioned rather than criminalized. International pressure exists to criminalize domestic violence, but the law-enforcement capability to do so is not strong in many developing countries and traditional attitudes persist, making reduction of this behavior problematic.

In the 20th century, global campaigns to prohibit behaviors such as drug use have involved coordinated legal efforts between nations that have been mediated by international organizations such as the United Nations. Typically, such documents as the UN Convention on Human Rights have sought to establish global prohibition norms. Global prohibition campaigns have included efforts to end drug and human trafficking, money laundering, antiterrorism, and piracy (Andreas and Nadelmann, 2006).

Transnational moral entrepreneurs (Andreas and Nadelmann, 2006; Becker, 1963) are people and the supporting organizations that seek to establish universal ethics to eliminate activities they consider to be evil. Western feminists have mobilized to give refuge to women negatively impacted by female genital mutilation (FGM). They have formed transnational advocacy networks (Keck and Sikkink, 1998; Khagram et al., 2002) to oppose violence against women. The ascendancy of this effort reflects the increasing status of women in developed Western societies during the past century.

Global prohibition norms seek to restrict the circumstances in which nation-states can authorize and participate in specified activities such as FGM. Nation-states that fail to enforce rulings against proscribed behavior are condemned and subject to international sanctions. Because the West is developed, they have been in a social and economic position to try to bring "universal" standards to the developing world. The evolving "international society" of international agreements is based primarily in Western European jurisprudence and, during the 20th century, the views and actions of the United States (Andreas and Nadelmann, 2006; Bull, 1984; Buzan, 2004; Wight, 1966).

Because standards of morality are not fully internationalized (and perhaps may never be fully consistent), and because these standards are externally imposed on the developing world, these efforts are not fully backed or enforced. The developed Western nations have pursued two paths toward changing prohibited behaviors: (1) adoption of refugee and asylum procedures that permit entry of individuals fleeing persecution due to said prohibited behavior; and (2) the criminalization of such behaviors within their societies (Andreas and Nadelmann, 2006). International adoption of standards has resulted in attempts to encourage criminalization of prohibited behaviors in developing nations that may be only loosely enforced, if at all.

In a social context accepting of what might otherwise be considered aggravated assault and rape outside of the family, it is not surprising that women, outside of the family, are frequent victims of violence committed by individual predators or organized crime. Internationally, forms of violence against women include femicide, domestic violence and homicide, genital mutilation, honor killings, and mass rape in wartime.

Femicide

The Americas is a place of patterned violence against and murders of women and girls. This is known as femicide. Marcela Lagarde y de los Rios (2010: xxiii) defines femicide as: "one of the extreme forms of gender violence; it is constituted by the whole set of violent misogynistic [woman-hating] acts against women that involve a violation of their human rights, represent an attack on their safety, and endanger their lives. It culminates in the murder of girls and women." She considers that femicide occurs because of authorities who are "omissive, negligent, or acting in collusion with assailants" who block institutional access to justice. Gendered violence is recognized as a human rights violation by the international community, and Mexican researchers (Lopez, Cabellero, and Rodriguez, 2010: 158; Monarrez Fragoso, Diaz de la Vega Garcia, and Morales Castro, 2006) have differentiated between types of femicide. Intimate homicide is "committed by men with whom the victim had or in the past had an intimate, familial, household, or other similar sort of relationship" (Cardoso and Sagra, 2002). This type includes child femicide, murder of a girl by a male or female in a social relationship of trust, responsibility, or power over a child because of that person's status as an adult in relation to a minor child (Lopez, Cabellero, and Rodriguez 2010: 158). Familial femicide involves death of one or more members of a family by a man who is in a familial relationship with the victims. In contrast to intimate femicide, "femicide of stigmatized occupations" refers to murder of women because of their occupation in jobs that carry low cultural status. Examples would include women working in bars or nightclubs as drink servers, dancers, or prostitutes.

The ongoing murder of women in locations such as Ciudad Juarez, Mexico, has been identified as systemic sexual femicide. Lopez, Caballero, and Rodriguez (2010: 158) define systemic sexual femicide as "the assassination of women who are kidnapped, tortured and raped. Their nude or semi-nude corpses are left in the desert, empty lots, in sewer pipes, in garbage dumps, and on train tracks. Through cruel acts, the assassins strengthen the unequal gender relations that distinguish the sexes." Systematic sexual femicide can be organized or unorganized. The organized form involves a network in which assassins consistently and systematically use a method of death aimed at erasing the identity of girls and women that is sustained over time. The unorganized form involves the killing of women often including kidnapping, rape, torture, and body disposal. These victims may be killed by family members, close friends, or strangers, and they are left in their homes, hotels, or remote places when dead. Researchers have identified employment in Mexican factories (*maquiladoras*), a large migrant population from the interior of Mexico, gangs, drug trafficking, and cartels as factors associated with a high rate of systemic sexual femicide in Ciudad Juarez and other areas of Latin America, which include Guatemala, El Salvador, Honduras, Costa Rica, Bolivia, Argentina, and Colombia. The violent murders of women are deemed misogynistic (woman hating) because of rape, torture, and mutilation, which occur before assassination. Unfortunately, systematic femicide is committed with impunity because of lack of effective law enforcement. Ciudad Juarez, Mexico, located across the border from El Paso, Texas, is the first Latin American location to be brought to international attention because of the disappearance and recovered bodies of women and girls. In 1993, there were 24 homicides of women and girls in Ciudad Juarez (Ibid.). This increased to 34 by 2005. From 1993 to 2005, there have been 442 recorded femicides. Total cases are classified as intimate femicide (28.5%), systemic sexual femicide (33.9%), femicide based on sexually stigmatized occupations (5.7%), organized crime and narcotics-trafficking assassinations (9.3%), community violence (12.4%), and negligence (2%), and 8.1 % could not be classified (Julia Monarrez Fragoso elaboration of Femicide Database, 1992–2005, El Colegio de la Frontera Norte, cited in Lopez, Caballero, and Rodriguez, 2010: 164–165). In response to this gender-specific homicide, the Mexican police are ineffective, losing murder case reports, mysteriously closing cases, and providing "solutions" that do not deal with the problem (Staudt, 2008). When mothers repeatedly visit police for information on daughters who have disappeared, sometimes for years, they are denied access and harassed. The *testimonio* (testament) of Eva Arce (Koopman, 2010: 47), whose daughter vanished on March 11, 1998, from Ciudad Juarez, gives evidence:

I've investigated a lot, but it hasn't done me any good, because I tell them everything, and they don't do anything. Neither the prosecutor or the federal attorney's office—it's the same thing: They don't do anything. I keep asking what they have done and it's the same story. The years go by and the prosecutors come and go, and the only thing they do is tell us nothing, and they refuse to meet with us when we ask for appointments. . . . I don't know what they have against me, because always wherever I go they have me totally under surveillance.

In 2003, they beat me and surrounded my house. They have followed me and called me on the phone to threaten me. They've tried to pick me up, too. Once they left me a message to go to the Hotel Lucerna to identify the body of my daughter, Silvia, but I didn't go. They wanted to put one over on me, and I thought, I'm not going, they'll disappear me, just like they did my daughter, Silvia.

Explanations of the Ciudad Juarez femicides vary from attacks by multiple serial killers or gangs, drug traffickers' "sport," spoiled sons of the wealthy, sex traffickers, snuff film production for American citizens, and the black market in body parts. International and Mexican organizations, including many women's organizations in Ciudad Juarez, are trying to end this violence but are encountering difficulty with law enforcement. Political scientist Kathleen Staudt views women's activism as part of the answer in addressing a gendered culture of violence against women on both sides of the border.

Domestic Violence and Homicide

In the 1990s, a worldwide study (Heise, Ellsberg, and Gottemoeller, 1999) estimated that between 10% and 50% of women, depending on the country, had been beaten by their spouse/partners. Wife beating is common in countries ranging from Bangladesh to Norway (Parrot and Cummings, 2006: 152). Southeast Asian women are at high risk of domestic violence. Human Rights Watch (1999b) reported that, in Sri Lanka, 60% of women have been beaten, 61% with a weapon. Among Pakistani women, 70% to 90% experience domestic violence. Parrot and Cummings (2006: 153) indicate: "It is generally agreed that intimate partner violence is a leading cause of injury among women of reproductive years, making it a global public health issue." Although known to be pervasive, issues exist in documenting the extent of the problem:

> The challenges to making cross-cultural estimates of the number of women beaten in their homes demonstrates the cultural complexities of the problem; in many countries, the extent of the violence is difficult to determine. Some cultures would deem any public disclosure of battering offensive so it remains a hidden problem. Many countries do not engage in any research to determine the extent of the problem. Due to social or religious beliefs, many cultures do not define battering as a problem. Some countries support wife-beating in an attempt to control women, The women themselves sometimes expect battering as an inevitable part of an intimate relationship. (Parrot and Cummings, 2006: 154)

In Southeast Asia, including Bangladesh, Burma, Cambodia, India, and Pakistan, acid attacks occur against attractive young women (Parrot and Cummings, 2006: 155). Men experiencing rejection or loss of dowry are known to attack women. Unapproved love relationships are often a cause of acid attacks against the face, neck, and upper part of the body. Rejection of a marriage proposal can lead to acid being thrown at the body and sex organs. In India, the practice of dowry, the giving of a payment to the groom (Caleekal, 2001), has led to "dowry deaths," disfiguring assaults on women with the intent to kill. "Kitchen fires" are blamed for women's deaths when they have kerosene deliberately thrown on them and are set alight for the purpose of keeping a dowry and gaining the possibility of another through marriage. Although the 1961 Dowry Prohibition Act was added to India's Penal Code, the number of dowry deaths in India has been increasing (Amnesty International, 2001). In 2005, India passed additional legislation to criminalize and prevent dowry deaths and violence against women. In India, Population Communications International collaborated with Indian social media to create a radio soap opera called *Tinka Tinka Sukh* (*Little Steps to a Better Life*), which addressed community and women's issues such as dowry death. It started community discussion of these gendered cultural practices although its impact has not been estimated (Sood, 2002).

Female Genital Mutilation

The World Health Organization (2008: 1) defines female genital mutilation (FGM) as: "All procedures involving partial or total removal of the external genitalia or other injury to the female genital organs for non-medical reasons." FGM, a type of operation to modify or remove female genitalia, is extensively practiced in sub-Saharan Africa and Egypt. It is becoming recognized as an act of violence against women. Feminists and Westerners have conducted a human rights and criminalization campaign in order to prohibit the practice in the West—an aspect of a "clash of civilizations." In the developed world, the concept of human rights abuse and right to asylum has been expanded to include violence against women. This is a result of a global prohibition campaign that has evolved into an international regime (Keohane, 1984; Krasner, 1983) based on international conventions and nation-state's refugee/asylum law and criminal law.

What term to use to describe female genital surgery—"mutilation" or "circumcision"—is controversial. The efforts to establish FGM as a refugee category under asylum statutes has led to the use of the term "female genital circumcision" (FGC) by academicians. In contrast, the term "female genital mutilation" is often used by change advocates, including the United Nations and World Health Organization, and emphasizes the trauma, health, and psychological impact of these operations. The use of the term "circumcision" by fieldworkers and researchers reflects a desire to be inoffensive and nonjudgmental. The term FGC has also been criticized because female circumcision is a much more invasive internal surgery than removal of the male foreskin. It has health, psychological, and reproductive consequences far beyond that of the operation given to males.

The World Health Organization (2001) estimates that 100–140 million women are exposed to FGC and classifies female genital mutilation into four categories. Type I includes removal of the layer of skin covering the clitoris (the prepuce), with or without the removal of all or part of the clitoris. Type II includes removal of the clitoris with partial or total excision of the labia minora (the two small folds of skin that lie immediately inside the labia majora of women and join at the front to form the hood of the clitoris). Types I and II might fall under the category of the sunnah circumcision and considered to be less severe than types III and IV or the pharonic circumcision. *Sunnah* refers to tradition or duty.

Types III and IV fall under the category of the more severe pharonic circumcision or infibulation. Type III is a more extreme form and involves the partial or total removal of the external genitalia and infibulation. Infibulation is the stitching together of the vulva in order to close it; only a small opening is left for the passage of urine and menstrual blood. Type IV covers a variety of procedures including the scraping of the tissue around the vaginal opening known as *angurya cuts*, posterior cuts from the vagina into the perineum known as gishri cuts, stretching of the clitoris and/or labia, cauterization by burning of the clitoris and surrounding tissue, and introduction of corrosive substances into the vagina (Communication Impact, 2005, No. 18). WHO is reviewing this classification and considering a Type V: ritual bloodletting based on small nicks to the clitoris, a very sensitive female organ.

Western feminists were the moral entrepreneurs who initially used medical reasons and concern about female sexual expression as the reasons for taking a universal ethical position against FGC. Medicalization, indicating the harm to health of FGC, has provided the initial primary reasoning behind a prohibitory campaign. In developing societies, FGC is done with knives, razor blades, metal, or broken bottles, without anesthetic and under unsanitary conditions. Teenaged and younger girls may experience shock and even die from this operation. Afterward, the vaginal opening may be the size of a match stick. Those who consider FGC harmful point out that it can have severe long-term health and psychological consequences. The more severe the procedure, the greater the threat to reproductive health and life will be. The physical impact of the operation includes unmitigated and severe pain, repeat bleeding throughout the life cycle, being unable to easily pass urine or retaining it, a greatly increased risk of infection, injury to the urethra and anus, menstrual difficulty, and fertility issues that include becoming sterile due to the practice. Women who have experienced FGM are also more likely to contract HIV infection.

Although labeled as Islamic, female genital circumcision is a cultural practice performed on young women as a rite of passage. Most countries practicing FGC are located in sub-Saharan Africa, with some in the Middle East and Asia. The highest rate is in Egypt. Additional countries with very high rates are Ethiopia, Kenya, Nigeria, Somalia, and Sudan. Older female relatives, particularly grandmothers and great-grandmothers, most often perform the operation. Female genital circumcision is represented to girls as a coming-of-age ritual. It is an aspect of traditional femininity, which is thought necessitated by family honor. Control over female sexuality is an objective. In the United States, the Centers for Disease Control estimates that 150,000 girls and women are at risk of FGM or have been circumcised.

The prohibition of FGC has involved feminist activists from developed and developing countries who became transnational moral entrepreneurs. Because FGC is painful and has numerous health consequences, feminists and political activists sought to define a behavior that was considered "normal" and define it as "deviant." The relative absence of such practice in the West and horrific reaction to it led to proselytizing for its prohibition.

Novelists have performed a function as moral entrepreneurs to create awareness of FGC. Prior to the development of human rights conventions, Alice Walker's 1992 novel, *Possessing the Secret of Joy*, drew attention to the issue of female genital cutting (FGC). Walker's book details the life of the fictional character Tashi, whose life suffers immensely due to the procedure. She is unable to enjoy intercourse and in marriage suffers greatly. Tashi's sexuality is contrasted when her husband has an affair and the woman does experience orgasm. Later in the novel, her child is born deformed due to complications from birth brought on by FGC. It is important to note that in Walker's novel, the fictional character Tashi chooses to have her operation done as an adult.

Women activists from the developed countries have encountered resistance from some international feminists who are struggling for broad-based social and economic rights in the aftermath of colonialism. Raising the standard of living to subsistence or above that level and achieving gender equality are seen as primary goals. On the other hand, the severity of FGC implies that women who undergo it do not have a high status. Integrating efforts to increase the social position of women with a strategy to reduce FGC through preventative education is a possible strategy.

After World War II, the United Nations and other international organizations have sought to establish conventions for the treatment of all humans that set precedents for organizing against FGC. In 1948, the United Nations passed the Universal Declaration of Human Rights. Article 25 specifies that all human beings have a right to good health and health care. This international accord has been cited as a reason to end FGC. In

1966, the International Covenants on Civil and Political Rights and on Economic, Cultural and Social Rights reinforced the right to health.

In 1979, the Convention on the Elimination of All Forms of Discrimination against Women (CEADAW) urged nation-states to: "take all appropriate measure to modify or abolish customs and practices which constitute discrimination against women" (art. 2f); and to "modify social and cultural patterns of conduct of men and women, with a view to achieving the elimination of prejudices and customary and all other practices which are based on the idea of the inferiority or the superiority of either of the sexes" (art. 5a). This was followed by CEADAW General Recommendation 14 (1990), in which nation-states were directed to take measures to end FGC; and General Recommendation 24 (1999), which emphasized that FGC operations have high risk of death and disability and that laws against FGC should be enforced.

After asylum law began a cycle of prohibition norm creation to protect women who were primarily from developing countries, the developed countries initiated their own set of anti-FGC laws. The arena of asylum law often connects with criminalization efforts in countries receiving asylum applicants. Globalization has brought the practices of varying social groups to international attention, and immigration can bring practitioners of FGM into a culture.

The policing of international crime has evolved into an increasingly highly organized body of law and enforcement institutions (Andreas and Nadelmann, 2006). Yet FGC is low on the list of international priorities compared to terrorism and drug and human trafficking. Because most laws against female circumcision are unenforced, a legal approach appears unlikely to be successful, with the exception of countries in which only small local communities practicing it (Althaus, 1997).

The drive to eradicate FGM has largely symbolic pressure from the West, where the many who are aware, if not all, consider it an ill-informed and inhumane practice in contradiction of women's rights.

United States

Criminalization efforts have led to the passage of laws in the West, including the United States. As part of the Immigration Reform and Immigrant Responsibility Act of 1996, the United States created a requirement that the Immigration and Naturalization

Service make immigrants aware of the illegality of FGM (Veazey, 2009: 203).

Representative Patricia Schroeder (Democrat, Colorado) was instrumental in the approval of the Federal Prohibition of Genital Mutilation Act (FPGMA) of 1995 (September 1996). This law stipulates imprisonment for up to five years for an individual who "circumcises, excises or infibulates the whole or any part of the labia majora or labia minora or clitoris of another person who has not attained the age of 18."

The reasons for passing anti-FGM legislation by the U.S. government seem to be related to concerns for setting the moral high ground in the international community and avoiding the embarrassment connected with the imprisonment of the asylum seeker (Boyle and Preves, 2000). In the 1980s, there was some discussion that making female genital cutting medically safe was satisfactory; however, this would have medicalized the procedure instead of medicalizing opposition against it. Thus, by the 1990s, the international community was only willing to accept a complete eradication of the practice, and all forms were banned.

In the United States, FGC operations may be given to children of immigrants from FGC origin countries in the Middle East, Africa, Indonesia, or Asian Muslim nations. Certain states have followed the federal government in criminalizing FGC. The FPGMA took effect in March 1997, and arrests were made in 2003 in California (Costello, 2004). The FBI conducted a sting, netting two individuals seeking to set up FGC operations. The states of California, Minnesota, North Carolina, Rhode Island, and Tennessee have passed laws against FGC. In the United States, it is difficult to find medical personnel willing to perform FGC. This can encourage illegal home operations.

The National Women's Health Center indicates that U.S. efforts to prevent FGC operations are problematized by "cultural adaptation, immigration status, economic issues, isolation and access to education and health care services." Immigrants may not seek health care for FGC conditions because of a fear of the legal consequences and inability to manage the cost.

European Union
Many countries in Europe have criminalized FGC, but the approaches utilized may vary from that of the United States. The 1979 Convention on the Elimination of All Forms of Discrimination against Women (CEDAW) identified FGC as an act of

violence against women which violates their human rights. The 1989 Convention on the Rights of the Child (CRC) identifies CRC as a form of child abuse. All member states of the EU have laws against FGM as a criminal act, an act of bodily harm or injury or for child protection.

Kyle et al. (2007) found that in Belgium, Spain, and the United Kingdom, health officials and police did not have sufficient knowledge about FGC or the law. This reduced reporting rates and follow-up. In the European Union countries, another issue in reporting FGC was the fear of being labeled a racist or culturally insensitive. Even in Western democracies, it has been difficult to enforce the law. FGC is perpetrated within families against minor girls, which make it unlikely that cases will be reported.

An aspect of criminal case procedure impeding implementation is the difficulty in finding evidence against a perpetrator. In families, secrecy may be maintained, and if girls are operated on abroad, there is a need for cross-border judicial cooperation. When child protection laws target FGC, compulsory measures to protect at-risk girls such as withholding of a passport are used only as a last measure after counseling the family. Seizing a passport intrudes upon the privacy of the family and raises concerns about enforcement.

The criminalization of FGC appears to lack clear strategies for implementation, which make protecting at-risk girls and convictions difficult. Public education campaigns about FGC are recommended, as many immigrants are not aware that the practice is outlawed. Examination of girls has been suggested as a way of detecting FGC, but it is after the fact and raises privacy issues. Modification of the laws to clarify implementation strategies may help.

Great Britain and other colonizing countries were among the first to criminalize FGM in Egypt and Africa. In Kenya, it is considered that such prohibition strengthened tribes' resistance to British rule. In Egypt, Great Britain did not enforce the law due to concern about rebellion. Today heightened awareness among impacted women has led to stands advocating for or against the traditional practice. The following 18 African countries have criminalized FGM: Benin, Burkina Faso, Central African Republic, Chad, Côte d'Ivoire, Djibouti, Egypt, Eritrea, Ethiopia, Ghana, Guinea, Kenya, Mauritania, Niger, Senegal, South Africa, Tanzania, and Togo. Sentences range from three months to life in prison.

Certain countries levy fines. Prosecutions have occurred in Burkina Faso, Egypt, Ghana, Senegal, and Sierra Leone. In Egypt, the heavily publicized death of a 12-year-old girl from the operation led to passage of prohibitory legislation.

When the FPGMA of 1996 was passed, it contained a requirement that the U.S. representative to the World Bank and related financial institutions oppose loans to countries in which FGC is prevalent and where there are no counter-FGC educational programs. The World Health Organization has also campaigned to raise awareness of the issue. Table 6.9 in Chapter 6 gives a list of countries that have passed laws regulating FGC. It shows that this legislation has come about since the U.S. law's passage. The overall impact, however, may not reflect the desire of foreign governments or FGC population constituencies to regulate the practice. As shown in the table, although some arrests have occurred, international information does not indicate extensive efforts to enforce the law, especially against the probable will of the general populace or select ethnic groups.

Law and Gender Equality

Government policy declarations may not be as effective as public information campaigns and counseling in countries in which it is thought to serve the common good. The negative impacts of criminalization of FGM can have unexpected consequences. It can force perpetrators underground. Victims may be reluctant to seek medical care because of fear of implicating their family. In Great Britain, immigrant families are known to send their daughters temporarily to home countries in order to have the traditional operation.

Ultimately, changing the social status of women by reducing the socioeconomic dependency of women on men through education and income generation may be more successful than prohibition and criminalization campaigns. In Senegal, outreach workers have achieved success in persuading communities to give up the practice through counseling and education.

Honor Killings

Honor killings are perpetrated by family members and relatives against rape victims and women considered to have engaged in premarital sex or accused of adultery. Taking virginity or sex outside of marriage is considered to diminish family honor. The

United Nations Population Fund (UNFPA) estimates that every year, over 5,000 women are killed in the name of honor. Honor killings are known to have occurred in Pakistan, Turkey, Jordan, Syria, Egypt, Lebanon, Iran, Yemen, Morocco, and other countries of the Mediterranean and Gulf regions (UNWomen, 2010). International immigration is associated with honor killings that have occurred in the United States, United Kingdom, France, and Germany.

In the United States, honor killings are prosecuted as homicides and linked to family violence. There are 50 documented cases of honor killings in the United States (see Chesler, 2009). Psychiatrist Phyllis Chesler (2009) has argued that the United States lags behind the European Union in recognizing that honor killings are distinct from domestic violence–related murders such as spousal killings. In the United States, Islamic advocacy organizations protest that murders of women by family members should be construed as domestic violence. Instead, Chesler (2009) argues, honor killings can be differentiated from domestic violence because they have eight different traits. First, honor killings are primarily committed by Muslims against Muslim girls and young women, while domestic violence is an act of men of all faiths typically against adult women. Second, honor killings involve fathers who kill their teenage daughters or daughters in their early 20s, although wives and older daughters are sometimes killed. Domestic violence is committed by adult male spouse/partners against an adult female spouse/partner. Third, an honor killing is carefully planned and death threats function as a means of social control, while intimate partner homicide is mostly unplanned and spontaneous. Fourth, multiple family members may take part in an honor killing, while intimate partner homicide is committed by one man. Fifth, girls and women are killed to end family dishonor; while domestic homicide does not involve honor, but a set of reasons ranging from suspected infidelity to a disliked meal. Sixth, honor killings involve extreme violence: rape, stoning, being burned alive, throat cutting, multiple stabbing, decapitation, etc. Domestic homicide may involve a man beating a woman to death or shooting or stabbing her. Seventh, honor killings are socially accepted, while domestic violence and homicide are increasingly viewed as crimes. Finally, honor killers do not show remorse, while those who commit intimate partner homicide sometimes do.

Chesler (2009) suggests that American battered-women's shelters do not meet the needs of battered Muslim, Hindu, or Sikh girls and women who are afraid of honor killing. Chesler's data indicate that 90% of honor killings in the West (United States and the European Union) are committed by Muslims against Muslims. She suggests that religious education could pinpoint the ethnic cultural basis of this behavior and indicate that the Koran and Islam do not promote the killing of women—including based on their sexual behavior. Regarding law enforcement, Chesler suggests that immigration officials should inform new-comers that: (1) domestic violence is against the law; (2) an honor killing is considered to be a crime of homicide; and (3) both the murderer and accomplices will be charged. As the problem of honor killing comes to be recognized in the United States, further legislation may be developed, as happened in the case of female genital mutilation.

Mass Rape in Wartime

This refers to patterned acts of rape of civilian women by military personnel rather than individual soldiers. Kathryn Farr (2009: 6) defines wartime rape as: "regularized, war-normative acts of sexual violence accompanied by intentional serious harm, including physical injury, physical and psychological torture, and sometimes murder." During World War II, U.S. soldiers in France and Germany are documented as committing mass rape (Brownmiller, 1975; Morris, 2000). In the 20th century, the following countries experienced conflict in which mass rape occurred: Belgium and Russia (World War I); Russia, Japan, Italy, Korea, China, the Philippines, and Germany (World War II); Afghanistan, Algeria, Argentina, Bangladesh, Brazil, Burma, Bosnia, Cambodia, Congo, Croatia, Cyprus, East Timor, El Salvador, Guatemala, Haiti, India, Indonesia, Kuwait, Kosovo, Liberia, Mozambique, Nicaragua, Peru, Pakistan, Rwanda, Serbia, Sierra Leone, Somalia, Turkey, Uganda, Vietnam, Zaire, and Zimbabwe (Gottschall, 2004). Public awareness of mass rape was first heightened during the conflicts in Kosovo and Rwanda (Gottschall, 2004).

In both the past and the present, it has been difficult for wartime rape victims to speak out because of disbelief and rape stereotypes. Those accused deny the crime. Nicola Henry, a wartime rape researcher, has provided the following quote from a soldier in wartime Yugoslavia to indicate how a victim can be demeaned when she makes a wartime rape accusation. The soldier stated: "I take full responsibility that there was no rapes, least of all did I try to rape [X]. Why would I do that? She's 45, and I'm only 26. Especially since the woman was unattractive. The way she was, I wouldn't lean my bike against her, let alone rape her" (Boyd, 2008: 1).

In the 21st century, active conflicts in which mass rape is being perpetrated include: The Democratic Republic of the Congo (formerly Zaire), Liberia, the Darfur region of Sudan, Chad, and Cote d'Ivoire (formerly Ivory Coast) (Casanas, 2010). In 2008, the UN Security Council passed a resolution recognizing rape as a war tactic reducing chances for peace. The United Nations has undertaken an initiative against sexual violence in conflict. Margot Wallstrom has served as the UN Special Representative on Sexual Violence. She has stated that mass rape "is no more inevitable than, or acceptable than, mass murder" (Casanas, 2010). "It is one of the great peace and security initiatives of our time," Wallstrom has indicated, but "it has been the least condemned and most silenced war crime" (Casanas, 2010).

Border Crossing and Rape

In the 21st century, the U.S.-Mexico border is increasingly recognized as a site in which smugglers, traffickers, and bandits practice sexual violence against undocumented women and girls. Arizona has become a site of "rape trees" (Vanderpool, 2009). Drug cartel members and human smugglers have been raping women and girls while they are in transit as undocumented entrants. Afterwards, they hang female undergarments on a tree to mark their activity. Michelle Brane of the Women's Commission for Refugee Women and Children states: "Nonprofit groups and even the U.S. Office of Refugee Resettlement—which has custody of unaccompanied children—estimate that the vast majority of women and female children encounter some sort of sexual assault en route to the United States. It's become the norm, and in many cases with female children, they just assume that there's been some sort of incident" (Vanderpool, 2009).

Social Harm and Human Rights Solutions

There is a history of failure to recognize social harms against women (Cain and Howe, 2008). Maureen Cain and Adrian Howe (2008: 150), British criminologists, stress: "Social harms against women . . . are quite frequently not defined as crimes and when they are so defined it may well be on terms that do not adequately redress the injury." Major efforts have occurred in classifying and developing strategies to identify, prosecute, and prevent crimes against women such as domestic violence. Recent legislation in 10 states ending the shackling of pregnant women during birth are a promising beginning toward ending mistreatment and recognizing the special needs of women prisoners. Globalization has generated the interconnections that can result in the transfer of cultural practices like female genital mutilation or the renewal of enslavement, especially of women. The new immigration has brought certain ethnic cultural practices involving social harm for women to Western nations. The United States and European countries have responded by criminalizing practices like female genital mutilation and strengthening penalties against honor killing.

The interconnection of formerly separated cultures within nations brings new challenges for law enforcement. New categories of women offenders, including drug mules and traffickers, have emerged to operate across borders. Borders are connected to violent crimes against undocumented women and girls.

References

Althaus, Frances A. 1997. "Female Circumcision: Rite of Passage or Violation of Rights?" *International Family Planning Perspectives* 23(3). http://www.guttmacher.org/pubs/journals/2313097.html

Amnesty International. 2010. *Human Rights in the United States of America*. London, UK: Author. http://www.amnesty.org/en/region/usa/report-2010

Amnesty International. 2007. *Human Rights in the Republic of India*. London, UK: Author. http://www.amnesty.org/en/region/india/report-2007

Amnesty International. 2001. *India: The Battle against Fear and Discrimination: The Impact of Violence against Women in Uttar Pradesh and Rajasthan*. London, UK: Author. http://www.amnesty.org/en/library/asset/ASA20/016/2001/en/c23e3527-db7b-11dd-af3c-1fd4bb8cf58e/asa200162001en.html

Andreas, Peter, and Ethan Nadelmann. 2006. *Policing the Globe: Criminalization and Crime Control in International Relations*. New York, NY: Oxford University Press.

Aronowitz, Alexis A. 2009. *Human Trafficking, Human Misery: The Global Trade in Human Beings*. Westport, CT: Praeger.

Banks, Duran, and Tracey Kyckelhahn. 2011. *Characteristics of Suspected Human Trafficking Incidents, 2008–2010*. Washington, DC: Bureau of Justice Statistics.

Beittel, June S. 2009. *Congressional Research Report for Congress: Mexico's Drug-Related Violence*. http://www.fas.org/sgp/crs/row/R40582.pdf

Belfast Telegraph. 2008. "18,000 Women and Children Trafficked into UK Sex Trade." July 3. http://www.belfasttelegraph.co.uk/news/local-national/18000-women-and-children-trafficked-into-uk-sex-trade-13898385.html.

Boyd, Cameron. 2008. "Wartime Rape, Collective Memory and the Law: Interview with Nicola Henry." *ACSSA Newsletter* 19. http://www.aifs.gov.au/acssa/pubs/newsletter/n19pdf/n19_6.pdf

Bresler, Patrick. 2005. "Forced Labor and Human Trafficking: Estimating the Profits." Working Paper. Geneva: International Labor Organization (ILO).

Brownmiller, Susan. 1975. *Against Our Will: Men, Women and Rape*. New York, NY: Simon and Schuster.

Bull, Hedley. 1984. "The Emergence of an International Society." In Hedley Bull and Adam Watson (Eds.), *The Expansion of International Society*. New York, NY: Oxford University Press.

Bunker, Pamela L., Lisa J. Campbell, and Robert J. Bunker. 2010. "Torture, Beheadings and Narcocultos." *Small Wars and Insurgencies* 21(1): 145–178.

Buzan, Barry. 2002. *From International to World Society? English School Theory and the Social Structure of Globalization*. Cambridge, UK: Cambridge University Press.

Cain, Maureen, and Adrian Howe. 2008. "Introduction: Women, Crime and Social Harm: Towards a Criminology for the Global Age." In Maureen Cain and Adrian Howe (Eds.), *Women, Crime and Social Harm: Towards a Criminology for the Global Age* (pp. 1–20). Oxford, UK, and Portland, OR: Hart Publishing.

Caleekal, Amuppa, 2001. "Dowry Death: Its Gruesome Reality and Future Interface in a Digital Cultural Revolution." http://www.digitalism.org/artdoc/ddeath.html

Campbell, Howard. 2009. "Female Drug Smugglers on the U.S.-Mexico Border: Gender, Crime and Empowerment." *Anthropological Quarterly*: 233–267.

Carcedo, Ana, and Montserrat Sagot. 2002. *Femicide in Costa Rica, 1990–1999*. San Jose, Costa Rica: Centra Feminista de Informacion y Accion.

Casanas, Gabriel. 2010. "UN: Wartime Rape No More Inevitable, Acceptable Than Mass Murder." Atlanta, GA: CNN International Edition. http://edition.cnn.com/2010/WORLD/africa/08/12/un.wartime.rape/

Casteel, Steven W. 2003. "Narco-Terrorism, International Drug Trafficking and Terrorism—a Dangerous Mix." Statement before the U.S. Senate Judiciary Committee, May 20. http://www.usdoj.gov/dea/pubs/cngrtest/ct052003.html

Chesler, Phyllis. 2009. "Are Honor Killings Simply Domestic Violence?" *Middle Eastern Quarterly* 16(2): 61–69. http://www.meforum.org/2067/are-honor-killings-simply-domestic-violence

Chesney-Lind, Meda. 2006. "Patriarchy, Crime and Justice: Feminist Criminology in an Era of Backlash." *Feminist Criminology* 1(1): 6–26.

Collins, Patricia Hill. "New Commodities, New Consumers: Selling Blackness in a Global Marketplace." *Ethnicities* 6: 297–317.

De los Rios, Marcela Lagarde Y. 2010. "Introduction." In Rosa-Linda Fregoso and Cynthia Bejarano (Eds.), *Terrorizing Women: Femicide in the Americas* (pp. xi–xxvi). Durham, NC: Duke University Press.

Dworkin, Andrea. 1988. *Letters From a War Zone: Writings 1976–1989*, Part 3, *Take Back the Day: I Want a 24 Hour Truce in Which There Is No Rape*. http://www.visuality.org/feministtheories/twentyfourhour_truce_on_rape.pdf

Ebbe, Obi N., and Dillip K. Das. 2010. *Criminal Abuse of Women and Children: An International Perspective*. New York, NY: CRC Press.

Egan, Timothy. 1998. "Contact With Young Lover Lands Ex-Teacher in Prison." *New York Times*. February 7. http://www.nytimes.com/1998/02/07/us/contact-with-young-lover-lands-ex-teacher-in-prison.html?ref=mary_kay_letourneau

Ekberg, Gunilla S. 2004. "The Swedish Law That Prohibits the Sale of Sexual Services." *Violence against Women* 10: 1187–1218. http://action.web.ca/home/catw/attach/Ekberg.pdf

Farley, Melissa. 2006. "Prostitution, Trafficking and Cultural Amnesia: What We Must Not Know in Order to Keep the Business of Sexual Exploitation Running Smoothly." *Yale Journal of Law and Feminism* 18: 101–136.

Farr, Kathryn. 2009. "Extreme War Rape in Today's Civil-War-Torn States: A Contextual and Comparative Analysis." *Gender Issues* 26: 1–41.

Gottschall, Jonathan. 2004. "Explaining Wartime Rape." *Journal of Sex Research* 41(2): 129–136.

Heise L., M. Ellsberg, and M. Gottemoeller. 1999. *Ending Violence against Women*. Population Reports Series. Series L, no. 11. Baltimore, MD: Population Information Programs, Johns Hopkins School of Public Health.

International Center for Prison Studies. 2010. *World Prison Brief*. http://www.prisonstudies.org/info/worldbrief/

Keck, Margaret E., and Kathryn Sikkink. 1998. *Activists beyond Borders: Advocacy Networks in International Politics*. Ithaca, NY: Cornell University Press.

Kempadoo, Kamala, and J. Doezama. 1998. *Global Sex Workers: Rights, Resistance, and Redefinition*. New York, NY: Routledge.

Keohane, Robert O. 1984. *After Hegemony: Cooperation and Discord in the World Political Economy*. Princeton, NJ: Princeton University Press.

Khagram, Sanjeev, James V. Rikker and Kathryn Sikkink. 2002. *Restructuring World Politics: Transnational Social Movements, Networks and Norms*. Minneapolis: University of Minnesota Press.

Koopman, Sara. 2010. "Testimonio: Eva Arce, Mother of Silvia Arce, Disappeared on March 11, 1998." In Rosa-Linda Fregoso and Cynthia Bejarano (Eds.), *Terrorizing Women: Femicide in the Americas* (pp. 45–48). Durham, NC: Duke University Press.

Krastner, Stephen D. (Ed.). 1983. *International Regimes*. Ithaca, NY: Cornell University Press.

Kruttschnitt, Candace. 2010. "The Paradox of Women's Imprisonment." *Daedalus* 139(3): 32–42.

Kunze, Erin I. 2010. "Sex Trafficking via the Internet: How International Agreements Address the Problem and Fail to Go Far Enough." *Journal of High Technology and Law* 10: 241–289.

Kyckelhahn, Tracey, Allen J. Beck, and Thomas H. Cohen. 2009. *Characteristics of Alleged Human Trafficking Incidents, 2007–2008*. Washington, DC: U.S. Bureau of Justice Statistics. http://bjs.ojp.usdoj .gov/content/pub/pdf/cshti08.pdf

Liptak, Adam. 2008. "U.S. Prison Population Dwarfs That of Other Nations." *New York Times*, April 23. http://www.nytimes.com/2008/04/ 23/world/americas/23iht-23prison.12253738.html

Lopez, Adriana Carmona, Alma Gomez Caballero, and Lucha Castro Rodriguez. 2010. "Femicide in Latin America in the Movement for Women's Human Rights." In Rosa-Linda Fregoso and Cynthia Bejarano (Eds.), *Terrorizing Women: Femicide in the Americas* (pp. 157–176). Durham, NC: Duke University Press.

Monarrez Fragoso, Julia, Pedro Diaz de la Vega Garcia, and Patricia Morales Castro. 2006. "Sistema Socioeconomica y Geo-referrencial Sobre la Violencia de Genero en Ciudad Juarez, Chihuahua: Propuestas Para su Prevencion." Comision para Prevenir y Eradicar la Violencia contra las Mujeres en Ciudad Juarez, El Colegio de la Frontera Norte, and Instituto Nacional de Estadistica, Geographia y Informarica, Ciudad Juarez, July.

Morris, M. (2000). "In War and Peace: Rape, War and Military Culture." In A. Barstow (Ed.), *War's Dirty Secret: Rape, Prostitution and Other Crimes against Women*. Cleveland, OH: The Pilgrim's Press.

Parrot, Andrea, and Nina Cummings. 2006. *Forsaken Females: The Global Brutalization of Women*. Lanham, MD: Rowman & Littlefield.

Payan, Tony. 2006. *The Three U.S.-Mexico Border Wars: Drugs, Immigration, and Homeland Security*. Westport, CT: Praeger Security International.

Russell, Diana E. H. 2001. "Defining Femicide and Related Concepts." In Diana E. H. Russell and Roberta A. Harmes (Eds.), *Femicide in Global Perspective* (pp. 12–28). New York, NY: Teachers College Press.

Sack. Kevin. 2001."AIDS Epidemic Takes Toll on Black Women." *New York Times*, July 3. http://www.nytimes.com/2001/07/03/health/03AIDS.html

Sood, A. 2002. "Audience Involvement and Entertainment-Education." *Communications Theory* 12(2): 153–172.

Staudt, Kathleen. 2008. *Violence and Activism at the Border: Gender, Fear and Everyday Life in Ciudad Juarez*. Austin: University of Texas Press.

Sudbury, Julia. 2002. "celling black bodies: black women in the global prison industrial complex." *Feminist Review* 70: 57–74. http://www.mills.edu/academics/faculty/eths/jsudbury/Celling_black.pdf

Sudbury, Julia (Ed.). 2005. *Global Lockdown: Race, Gender and the Prison-Industrial Complex*. New York, NY: Routledge.

Sutherland, Edwin H. 1949. *White Collar Crime*. New York, NY: Holt, Rinehart and Winston.

United Nations. 2010. "United Nations Rules for the Treatment of Women Prisoners and Non-custodial Measures for Women Offenders (the Bangkok Rules)." New York, NY: Author. http://www.ihra.net/files/2010/11/04/english.pdf

United Nations Population Fund. 2000. *The State of the World's Population*. http://www.unfpa.org/swp/2000/english/index.html

UN Women. 2010. "Facts and Figures on Violence against Women." http://www.unifem.org/gender_issues/violence_against_women/facts_figures.php?page=4

U.S. Department of State. 2010. *Trafficking in Persons Report* (10th ed.). http://www.state.gov/documents/organization/142979.pdf

U.S. Office of the Attorney General. 2010. *Attorney General's Annual Report to Congress and Assessment of U.S. Government Activities to Combat Trafficking in Persons: Fiscal Year 2009*. Washington, DC: Author. http://www.justice.gov/ag/annualreports/tr2009/agreporthumantrafficking2009.pdf

U.S. State Department, Office to Monitor and Combat Trafficking in Persons Website. "Hillary Clinton Quotation." http://www.state.gov/g/tip/index.htm

Vanderpool, Tim. 2008. "Price of Admission." *Tucson Weekly.*

Veazey, Linda. 2009. "When Ignorance May Be the Defense: Immigrants and Knowledge of U.S Law." *Judicature* 92(5): 202.

Victims of Trafficking and Violence Protection Act of 2000. Public Law 106-386-OCT 28, 2000. http://www.state.gov/documents/organization/10492.pdf

Walmsley, Roy. 2009. *World Imprisonment List* (8th ed.). London, UK: King's College London, International Center for Prison Studies.

Walmsley, Roy. 2006. *World Female Imprisonment List.* London, UK: King's College London, International Center for Prison Studies. http://www.prisonpolicy.org/scans/Worldfemaleimprisonmentlist.pdf

Waltman, Max. 2010. "A Working Paper: Prohibiting Purchase of Sex in Sweden: Impact, Obstacles, Potential and Supporting Escape." http://www.prostitutionresearch.com/Waltman2010ProhibitingPurchaseOfSexInSweden_WORKING_PAPER-3.pdf

Wight, Marvin. 1968. *Western Values in International Relations: Diplomatic Investigations.* Boston, MA: Harvard University Press.

World Health Organization. 2008. *Eliminating Female Genital Mutilation: An Interagency Statement—OHCR, UNAIDS, UNDP, UNECA, UNESCO, UNFPA, UNCHR, UNICEF, UNIFEM, WHO.* http://whqlibdoc.who.int/publications/2008/9789241596442_eng.pdf

4

Chronology

Antiquity and the Origins of Patriarchy: 10,000 BCE–500 BCE

380 BCE   Greek women are designated as having no legal status independent of men.

Republican Rome: 509 BC–27 BC

49   The *lex Iulia de vi* establishes that rape is forcible intercourse, but that only an individual with freeborn status can bring the charge.

Dominate: AD 284–476 (Western Empire); AD 284–565 (Eastern Empire)

320   Constantine passes a *raptus* law punishing the abduction of a girl, which could include rape.

538   The Codex Justinianus defines *raptus* as the abduction, seduction, or rape of a woman regardless of her social standing and whether or not she is enslaved.

Middle Ages: 501–1500

600   Women in England may be punished in public as "scolds."

Early Modern Period: 1501–1800 (Colonial and Early America)

1619   Twenty men and women from Africa are brought on a slave ship to Jamestown and were sold in the first North American slave auction. British and international custom allows servitude for life. White Christians who come as indentured servants serve for a limited and defined term.

1638   The Massachusetts Bay colony expels Anne Hutchinson.

1640   Massachusetts legalizes slavery. English common law is changed because it is specified that a child inherits the status of the mother. This permits intergenerational slavery.

1662   Virginia legislates that the child of a nonwhite mother cannot be born free, contrary to English common law in which a child inherits the father's status.

1663   Maryland enacts a law that permits enslavement of white women who marry black slaves. The children of white-black interracial unions are considered slaves.

1664   Maryland becomes the first state to make marriage between a white woman and a black slave illegal.

1667   Virginia enacts a law that prevents baptized "slaves by birth" from being free.

1692   The Salem witch trials condemn 19, mostly women, to die.

1711   A Pennsylvania act outlawing slavery is rejected by Queen Anne of England.

1765–1769   William Blackstone publishes Commentaries on the Laws of England.

1769   The American colonies adopt English common law. It treats a husband and wife as one person. Women have no legal status apart from their husbands.

1777   Vermont, not yet officially recognized as a state, outlaws slavery.

1780   Massachusetts passes an antislavery law and gives African American men, but not women, the right to vote.

Pennsylvania passes a law requiring the gradual abolition of slavery.

1787   Thomas Jefferson's daughter Mary and Sally Hemmings, his enslaved mistress, accompany him to Paris

1792   Englishwoman Mary Wollstonecraft publishes *A Vindication of the Rights of Women*.

The Spread of Industrialization: 1801–1890

1802   Ohio adopts a constitution that abolishes slavery but does not permit African American men to vote.

Thomas Jefferson is accused by the *Richmond Recorder* of keeping Sally Hemmings "as his concubine, one of his own slaves."

1804   The Napoleonic Code of France specifies that women, children, and the insane are legal minors.

1807   New Jersey revokes the right of women to vote, a right they were granted by the Constitution of New Jersey in 1776.

1808	Importing slaves to the United States is federally out-lawed. Estimates are that 250,000 African men and women were imported after it became illegal.
1824	The Missouri Supreme Court rules that a husband can beat his wife.
1837	The Mississippi State Supreme Court rules that Betsy Allen, a Chicasaw, could protect her property from her white husband's creditors.
1831–1861	The Underground Railroad facilitates the escape of African American men, women, and children to free-dom in the northern states or Canada.
1832	African American women establish an antislavery society in Salem, Massachusetts, on behalf of enslaved African American women.
1833	The American Anti-Slavery Society is founded (AASS).
	Lucretia Mott and others found the Philadelphia Female Anti-Slavery Society.
1837	Women hold an American Women's Anti-Slavery Convention in New York.
1839	Maryland passes the first Married Women's Property Act.
1840	Women delegates are refused admittance to an international Anti-Slavery Convention in London. An initial women's rights convention is called by Lucretia Mott and Elizabeth Cady Stanton.
1843	Dorothea Dix's reports about the condition of the insane in prison lead to reform.
	Sojourner Truth begins her abolitionist work.
1848	The Seneca Falls Women's Rights Convention begins the American women's suffrage movement and

adopts a Declaration of Sentiments, which parallels the Bill of Rights. Frederick Douglas and other prominent male and female antislavery activists attend. Sixty-eight women and 32 men sign the Declaration of Sentiments.

New York adopts the Married Women's Property Act, which allows women some control over earnings and property.

Harriet Tubman escapes enslavement and returns to free over 300 slaves in repeat tries.

1850   Congress passes the Fugitive Slave Act.

1851   Sojourner Truth's speech "Ain't I a Woman?" is given in Akron, Ohio.

1857   The U.S. Supreme Court *Dred Scott* decision determines that African Americans do not have the right of citizens.

1861   Harriet Jacobs's autobiography, *Incidents in the Life of a Slave Girl*, is published and describes the sexual exploitation of African American enslaved women.

1862   Congress abolishes slavery.

            The Emancipation Proclamation frees slaves in territories of the Union.

1865   The Thirteenth Amendment to the Constitution abolishes slavery in the United States.

            Elizabeth Cady Stanton, Susan B. Anthony, Frederick Douglas, Lucy Stone, and others begin the American Equal Rights Association to work for equal rights for women and African Americans.

1866   All Southern states have legislatively passed Black Codes to restrict the right of African Americans to vote, serve on juries or testify against whites in court.

1868   Myra Bradwell begins publication of the *Chicago Legal News*. In the second issue, she adds a column on "Law Relating to Women," advocating that women be allowed to vote and reporting on women practicing law in an era before women were admitted to the bar.

The American Equal Rights Association splits over which group, women or African Americans, should be prioritized in working for equal rights.

The Fourteenth Amendment to the Constitution grants African American men the right to citizenship.

1869   In Great Britain, women gain the right to own property.

Arabella Mansfield of Iowa becomes the first woman admitted to the bar to practice law in the United States.

Myra Bradwell applies to the Illinois Bar but is denied due to her sex.

The *Chicago Legal News* reports that Mary E. Magoon has a law office in North English, Iowa. Although not admitted to the bar, she was able to practice at the county level.

Lema Barkaloo becomes the first woman admitted to a law school at Washington University in Saint Louis. She did not complete the degree, but passed the Missouri Bar exam after studying for a year.

The Prohibition Party is founded to lobby against the sale and drinking of alcohol.

Elizabeth Cady Stanton and Susan B. Anthony found the National Woman Suffrage Association.

Lucy Stone found the American Woman Suffrage Association.

The Wyoming Territory grants suffrage to women.

1870   The Fifteenth Amendment to the Constitution provides for voting rights regardless of "race, color, or previous condition of servitude," yet did not include women.

Lema Barkaloo begins law practice but passes away from typhoid at age 22.

Ada Kepley becomes the first women to receive a formal law degree. She graduates with an LLB from Union College of Law in Chicago, now known as Northwestern.

Esther McQuigg Morris becomes the first woman judge when she receives an appointment as justice of the peace in a Wyoming mining town.

Utah grants suffrage to women.

1871   Belva Ann Lockwood enters the National University Law School.

Alabama and Massachusetts courts overturn legal precedent that a husband can beat his wife.

1872   Charlotte E. Ray becomes the first African American woman admitted to the bar to practice law in the District of Columbia.

Myra Colby Bradwell is denied the right to practice law because she is considered a legal extension of her husband.

Victoria Clafflin Woodhull founds the Equal Rights Party. Its principles feature socialism and sexual and racial equality. She runs for president.

1874   The Woman's Christian Temperance Union is founded.

1889   Jane Adams and Ellen Gates Star found Hull House, the first settlement house in the United States.

The Progressive Era: 1890s–1930

1891   Marie Owens hired as a police officer in Chicago.

1893   The Anti-Saloon League is founded in Oberlin, Ohio, in support of prohibition of.

         Colorado grants suffrage to women.

1895   The Anti-Saloon League becomes national.

1896   Idaho grants suffrage to women.

1900   All states have passed laws allowing married women some control over earnings and property.

1905   The position of policewoman is established.

1907   Congress begins an investigation of the trafficking of women into the United States for prostitution.

1909   Iowa is the first state to allow closure of a brothel by court injunction.

1910   The U.S. Congress passes the Mann Act (also known as the "White Slave Act"), made forced prostitution, harboring immigrant women prostitutes, and transport of prostitutes across state lines federal offenses.

         Alice Stebbens Wells becomes the first woman to work as a police officer.

1914   The Harrison Act criminalizes narcotics possession and sales.

1917   The U.S. Congress passes the Selective Services Act of 1917. It includes Section 12, the sale of alcohol to soldiers and establishing dry zones around camps. Section 12 authorizes the secretary of war to remove brothels from around the camps.

1919   The Eighteenth Amendment to the Constitution outlaws manufacture, transportation, and sale of alcohol.

               The Volstead Act authorizes federal enforcement of Prohibition but receives little assistance from urban law enforcement.

1920   Women receive the right to vote as guaranteed by the Nineteenth Amendment to the U.S. Constitution.

1926   Violette N. Anderson is the first African American woman attorney to present a case before the U.S. Supreme Court.

The Medical Model and Treatment Era: 1930s–1970

1933   The Twenty-first Amendment to the Constitution repeals Prohibition. States are allowed to establish their own liquor laws.

1945   The end of World War II is marked by prostitution near military bases.

1948   The United Nations passes the Universal Declaration of Human Rights. Article 25 specifies that all human beings have a right to good health and health care. This international accord has been cited as a reason to end all forms of violence against women

               The United Nations passes the Convention for the Suppression of the Traffic in Persons and of the Exploitation of the Prostitution of Others.

1950   Harvard Law School admits women.

1952   Congress passes the Boggs Act and establishes mandatory federal minimum sentences for drug offenses.

1956   Congress passes the Narcotics Control Act and con-
            tinues to add to federal mandatory minimum drug-
            offense guidelines.

1961   The American Law Institute proposes punishment
            for individuals who purchase sex.

1963   Ellen Ash Peters is the first woman to be granted ten-
            ure at Yale Law School.

            The Equal Pay Act is passed by Congress. It requires
            equitable wages for equal work regardless of race,
            creed, national origin, or sex.

1964   The U.S. Civil Rights Act of 1964 prohibits discrimi-
            nation in employment on the basis of race, creed,
            national origin, or sex.

1965   President Lyndon Johnson establishes the President's
            Commission on Law Enforcement and the Admin-
            istration of Justice to suggest reform for the criminal
            justice system.

1966   The United Nations passes the International Cove-
            nants on Civil and Political Rights and on Economic,
            Cultural and Social Rights reinforced the human
            right to health.

1967   The Report of the President's Commission on Law
            Enforcement and the Administration of Justice pub-
            lishes 200 recommendations for changing criminal
            justice practices.

1968   The first woman police officer is assigned to patrol in
            the community.

            Executive Order 11246 requires affirmative action
            plans to hire women and prohibits sex discrimination
            by federal contractors.

1969   The Seventh Circuit Court of Appeals rules in *Bowe v. Colgate-Palmolive Company*, 416 F.2d 711 (7th Cir. 1969), that women who meet physical requirements can work in many previously male-only jobs.

Community-Based Era: 1967–1980

1970   Repeal of most mandatory minimum sentences occurs, as they are recognized as ineffective and too harsh.

1971   The first hotline for battered women is established.

Nevada becomes the only state to legalize brothels.

California's legislature rejects a bill to allow particular counties to permit brothels.

1972   The U.S. Supreme Court rules in *Furman v. Georgia* that the death penalty is "cruel and unusual punishment" and voids 40 state laws.

1973   The U.S. Supreme Court rules in *Roe v. Wade* that a woman has a constitutional right to abortion.

1973   Margo Saint James organizes Call Off Your Old Tired Ethics (COYOTE), which is pro–sex work.

1974   Congress passes the Juvenile Justice and Delinquency Prevention Act (JJDPA). It stipulates that status offenders should not be placed in secure detention.

Michigan passes Public Act 266, which reforms rape law, influencing other states. It identified victims as male or female, specified degrees of sexual assault, made marital rape a crime, and did away with a requirement to prove victim resistance.

1975   The U.S. Supreme Court rules that juries cannot exclude women on the basis of their sex.

1975 (*cont.*)	Freda Adler introduces the "liberation hypothesis," which predicts that women will commit more crime as economic opportunity increases.
1976	The U.S. Supreme Court rules in *Gregg v. Georgia* that the death penalty can be applied, reinstating it.
1979	United Nations Convention on the Elimination of All Forms of Discrimination against Women (CEDAW) is passed. It identifies female genital mutilation as an act of violence against women, which denies their human rights.
1977	Oregon is the first state to require mandatory arrest in cases of domestic violence.
1978	Minnesota is the first state to allow warrantless arrests in cases of domestic violence.
1980	The U.S. Equal Employment Opportunity Commission receives guidelines on prohibiting sexual harassment.

Crime Control and Prison Warehousing Era: 1980s–Present

1981	Sandra Day O'Connor is appointed the first woman justice of the U.S. Supreme Court. The Massachusetts and New Jersey Supreme Courts rule that a husband can be charged with marital rape.
1982	President Ronald Reagan declares the War on Drugs.
1984	Congress passes the Sentencing Reform Act as part of the Comprehensive Crime Control Act. It authorizes the U.S. Sentencing Commission. Congress passes the Family Violence Prevention and Services Act and the Victims of Crime Act, which provides funding for shelters and domestic violence interventions.

Velma Barfield becomes the first woman executed after reinstatement of the death penalty.

Thurman v. City of Torrington (Connecticut) results in a $2.3 million award to Tracey Thurman due to prolonged police response time to her domestic violence call.

The Minneapolis Experiment provides data indicating that mandatory arrest is more effective than police counseling in preventing repeat domestic violence.

1985   The U.S. Surgeon General indicates that domestic violence is a public health problem.

Prominent Securities and Exchange Commission attorney John Fedders is forced to resign by President Ronald Reagan after his wife cites being repeatedly beaten for 18 years as grounds for divorce.

1986   Congress passes the first Anti-Drug Abuse Act. It provided for mandatory minimum prison sentences for drug possession and sales, eliminated probation or parole for certain categories of drug offenders, and increased fines.

Subtitle B of the Anti–Drug Abuse Act, the Drug Possession Penalty Act establishes criminal penalties for simple possession or a controlled substance.

The U.S. Supreme Court upholds race- and gender-based affirmative action.

1987   The U.S. Congress passes the Sentencing Reform Act. It provided sentencing guidelines for federal trial judges. Violent, repeat and white collar crimes were targeted for more severe penalties. Over 1 million sentences have been given since the act took effect, and it started the trend of a growing prisoner population including among women of diverse backgrounds.

The U.S. Supreme Court rules in *McCleskey v. Kemp* that racial disparities need not be recognized as violation of constitutional "equal protection under the law" unless intentional racial discrimination against a female or male defendant can be shown.

1988   Congress passes the second Anti-Drug Abuse Act. It provides for more severe penalties for possession of crack cocaine as opposed to powder cocaine and mandatory imprisonment for simple possession of more than five grains of crack. It results in increased imprisonment of minority women and men.

1989   The United Nations passes the Convention on the Rights of the Child (CRC), which identifies female genital mutilation as a form of child abuse.

The number of imprisoned blacks surpasses the number of imprisoned whites.

1990   The United Nations passes CEDAW General Recommendation 14, directing nation-states to take measures to end female genital mutilation.

1991   The Joint Commission on Accreditation of Hospitals mandates that emergency room personnel receive training to identify battered women.

1992   The American Medical Association and the U.S. Surgeon General suggest that women receiving medical care be screened for domestic abuse.

1993   Janet Reno is appointed the first U.S. female attorney general.

Ruth Bader Ginsberg is appointed to the U.S. Supreme Court by President Bill Clinton, becoming the second woman to serve.

1994   Congress passes the Violent Crime Control and Law Enforcement Act. It provides funding for 100,000 new police officers, prison expansion, and crime prevention programs. Other initiatives include the prohibition of firearms purchase and ownership by persons subject to a family violence restraining order; specification that states must recognize and enforce family violence restraining orders across interstate lines; enhanced penalties for immigration related crimes including expedited deportation for unauthorized aliens and aliens convicted of aggravated felonies; and requiring states to enact laws or regulations requiring those convicted of sexually violence crimes to register with agencies for 10 years after release.

Congress passes the Violence against Women Act (VAWA), which provides funds for rape and domestic violence victims, establishes a 24-hour hotline for battered women, permits women to litigate civil rights remedies for gender-related crimes of victimization, and authorizes gender sensitivity training for police and the judiciary. This law makes crossing state lines to commit domestic violence a federal crime.

Congresses passes the Gender Equity in Education Act for gender sensitivity training for educators, improving math and science training for girls, pregnant teen counseling, and sexual harassment prevention.

Congress passes the Jacob Wetterling Act requiring all states to keep a registry of sex offenders and provide the information to a National Sex Offender Registry.

California passes "Three Strikes" legislation. This initiative, which increased penalties after a third arrest, sends many California women drug users to prison.

New Jersey passes Megan's Law and requires notification of the presence of convicted sex offenders in communities.

1995   The Violent Crime Control and Law Enforcement Act results in ending education Pell grants for imprisoned women and men.

1996   Congress passes the Prison Litigation Reform Act (PLRA) and limits prisoner litigation. Women prisoners, lacking an extensive history of litigation unlike male prisoners, are very impacted.

Congress passes the Illegal Immigration Reform and Immigrant Responsibility Act (IIRIA), increasing Immigration and Naturalization Service authorization for alien detention. Immigrant women and men begin to increase in the federal prison population. IIRIA includes a provision that the Immigration and Naturalization Service make immigrants aware that female genital mutilation is a crime in the United States.

Congress passes the Federal Prohibition of Genital Mutilation Act (FPGMA) of 1995.

In *People v. Superior Court*, the California Supreme Court rules that judges may dismiss prior felony allegations in second- and third-strike cases "in the interest of justice."

A document on female genital mutilation urges international legal action.

1998   Sweden passes the Act Prohibiting the Purchasing of Sexual Services.

1999   The United Nations passes CEDAW General Recommendation 24, noting that female genital mutilation operations have a high risk of death and disability, and stressing that laws against female genital mutilation should be enforced.

The number of U.S. prisoners expands beyond 2 million.

2000   The Palermo Protocol Convention for the Suppression of Trafficking in Persons and of the Exploitation of the Prostitution of Others is passed.

Women are 13% of all police officers.

The Violence against Women Act is reauthorized with dating violence and stalking provisions.

The Supreme Court invalidates a portion of the Violence against Women Act ruling that rape and domestic violence victims cannot sue attackers in federal court.

2001   In response to the second World Trade Center attacks, Congress passes the USA Patriot Act.

2004   The Supreme Court rules in *Blakely v. Washington* that judges should not use judicial discretion to enhance sentences. Advocates believe this decision will impact the federal mandatory sentencing guidelines, especially as they pertain to the nonviolent drug crimes that are a major reason for women's and men's increased imprisonment.

2005   The Violence against Women Act is reauthorized with provisions to cover teen dating and prevention funds.

The Supreme Court rules that a domestic violence victim cannot sue a police department if a restraining order is not enforced.

2008   The United Nations' Security Council passes a resolution citing rape as a wartime tactic and deterrent to peace.

New York passes the Safe Harbor for Exploited Youth Act and becomes the first state to treat prostituted minors as victims, not criminals.

2009   Sonia Sotomayor is appointed to the U.S. Supreme Court by President Barack Obama, becoming the third woman to serve and the first Hispanic.

2010   Congress passes the Tribal Law and Order Act. Among the criminal justice issues the act addresses,

2010   it provides for programs that deal with high rates of
(*cont.*)   rape and sexual violence among American Indian
               and Alaskan Native women.

               Elena Kagan is appointed to the U.S. Supreme Court
               by President Barack Obama, becoming the fourth
               woman to serve.

               Jaycee Lee Dugart, abducted and kept in captivity for
               18 years, bearing two children, is awarded $20 million
               for lapses in duty by law enforcement of the state of
               California.

2011   The Violence against Women Act and the Family Vio-
               lence Prevention and Services Act are to be consid-
               ered for reauthorization in a harsh fiscal climate

               A petition to establish Caylee's Law, making it a
               felony for parents or guardians not to report a miss-
               ing child, is started.

5

Biographies

Freda Adler (1934–)

A leading theorist in the area of women and crime, criminologist and educator Freda Adler received a BA in sociology, an MA in criminology, and a PhD (1971) from the University of Pennsylvania. In 1975, she received attention for introducing the "Liberation Theory of Female Criminality," also known as the liberation hypothesis, which predicted that the women's movement would lead to a higher crime rate for women due to increased opportunities and the associated motivation. The new theory contradicted traditional pathological explanations of women's offending. Her book, *Sisters in Crime: The Rise of the New Female Criminal* (1976) has been followed with a prolific publication record: 12 additional books (author or coauthor), nine edited or coedited books, and more than 100 peer-reviewed journal articles. During her career, Adler has been president of the American Society of Criminology (1994–1995) and also served as a consultant to the United Nations on criminal justice issues. She is currently a professor emeritus at Rutgers University. She has received the Beccaria Medal from the Deutsche Kriminologische Gesellschaft of Germany, Luxembourg, and Switzerland; the Chi Omega Sociology Award; the American Society of Criminology International Division Award; and the Academy of Criminal Justice's Founders Award.

Polly Adler (1900–1962)

Born in Yanow, Russia, Polly Adler immigrated to the United States as a teenager. After working in a sewing sweatshop, she became madam of a brothel by age 24. From 1930 through the 1940s, she expanded her business all over Manhattan, catering to an upper-class clientele and also selling liquor, including during prohibition. The club offered a congenial atmosphere, and writers Dorothy Parker and Robert Benchley would come by for lunch. During the Depression, Adler was able to bribe officials and said to have the protection of gangsters. In the 1930s, Adler was repeatedly arrested, often before elections, but no charges ever stuck. In 1930, she was called to testify about political corruption and fled to Florida rather than betray clients. Finally, in 1935, she was arrested and given 30 days. She wrote an autobiography, *A House is Not a Home* (1953; reprint, 2006, University of Massachusetts Press).

Casey Anthony (1986–)

The daughter of two law enforcement workers, Casey Anthony was tried for murder in the death of her two-year-old daughter, Caylee Anthony. The trial of a mother accused of killing a child became a media sensation, as had the prior cases of Andrea Yates and Susan Smith. During news coverage, a profile of Casey Anthony as a habitual liar developed. For example, she invited her parents, George and Cindy Anthony, to her high school graduation, but she did not actually graduate as she had stopped attending classes late in the year. At age 19, Casey Anthony began to gain weight, but denied that she was pregnant and said that she was a virgin. At seven months, she finally told her parents. Caylee Anthony was born on August 9, 2005. Casey had been having sex with several men and could not identify the father. She wanted to give up the baby, but her mother discouraged her. Casey did not fit the profile of a mother who would form a strong attachment to her child.

Her fiancé, Jesse Grund, acted as the baby's father, and Casey and Caylee lived with her parents. In 2008, Cindy Anthony, her mother, viewed an online photograph of Casey at a "no clothes party" and accused her of being an unfit mother. After Cindy

Anthony threatened to take custody of Caylee, Casey took Caylee and moved out, stating that she would take a job at Universal Studios in another locale. When contacted, she would state that Caylee was with a babysitter, Zenaida Fernandez-Gonzalez. After Casey's car turned up in a tow yard with her purse, Caylee's toys, and an odor of decomposition, her parents confronted her. A tearful Casey told them that the babysitter, Zenaida Fernandez-Gonzalez, had kidnapped Caylee.

Thirty-one days after leaving, Casey reported Caylee Anthony as missing and told her story to police. False statements were identified. The babysitter did not exist, and Casey was not working at Universal Studios. She was arrested and a search was organized to look for Caylee Anthony. Casey was identified as a partier and as getting a "Bella Vita" (Life is beautiful) tattoo. Bounty hunter Leonard Padilla posted a $500,200 bond, and Casey was released. He hoped that she would provide clues but was disappointed. Casey was soon returned to jail for check forgery and using a friend's credit card. A meter reader found Caylee's remains in a wooded area near the Anthonys' home. Duct tape attached to the skull suggested homicide.

The Casey Anthony case came to trial in June 2011 and was broadcast live on cable television. The prosecution made a case that Casey was a promiscuous woman who was detached from her child. In her parents' home, a search about chloroform was found on a computer. Traces of chloroform were obtained from Casey Anthony's vehicle. Casey Anthony's defense attorney, Jose Baez, presented an alternate version of Caylee's death, stating that she had drowned in a swimming pool and that her father, George Anthony, had tried to cover it up to prevent child neglect charges. In addition, Baez alleged that George Anthony had sexually abused Casey and that her brother Lee had made advances. Ultimately, the jury accepted the alternate version and found Casey Anthony not guilty of first-degree murder, aggravated manslaughter, and aggravated child abuse. Instead, she was convicted on four counts of giving false information to the police. She received one year in jail and a $1,000 fine. She received credit for time served and good behavior and was released on July 17, 2011. Public dismay over the verdict in her case has resulted in a petition for Caylee's law: to make failure of a parent or guardian to report a missing child a felony offense.

Kevin Bales (1952–)

A leading antislavery expert, Kevin Bales received a PhD from the London School of Economics. He is emeritus professor of sociology at Roehampton University in London and a visiting professor at the Wilberforce Institute for the Study of Slavery and Emancipation, University of Hull, and he serves on the board of directors of the National Cocoa Institute. Bales's 1999 book *Disposable People: New Slavery in the Global Economy* earned a Pulitzer Prize nomination and has been translated into 10 languages. Revised in 2005, this work received the designation as a top "World Changing Discovery" on a list of 100 created by an association of British universities. The Italian edition of this book was given a Premio Viareggio for humanitarian service in 2000. A documentary that Bales cowrote, *Slavery: A Global Investigation*, won a Peabody Award in 2000 and, in 2002, two Emmy awards. In 2004, Bales received the Judith Sargent Murray Award for Human Rights followed by the University of Alberta Human Rights Award in 2005.

Bales is president of Free the Slaves, an affiliate of Anti-Slavery International, for which he is a trustee. He is director of the Alliance to Stop Slavery and Stop Trafficking and a UN Global Program on Trafficking in Human Beings consultant. He has advised the U.S. government on slavery and human trafficking policy. Bales edited a UN anti-trafficking toolkit and has authored a report on forced labor for the Human Rights Center at the University of California at Berkeley. For the National Institute of Justice, he researched human trafficking to the United States for two years. He is active in the international chocolate industry seeking to end child labor. Additional books he has authored include *New Slavery: A Reference Handbook* (revised 2nd ed., 2005), and *Ending Slavery: How We Free Today's Slaves* (2007). In 2008, with Zoe Trod, *To Plead Our Cause: Personal Stories by Today's Slaves*, and *Documenting Disposable People: Contemporary Global Slavery* with Magnum photographers, were published. In 2009, he coauthored *The Slave Next Door: Modern Slavery in the United States* with Ron Soodalter.

Arizona Donnie Clark Barker (1872–1935)

"Ma Barker" was a member of the Barker-Karpis gang. Her exact role is disputed, and she is viewed as either a decision maker or a member who was not involved in planning. Ma Barker was married to George Barker, and they had four sons who became increasingly involved in crime from a young age. Ma Barker believed that her sons were innocent and picked on by the police. The Barker sons became members of the Barker-Karpis gang, committing murder, kidnapping, robbery, and burglary. Ma Barker traveled with her sons and, not considered very intelligent, is thought to have provided a cover for the gang. In 1931, Freddie Barker and Alan Karpis killed a police officer, triggering rewards for bringing them in. Even a small reward was offered for Ma Barker. All of her sons were imprisoned for criminal acts, and each died violently. Ma Barker was very likely guilty only of aiding and harboring her fugitive sons and was never arrested. In 1934, a dying Barker-Karpis gang member alerted the Federal Bureau of Investigation (FBI) about the gang's structure, and Ma Barker was accused of accompanying her sons. The FBI, directed by J. Edgar Hoover, represented her as a criminal mastermind directing the gang, and she became a legend. In 1935, she was killed in an FBI raid on the gang. The FBI continues to represent Ma Barker as a major criminal in its publications, and the Baker-Karpis gang was the subject of four sensationalized movies including *White Heat* (1949), in which an overly loving mother has a gangster son (played by James Cagney).

Sandra "La Reina del Pacifico (Queen of the Pacific)" Avila Beltran (1960–)

Sandra Avila Beltran was born in the state of Sinaloa, Mexico. Her uncle was Miguel Angel Felix Gallardo, a key Mexican drug trafficker. Her relationship with Juan Diego Espinoza Ramirez, a Columbian cocaine trafficker, is thought to have led to drug trafficking involvement. In 2001, nine tons of cocaine were found in the Manzanillo, Colima Pacific port. It was traced to Beltran and Juan Diego Espinoza. They were arrested on September 28, 2007. She is accused of organized criminal activity, trafficking in drugs, and money laundering in both Mexico and the United States, which has requested extradition. Beltran is considered the most successful female trafficker worldwide.

Mukhtaran Bibi (1972–)

Mukhtar Mai ("respectful big sister") successfully challenged being gang-raped in Punjab, an eastern province of Pakistan. Her family was punished for a "crime of honor" committed by her brother. He allegedly had sexual relations with a high-caste woman from a high-ranked clan, and they retaliated against his sister. In addition, her brother was sodomized by a member of the woman's family to further punish him. Mukhtar Mai was a victim of clan reprisal against her brother and faced stigmatization after being raped and not meeting the cultural expectation that she commit suicide. Mai did not remain silent and defied religious and cultural tradition by taking her assailants to court. It took many years and attempts in varying courts to bring her case to the attention of higher government. In Pakistan, Mai symbolized the global efforts of women to challenge rape stigmatization. In 2005, she won her case in Pakistan's Supreme Court and received reparations. All 14 rapists and accomplices to sexual assault were convicted and imprisoned. A financial award that surpassed annual Pakistani salaries by 20% was granted.

Mai was named *Glamour* magazine's 2005 Woman of the Year. *In the Name of Honor: A Memoir* (2007) was published in the United States and is available in 23 languages. In 2007, she received the Council of Europe's North-South Prize. She is internationally known for her advocacy and has addressed the United Nations about the stigmatization of rape victims. Further defying tradition in a society where few raped women ever marry, Mai married the police officer, Nasir Abbas Gabol, who was assigned for her protection. Initially, she turned Gabol down because he was already married, but Gabol threatened suicide and his first wife convinced her. Although Mukhtar Mai was not allowed to attend school herself, she runs a school for young women and a shelter for abused women. She began the Mukhtar Mai Women's Welfare Organization in Pakistan and remains active in advocacy against honor killings and the stigmatization of women who have been raped.

Sidney Biddle Barrow (1952–)

Known as the "Mayflower Madam," Sidney Biddle Barrow was descended from ancestors who came on the *Mayflower*. First in her class with a business degree from the Fashion Institute of Technology in 1972, she traveled to Europe and then took a job with the A & S Department Store chain, which later went out of business. Going by the name Sheila Devin, she ran a profitable prostitution ring based in New York. Her Cachet escort service brought in from $400 an hour to $2,000 a night. In 1984, she was arrested but kept client confidentiality and pled guilty only to the charge of promotion of prostitution. She was sentenced to one year in jail and served three years on probation. In addition, she paid a $5,000 fine. The title of her memoir is *Mayflower Madam*.

Myra Colby Bradwell (1831–1894)

Seeking to bring women into legal education and the law, Myra Bradwell was a woman's activist and publisher. Historically, she was the first woman to be admitted to the Illinois Bar and became a practicing lawyer in Illinois in 1882. After receiving formal education, including attending the Elgin Female Seminary, in 1855, she began teaching school. Married to James B. Bradwell, she was exposed to the law as he was elected to the Chicago Bar and was a successful lawyer, judge, and general assemblyman. Myra Bradwell studied the law under her husband and apprenticed in his office. In 1866, she applied for a license, but her application was denied because married women could not enter into legal contracts. She was again denied on the basis of sex in 1870. Myra Bradwell appealed to the Illinois Supreme Court, based on the claim that denial of admission to the bar as a female violated her Fourteenth Amendment rights. In 1872, her petition was rejected in a ruling that denied women the right to practice a profession because of expectations for their sex. She was again denied because of her gender by the U.S. Supreme Court in 1873. In 1890, the Illinois Supreme Court acted to approve her first application, and in 1892, she received a license to practice, although she did not ever use it. She is remembered for her advocacy of women's rights.

Pat Brown (1955–)

Criminal profiler Pat Brown received a BA degree from the University of the State of New York (1981) and a master's degree in criminal justice from Boston University (2007). Brown's professional interest developed after she rented a room to a murder suspect. She began investigating crimes through profiling and, in 1996, founded the nonprofit Sexual Homicide Exchange (SHE), which provides free services for law enforcement. It also hosts the Society for Investigative Criminal Profiling, which provides research on deductive profiling and is establishing practice standards for criminal profiling. In 2000, the Pat Brown Criminal Profiling Agency opened. Her work involves helping police and victim families with profiles of criminal behavior, possible motive, and suspects through examination of behavioral and physical evidence. Brown provides profiling and forensic analysis as a national and international media figure on television, including the four-year series *I, Detective* on Court TV. Brown coauthored, with Bob Andelman, *The Profiler: My Life Hunting Serial Killers and Psychopaths* (2010, Voice). She is a founder and contributes to the *Women and Crime Ink* blog.

Laura Bullion (1876–1961)

A member of the "Wild Bunch" gang connected to Butch Cassidy, Laura Bullion was a noted woman outlaw who was considered beautiful. Bullion's father had been an outlaw, and she met William "News" Carver and Ben Kilpatrick at age 13. William Carver became involved with her when she was age 15. She worked as a prostitute until 16 or 19. Later, Laura Bullion is thought to have worked as a prostitute in Madam Fannie Porter's brothel in San Antonio, a gang hideaway. Bullion was involved with both Carver and Kilpatrick. She fenced stolen goods and made connections for horses and other supplies. In 1901, Carver was killed by the law, and Bullion was captured with Kilpatrick and convicted of robbery. Kilpatrick served time while writing to her and was killed in 1912 during a train robbery. Bullion served three years and six months of a five-year sentence. Released in 1905, she moved to Memphis, Tennessee, in 1918 and worked as a seamstress.

Bonnie Campbell (1948–)

Beginning life as the daughter of a factory worker and single mother with five children, Bonnie Campbell milked cows as a child. She was an excellent student and took a civil service job in

Washington, D.C., after high school. She married coworker Ed Campbell and became politically involved. In Iowa, she joined the Democratic Party and attained a BA and a law degree from Cornell. A traumatic experience changed her life when her half brother Stephen Pierce raped and murdered a 16-year-old girl. She became interested in victims' rights and was stalked herself by a stranger. When she won election as Iowa's attorney general in 1990, she worked on antistalking and domestic violence laws and helped to establish shelters and domestic violence victim compensation programs. After the passage of the 1995 Violence against Women Act, President Bill Clinton appointed her director of the Office of Violence against Women. In 2000, toward the end of Clinton's second term, he nominated her to the Eighth Circuit Court vacancy, but she was never given a judicial hearing. Afterward, she has worked in private legal practice in Washington, D.C., and in Iowa. Campbell is a member of the Iowa State Board of Regents,

Hillary Rodham Clinton (1947–)

In 1969, Hillary Clinton received a bachelor's degree from Wellesley College and went on to attend Yale Law School, where she met her future husband, William Jefferson Clinton. In 1976, she followed her politically minded husband to Arkansas and joined the Rose Law firm. In 1978, she became first lady of Arkansas. In 1979, she became the first woman to receive partner status in the Rose Law firm. Beginning in 1993, for eight years, she was first lady of the United States. In 2000, she won election to the U.S. Senate for New York State and was reelected in 2006. In 2007, she began preparation to run for president and won the New Hampshire Democratic primary. She lost the Democratic presidential nomination to Barack Obama, who won the presidency in 2008.

Clinton accepted a position as secretary of state in the Obama administration, the third woman to serve. She is widely recognized as involved in women's advocacy and, since the 1990s, she has been active in efforts to end sex trafficking.

Meda Chesney-Lind (1947–)

Meda Chesney-Lind, PhD, has been referred to as the "mother of feminist criminology." She is a professor of women's studies at the University of Hawaii–Manoa. She is nationally recognized for her work on women and crime. She is the author of *Girls, Delinquency and Juvenile Justice* (Wadsworth, 1992) which received the American Society of Criminology's Michael J. Hindelang Award, and *The Female Offender: Girls, Women and Crime* (1997, Sage; 2nd ed., 2004, Sage). Chesney-Lind has received numerous awards for her research and advocacy for girls and incarcerated women. She has been instrumental in bringing public attention to expand and reform services for delinquent girls.

Sharon Cooper, MD (1952–)

Dr. Sharon Cooper is a neuroscience researcher and studies brain development of trafficked girls, Internet child and youth exploitation, and underage prostitution. She is executive director of Developmental Forensic Pediatrics, a consulting firm providing clinical services for disabled children and child maltreatment victims including those exposed to prostitution, cyber-enticement, and child pornography. She has testified about compliant victimization and exploitation of youths on the Internet. In addition, she is a forensic pediatrician at the Southern Regional Health Education Center, which provides services for nine North Carolina counties; a member of the faculty of the University of North Carolina–Chapel Hill School of Medicine; and an instructor and board member of the National and International Centers for Missing and Exploited Children and lead author of *Child Sexual Exploitation Quick Reference: For Health Care, Social Service, and Law Enforcement Professionals*, with Angelo P. Giardano and Nancy D. Kellogg (2006).

Dorothea Dix (1802–1887)

In the 1800s, Dorothea Dix, who was trained as a nurse, was active in improving the social condition of the mentally ill. In 1841, she visited a local jail and viewed mentally ill inmates unclothed and chained to a wall. In response, Dix began a campaign to improve the clothing, housing, and treatment of mentally ill inmates and patients in Massachusetts. In the 1800s, state hospitals and treatment programs for the mentally ill did not exist. Dix worked to establish legislation to help the mentally ill in Massachusetts, other states, and internationally. In 1845, she published *Remarks on Prisons and Prison Discipline in the United States*, which became an important historical public health document.

Jaycee Dugard (1980–)

Kidnapped at the age of 11 from South Lake Tahoe, California, Jaycee Dugard was the object of an intensive search. She was not located until August 2009, when Philip Garrido became an object of suspicion. Garrido was on parole for a sex offense, and when a meeting was requested, brought Jaycee Dugard along with his wife and two daughters born to Jaycee. At this meeting, Dugard announced who she was, Garrido was arrested, and Jaycee was reunited with her parents. Garrido and his wife, Linda, were arrested and charged with kidnapping and rape. Because Garrido was on probation and his home had been visited by deputies, although not the backyard compound where Jaycee and her daughters were kept, the California Office of the Inspector General found numerous lapses by the California Department of Corrections and Rehabilitation. The state of California gave Dugard a $20 million settlement. In 2011, Dugard published *A Stolen Life* (Simon and Schuster), which recounts her life in captivity.

Melissa Farley (1942–)

An outspoken advocate of the criminalization of prostitution and antipornography, radical feminist Melissa Farley is a clinical psychologist and researcher. She received a BA in psychology from Mills College (1964), an MS in clinical psychology from San Francisco State University, and a PhD from the University of Iowa in counseling psychology. Farley is director of the nonprofit Prostitution Research and Education. Her research has focused on the psychological effects of violent sexual victimization, prostitution, and being trafficked. In national and international studies of samples of prostitutes, she has repeatedly found high levels of violent encounters and post-traumatic stress disorder. She has authored *Prostitution and Sex Trafficking in Nevada: Making the Connections* (2007) and is editor of *Prostitution, Trafficking and Traumatic Stress* (2004). In addition, she is a coauthor of *Challenging Men's Demand for Prostitution in Scotland* (2008) with J. McLeod, L. Anderson and J. Golding, published by the Women's Support Project.

Lea Weingarten Fastow (1961–)

The wife of former Enron chief financial officer Andrew Fastow, Lea Fastow was director and assistant treasurer of corporate finance from 1991 to 1997. Brought up in the wealthy Weingarten family, she earned a BA from Tufts University and an MBA from Northwestern University. Enron was a natural gas company ranked in the top 10 of Fortune 500 companies with an increase in earnings from $13.3 billion in 1996 to $100.8 billion in 2000. It ranked as the seventh-largest U.S. corporation when bankruptcy was declared in 2001. The massive profits reported by Enron were created by illegal accounting procedures, which included kickbacks to Andrew Fastow. Lea Fastow, who became a housewife in 1997 after the birth of her first child, was the only woman indicted. While her husband faced 100 charges, she faced six. Both she and her husband were alleged to have laundered money from off-the-books partnerships. In a plea bargain, Lea pled guilty to filing a false tax report that did not include $47,800. She was convicted of a misdemeanor and given one year in jail. She entered jail on July 11, 2004, and was released to a halfway house on July 12, 2005.

Heidi Fleiss (1966–)

Known as the "Hollywood Madam," Heidi Fleiss was a child of privilege who partied, did drugs, and was unable to find a skill until she met "Madam Alex," who ran a high-end call girl business and put Heidi to work to pay off a gambling debt. In 1991, Heidi started a business on her own with high-end customers, letting college girls keep 60% of the payment at $1,500 a night. It is possible that a lack of discretion led the Los Angeles Police Department to arrest her in 1993. Among the clients who testified at her trial was Charlie Sheen, who had spent $54,000 in one year. The media extensively publicized her trial, and Fleiss started HeidiWear to finance her court costs. She was convicted of pandering and tax evasion. In 1997, she was sentenced to 37 months in a federal prison. She served 20 months of her sentence before being transferred to a halfway house for the remainder.

Mary Frith (1584–1659)

"Moll Cutpurse," a pickpocket, rose through the ranks to lead a gang that fenced goods. She was born to a family that could afford to send her to better schools, but feminine expectations and skills lost out to being with boys. She was reputed to be a bully. Frith fell in with a cutpurse who committed a variety of crimes including highway robbery. Eventually she left crime commission to professional thieves and robbers and fenced their goods, even selling them back to the victims. She lived to be 75 years of age.

Jean Harris (1923–)

Jean Harris served as head of the elite private Madeira school and graduated with honors from Smith College in 1945. Married to Jim Harris, with whom she had two children, she was a housewife until they divorced as their children came of age. Afterwards she quickly began a relationship with the "Scarsdale Diet Doctor" Herbert Tarnower, a confirmed bachelor who had sexual relationships with numerous women. Jean tolerated his affairs as long as they were not serious, and an intimate relationship continued for many years. Jean worked as a schoolteacher but then moved up by becoming the head of the Thomas School in Rowayton, Connecticut. As their careers advanced, Jean began to experience depression, and Tarnower prescribed Desoxyn, a drug with a similar chemical makeup to amphetamines. In 1974, Harris was removed from the position at the Thomas School. While unemployed, she helped Tarnower compile the Scarsdale Medical Diet Book. Then she was hired as the head of the Madeira School for Girls in Washington, D.C. By 1979, the school was considering dismissing her and she came to see her career and relationship as a failure, buying a gun. Jean Harris testified that she took the gun to Tarnower's house, intending to kill herself in the garden; but she entered into conflict with Tarnower, who was accidentally shot and killed. The prosecution alleged that Jean Harris broke into Herbert Tarnower's house and shot him four times. A jury found her guilty of second-degree murder. She was sentenced to 15 years to life in prison but Governor Mario Cuomo commuted her sentence after 12 years. She became an advocate for better conditions in women's prisons. She is the author of three books,

including *Stranger in Two Worlds* (1993, Zebra) in which she tells
her story.

Kamala Harris (1964–)

Recipient of a JD from the University of California Hastings
School of the Law (1989), Kamela Harris is an attorney who has
risen in the ranks of public service. From 1990 to 1998, she served
as deputy district attorney in Alameda County, California. Next,
she became managing attorney of the Career Criminal Unit in
the San Francisco District Attorney's Office. In 2003, Kamala
Harris was elected district attorney of San Francisco, and she
was reelected in 2007. After the 2010 California elections, she
became the first woman to be appointed as attorney general of
California. Harris is active in the prosecution of sex trafficking
and created the first human trafficking unit in a local prosecutor's
office. She cosponsored the California Trafficking Victims Protection Act of 2005 and increased penalties for sex offenders
targeting children.

Patty Hearst (1954–)

Unlikely to become known as an outlaw, Patty Hearst is the
daughter and heiress of the newspaper magnate William Randolph Hearst. She attended Menloe College and the University
of California at Berkeley. In 1974, she was kidnapped by the
radical Symbionese Liberation Army. This group is considered
to have had about 11 to 12 members and was led by Donald
DeFreeze. Patty Hearst was kept in unhealthy confinement in a
closet, repeatedly being humiliated and brainwashed. Under
these coercive conditions, she adapted by joining the group. Her
first actions were to make tape recordings about the "capitalist
crimes" of her parents. Next, the revolutionary group extorted
William Randolph Hearst into giving $2 million of food to the
poor. While with the group, Patty Hearst participated in two bank
robberies in Los Angeles and San Francisco. On May 17, 1974, six
members of the Symbionese Liberation Army were killed in a
police shootout and fire in Los Angeles. Patty escaped with William and Emily Harris and evaded the police while traveling in
the United States. On September 18, 1975, Patty Hearst, the

Harrises, and another member were captured by the FBI in San Francisco. Hearst was taken to trial and convicted of bank robbery and felony use of firearms. She was sentenced to seven years in prison but appealed her conviction. As a result, she was alternately imprisoned and free during appeals. In February 1979, Hearst was released and married her former bodyguard Bernard Shaw. Her book, *Every Secret Thing* (1982, Pinnacle Books) written with Alvin Moscow, provides an account of her experiences with the Symbionese Liberation Army.

Leona Helmsley (1920–2007)

Known as the "queen of mean," Leona Helmsley rose from an unprivileged background to become a real estate agent and ultimately wed Harry Helmsley (1909–1997), a real estate multibillionaire. Known for self-promotion, the "queen of the palace" very visibly ran Helmsley hotels and was alleged to be unkind to her staff and would not tolerate mistakes. In 1986, charges were raised that fraudulent business expenses had been used to cover for renovation to a Helmsley mansion. In 1988, a federal jury indictment named Harry and Leona Helmsley and two former company executives as having committed conspiracy, fraud, extortion, and tax evasion. A jury found Leona Helmsley guilty of 33 felonies. In the sentencing phase of the trial, Leona admitted guilt, hoping for leniency. She was sentenced to four years in prison, fined $7.1 million and ordered to pay $41.7 million in back taxes. At age 72, she served 18 months in prison and 3 months of home confinement. She appealed and was released early because of her age and her husband's ill health.

Shauntay Henderson (1982–)

Growing up in a disorganized family environment, Shauntay Henderson's mother died when she was very young. She grew up in the Charlie Parker Square Housing Project in Kansas City. She attended five different schools over a three-year period and earned only five to six credits per year. She is believed to have been the leader of the 12th Street gang, but this was not substantiated. She is alleged to have had a "hit list" of perceived "enemies" and considered to be involved in several shootings during a gang war because she was viewed as present at the scene, partly because of her penchant for dressing in a masculine way. Henderson was charged with the murder in the second degree of DeAndre M. Parker, shot and killed at a gas station. Henderson was present at the scene and went into hiding for months. Tips that she might have fled to Iowa led to her placement on the FBI's Ten Most Wanted Fugitives List, with a reward of $100,000 for her arrest. She was captured in less than 24 hours. At her trial, she pled self-defense and alleged that Parker had tried to run her over with his truck. She was acquitted of murder in the second degree and found guilty of armed criminal action, for which she received 3 years, and voluntary manslaughter, covered by probation for 10 years after release. Trial testimony indicated Parker had previously tried to kill Henderson. Released in 2010, Henderson was rearrested after a police car chase and charged with felony possession of a firearm, which would return her to prison.

Donna M. Hughes (1954–)

A professor of women's studies at the University of Rhode Island, Donna M. Hughes is active in combating prostitution and sex trafficking. She holds the Eleanor M. Carlson and Oscar M. Carlson endowed chair in women's studies. At Pennsylvania State University, she received a BA and MA in animal science before earning a PhD in genetics in 1990. Increasingly, however, feminist concerns began to dominate her life. Hughes has served as education and research coordinator for the Coalition against Trafficking in Women. She is published in the area of prostitution and sexual slavery in the United States, Russia, Ukraine, and Korea. From 2006 to 2009, she was a leader in the effort to end decriminalization of indoor prostitution in Rhode Island and a cofounder of Citizens against Trafficking (CAT).

Ruth Joan Bader Ginsberg (1933–)

Associate justice of the Supreme Court of the United States, Ruth Bader Ginsberg was appointed by President Bill Clinton in 1993 and is only the second women to ever serve. Reflecting the pioneering movement of women into the law during the second half of the 20th century, Ginsberg received a bachelor's degree from Cornell University (1954) and an LLB degree from Columbia Law School (1958). She began her career as a law clerk in 1959 under the Honorable Edmund L. Palmieri, judge of the U.S. District Court for the Southern District of New York. From 1963 to 1972, Ginsberg was a professor of law at Rutgers University, where she cofounded the *Women's Rights Law Reporter* (the first legal journal to focus on women's rights) and authored the first casebook on gender equality law. During the 1970s, she volunteered as a lawyer for the American Civil Liberties Union and became its general counsel in 1973 when she headed the Women's Rights project and argued several landmark cases before the Supreme Court. In 1972, she became a professor of law at Columbia Law School, becoming the first woman to achieve tenure and remaining in the position until 1980, when she was appointed by President Jimmy Carter as a judge on the U.S. Court of Appeals, D.C. Circuit. In 1993 she left the position to be on the Supreme Court. Ginsberg has been a major advocate for gender equality of citizenship status as a constitutional principle. In 2009, *Forbes* named her among the 100 Most Powerful Women.

Jessica Lenahan (formerly Gonzales; 1966–)

A battered woman, Jessica Gonzales had taken out a restraining order against her husband. In June 1999, her three daughters, aged 10, 9, and 7, were abducted by her estranged husband. Jessica repeatedly called the Castle Rocks (Colorado) Police Department, which did not respond. Her husband later drove to the police department, fired upon it, and was killed by return fire. Previously, he had killed his three daughters, who were found in the back of his vehicle. Gonzales sued the Castle Rocks Police Department in a case that went to the U.S. Supreme Court. In 2005, the Supreme Court ruled that that she had no constitutional right to sue based on lack of police enforcement of her protective order. Gonzales has filed a petition with the Inter-American Court on Human Rights. It represents the first time an American woman who was a victim of domestic violence has filed a petition in an international court alleging violation of her human rights.

Elena Kagan (1960–)

Appointed associate justice of the Supreme Court by President Barack Obama in 2010, Elena Kagan is the fourth female justice to serve. She received an AB in history from Princeton University (1981), attended Worcester College of Oxford University for a master of philosophy (1983), and earned a JD from Harvard Law School (1986), where she was supervisory editor of the *Harvard Law Review*. She clerked at the federal Court of Appeals (1987) and Supreme Court (1988) and then took a position in private practice at a Washington, D.C., law firm. She took a position as professor at the University of Chicago Law School (1991) and was tenured in 1995, but resigned to become White House counsel and deputy director of the Domestic Policy Council. A nomination to the U.S. Court of Appeals for the D.C. Courts was blocked and expired without action. In 1999, she became a professor at Harvard Law School, making full professor in 1991; and in 2003, she became the first woman to serve as its dean. In the Obama administration, she became solicitor general in 2009, again the first woman to hold the position. In 2010, she left to join the Supreme Court.

Sunitha Krishnan (1969–)

Dr. Sunitha Krishnan, a social activist from India, is the cofounder and executive of Prajwala, an Indian organization that has rescued over 3,000 women and girl sex trafficking victims and provided shelter. The organization operates transition centers for children born of mothers in prostitution. The goal is to provide education and training in carpentry, printing, and other occupations in order to remove women from brothels. In 2008, Dr. Krishna received the CNN-IBN network Real Hero Award. In 2009, she was a Vanitha Woman of the Year, and in 2011, she received a Global Leadership Award.

Somaly Mam (1970 or 1971–)

Born in Cambodia but uncertain of the year, Somaly Mam was an orphan who became a victim of sex trafficking. Sold into slavery and sexually abused until 12 years of age and married at age 14, she was sold to a brothel at age 16. Suffering forced sex and related abuse, she became involved with a French human rights worker and escaped to France. Four years afterward, she returned to Cambodia to take steps against sex trafficking. Posing as a nurse for Doctors without Borders, she distributed condoms to women in brothels. Becoming more involved, she founded an NGO that offers safe havens for women and girls who are victims of sex trafficking. These have been established in Cambodia, Thailand, Laos and Vietnam. It is estimated that 4,000 girls and women have been saved. In 2006, Mam's daughter was kidnapped, raped, and sold into sexual slavery. Reunited, she advised her daughter to use her suffering as a basis to help others. Mam heads the Somaly Mam Foundation, and her work has been recognized with the following honors and awards: *Glamour* Magazine Woman of the Year (2006); CNN Real Hero (2006); *Time* Magazine Most Influential People (2008); World Children's Prize for the Rights of the Child (2008); and the U.S. State Department Heroes of Anti-Trafficking Award (2009). She is the author of *The Road of Lost Innocence* (2007, Virago Press).

Blanche Moore (1933–)

Blanche Moore is a probable serial murderer who employed arsenic. Because she is alleged to be a repeat killer of men in boyfriend or marital relationships, she is classified as a Black Widow. Blanche Moore was apprehended because her second husband, the Rev. Dwight Moore, became ill, was hospitalized and was found to have ingested large amounts of arsenic over a period of one week, eventually surviving. This led to an investigation of the deaths of her former boyfriend, Raymond Reid, and her first husband, James N. Taylor. Forensic investigation of their exhumed remains revealed the cause of death as arsenic poisoning. Blanche Moore's father, P. D. Kiser, was an alcoholic who died of symptoms similar to those of arsenic poisoning. She was said to have a hatred of her father, who forced her into prostitution for income. This is a possible psychological factor in the commission of her crimes. Moore was convicted for the death of Reid. Trials for other wrongful deaths and suspected poisonings were withheld because she had already received the death penalty for Reid's death. Moore has proclaimed her innocence and sustained several appeals. At age 78 in 2011, she remains in the custody of the North Carolina Department of Corrections on death row.

Susan Murphy-Milano (1958–)

Susan Murphy-Milano is a battered women and children victim's rights advocate with the Institute for Relational Harm Reduction and Public Pathology Education. Susan's father, a Chicago Violent Crimes detective, committed murder-suicide, leaving her to find the bodies of her father and mother. Murphy-Milano reacted to this by resolving to learn about relationships and become a domestic violence advocate. In 1993, she was instrumental in passage of the Illinois Stalking Law, and in 1998, she worked on passage of the Lautenberg Amendment, which prohibits police officers with a domestic violence conviction from gun ownership. In addition, she established Project: Protect but stepped down and became head of Corporate-on-Site, Inc., which educates employers about workplace violence. Her books include *Defending Our Lives: Protecting Yourself From Domestic Violence and Stalking* (1996), *Times Up: A Guide on How to Leave and Survive Abusive and Stalking Relationships* (2010), and *Holding My Hand Through Hell* (2012). She airs the *Susan Murphy-Milano Show: Time's Up* on Zeus Radio.

Chouchou Namegabe (1978–)

From the Democratic Republic of the Congo (DRC), Chouchou Namegabe used radio broadcasts to notify people about a rape epidemic. She put rape victims on the air to document their stories. In 2003, Namegabe founded the Association des Femmes des Medias (Women's Media Association, or AFEM) in response to the DRC's civil conflict. She broadcasts women's rape testimonials, ending the silence of women experiencing mass rape in wartime and advocating against rape. It influences other women to seek help. Namegabe has visited the United States to testify before the Senate Foreign Relations Committee. In addition, Namegabe has testified—and women's recorded testimonials are being used as evidence—in the International Criminal Court located at The Hague, including against wartime leader Thomas Lubanga. In 2009, she received a Global Leadership Award from Vital Voices and a Knight International Journalism Award.

Sandra Day O'Connor (1930–)

Sandra Day O'Connor was the first woman to be appointed associate justice on the United States Supreme Court. She received a BA in economics from Stanford University (1950) and a law degree (1952). In the 1960s, O'Connor became an Arizona assistant attorney general, and in 1969, she was appointed by Governor Jack Williams to the State Senate, filling a vacancy. A conservative Republican, she was reelected twice before she was elected a judge in the Maricopa County Superior Court in 1974. In 1979, she was elected to serve on the Arizona State Court of Appeals. In 1976, President Ronald Reagan appointed her to the U.S. Supreme Court, establishing a historical precedent for women in the law. In turn, she provided the deciding vote in upholding reversal of the *Roe v. Wade* decision on abortion rights. O'Connor retired from the court in 2006. In 2009, President Barack Obama awarded her the Presidential Medal of Freedom.

Bonnie Parker (1911–1934)

Coming to adulthood in the Great Depression, the rural-raised Bonnie Parker became involved with the wrong men. She married her first husband, Roy Thornton, when she was 16. Roy was prone to long absences, and when he returned after another, she refused to take him back. He took part in a robbery and was jailed for five years. Parker did not divorce him, considering it unfair to do while he was in prison. Surviving on waitressing and housework, she met Clyde Barrow, who was subsequently given two years in prison for a robbery of a grocery store. Parker went regularly to see him at the prison and even smuggled a gun he used for a brief escape. Captured, Barrow went back to prison for two years and was paroled in 1932. Reunited with Parker, and with members of a gang, he robbed a series of banks from 1932 to 1934 and committed 12 murders, 9 of which were of law-enforcement officers. Banks were unpopular for foreclosing on homes and businesses, and Bonnie and Clyde developed a following. They cultivated a romantic outlaw image by sending photos and Bonnie's poems to news sources. Their pattern was to rob a bank and then make a getaway in a stolen car, sometimes taking a law-enforcement officer hostage and releasing them a distance away to embarrass them. Soon the gang began occasional killing during the robberies or getaways, murdering six civilians and six police officers. The police and vigilantes began to pursue them, and they were killed in an ambush staged at Ruston, Indiana.

Kathleen Reichs (1950–)

Forensic anthropologist Dr. Kathleen Reichs is a professor of anthropology at the University of North Carolina at Charlotte. She investigates human remains to determine the identity of victims and their manner of death. Families of missing persons receive closure, and the evidence is used in criminal cases. Reichs gave testimony in Rwanda regarding genocide and worked at Ground Zero for two weeks. She has also identified a three-time serial killer in Montreal who was arrested based on her evidence.

In 1995, Reichs created the fictional character Temperance Brennan, a forensic anthropologist and medical examiner featured in 13 mystery novels, on which the television program *Bones* is based. She also produced episodes of *Bones*. Reich's experience is a basis for her novels. *Déjà Dead*, her first novel, received the Albert Ellis Award for Best First Novel (1997).

Janet Wood Reno (1938–)

Appointed by President Bill Clinton, Janet Reno served as the first women U.S. attorney general from 1993 to 2001. She received a BS from Cornell University. In 1971, Reno became the Florida House of Representatives' director of the Judiciary Committee and was a major player in revising Florida's court system. In 1973, she became a prosecutor with the Dade County State's Attorney General Office and became a partner in a private law firm in 1976. Reno was appointed state's attorney for Dade County (now referred to as Miami–Dade County), and she was elected to this office four times. She used her powers to find and try child abusers. Reno prosecuted three child abuse cases in Miami-Dade County that were widely reported by the media. She established techniques for interviewing young children, and a law was passed permitting them to give testimony for courtrooms on closed-circuit television—without facing intimidation of suspected sex abusers.

As U.S. attorney general, Janet Reno dealt with religious cults, domestic and international terrorism, and undocumented immigration, through the seizure of Elian Gonzalez, a Cuban national. After serving under Clinton, she made an unsuccessful run for governor of Florida. She was given the Council on Litigation's Professionalism Award (2008) and the Justice Award (American Judicature Society).

Ethel Rosenberg (1915–1955)

The first woman to be executed as a spy, Ethel Rosenberg was convicted for treason, along with her husband, Julius Rosenberg. In 1939, she joined the Young Communist Party and married. During the development of nuclear weaponry during World War II, U.S. policy was that the atomic bomb specifications should not be allowed to become known to unaligned countries. During the Cold War between the United States and the Union of Soviet Socialist Republics (USSR), an era of anticommunism spurred by Senator Joe McCarthy, it was thought that Communist spies were actively seeking such intelligence to use to destroy the United States. It is now known that Soviet spies were active, but the guilty verdict for the Rosenbergs is questioned. They claimed their innocence and maintained that they were victims of political fanaticism and injustice. The evidence against them came from Ethel's brother, David Greenglass, and his wife Ruth, who claimed that he had transmitted a pencil sketch of the atom bomb to the USSR. Some consider that the Greenglass testimony may have been coerced.

Malika Saada Saar

Saar is the founder and director of the Rebecca Project for Human Rights, which worked for justice for families. She is an advocate for prevention of sexual abuse of girls and was active in the closure of the Craigslist "adult services" section, in which ads were being placed by sex traffickers to buy and sell underage girls. Previously, Saar began Crossing the River, a workshop in which women used written and spoken word to recover from violence and substance abuse. A member of the Presidential Advisory Council on HIV/AIDS, she has received *Redbook* magazine's Mothers and Shakers Award.

Robin Sax (1971–)

Robin Sax is a victim advocate, legal analyst, and former prosecutor for the Los Angeles District Attorney's Office specializing in sex offenses. She has a BA from the University of California–Santa Barbara (1993) and a JD from Pepperdine University School of Law (1997). In 1997, she joined the Riverside County District Attorney's Office, and from 1999 to 2009, she prosecuted sex offenders for the Los Angeles District Attorney's Office. She is a legal analyst for NBC News and a legal commentator for Nancy Grace, Fox News, and Larry King Live. She appears on *Good Morning America* and ABC News to debate controversial criminal cases. In 2009, she represented the parents of murdered teenager Amber Dubois and convicted John Albert Gardner. She regularly contributes to Women and Crime Ink and the Huffington Post. She is the author of six books, including *It Happens Every Day: Inside the World of a Sex Crimes D.A.* (2009, Prometheus Books); and *Predators and Child Molesters: What Every Parent Needs to Know to Keep Kids Safe* (2009, Prometheus Books), which received the Amber Alert Book of the Year Award.

Mana al Sharif (1979–)

Al Sharif has challenged the Saudi Arabian law prohibiting women from driving in cities. She has a driver's license but is allowed to drive only in rural areas. She posted a video on You-Tube asking interior minister, his Highness Prince Nayef bin Abdel Aziz, to permit women to drive in cities. She was detained on May 21, 2011, and released on May 30, 2011, due to international pressure. Her efforts have drawn attention to the fact that there is no written Saudi law banning women from driving. Senior clerics issued a fatwa, a form of religious edict. Al Sharif must rely on male relatives or live-in drivers to get around in cities. Saudi Arabia has blocked her Facebook and Twitter pages, but other Internet sites have supported her.

Rita J. Simon (1931–)

An author of 63 books, Rita J. Simon received her PhD in sociology from the University of Chicago in 1957. She has served on the faculty of the University of Illinois and she is a professor in the School of Public Affairs and Washington College of Law at American University. One of her 63 books is *The Crimes Women Commit and the Punishments They Receive* (1990, Lexington Books). She is an editor of *Gender News* and is often quoted in the media.

Sonia Maria Sotomayor (1954–)

Sonia Sotomayor is associate justice of the Supreme Court after an August 2009 appointment by President Obama. She is the court's first Hispanic and third woman to serve. Sotomayor received an AB from Princeton University (1976) and a JD from Yale Law School (1979), where she edited the *Yale Law Journal*. In 1979, she began as an assistant district attorney in New York and entered private practice in 1984. In 1992, she was appointed to the U.S. District Court for the Southern District of New York by President George H. W. Bush. In 1997, President Bill Clinton appointed her to the U.S. Court of Appeals for the Second Circuit. In the interim, she also taught at the New York University of Law and Columbia Law School. Sotomayor became a member of the Second Circuit Task Force on Gender, Racial and Ethnic Fairness in the Courts. She has received the Outstanding Latino Professional Award in 2006 by the Latino/a Law Students Association.

Susan Smith (1971–)

Susan Smith grew up in a stressful family environment. Her father, Harry, was 21 years old when he married 17-year-old Linda, who was pregnant with another man's son. They had two children together, Scotty and Susan. Harry had an alcohol problem and accused Linda of having affairs. In 1977, Linda divorced Harry, who soon committed suicide in 1978, depriving Susan of her father. Linda was remarried to Bev Russell, a well-off businessman. Russell sexually molested Susan Smith, but her mother refused to believe her. Susan started but did not finish college, and took a job at a Winn-Dixie grocery, slept with various men, becoming emotionally unstable to the point that she tried to commit suicide in 1988. She met David Smith, who was dating another woman. He married her when she became pregnant. Susan's marriage to David, her boss, was troubled by the affairs they both had and frequent separations. During this period, they had two children, Michael Daniel Smith and Alexander Tyler Smith. Susan Smith began an affair with Tom Findley and divorced. Tom Findley told Susan that he did not want to marry and raise another man's children, cutting her off at a time when she was drinking heavily and very depressed. At this point, she decided to commit altruistic filicide because she did not want to deprive her children of a mother after her own suicide. Susan took her Mazda, put the two boys in their car seats, and proceeded to drive it into the lake, changing her mind and leaving the vehicle to roll into the lake and drown her two children. Afterward, she perpetrated a hoax in which she alleged that her children had been kidnapped in a carjacking. After a week in which national media broadcast her pleas to find her children, Susan Smith broke down and confessed. At her trial, the prosecutor sought the death penalty, but when Smith was found guilty, she was given 30 years to life. Susan Smith will be eligible for parole in 2025.

Martha Stewart (1941–)

Business entrepreneur and head of Martha Stewart Omnimedia, magazine publisher, and media personality Martha Stewart was convicted for lying to investigators about an ImClone stock sale in 2004. She was convicted of insider trading, the criminal use of material and nonpublic information to realize profit or loss on a stock purchase or sale. Stewart sold her stock before an adverse Food and Drug Administration ruling blocked an ImClone product, reducing the value of the stock. The U.S. Securities and Exchange Commission proved in court that Stewart sold her 3,928 shares on December 27, 2001, to avoid a loss of $45,673 that occurred when the stock value fell 16% the next day. Extensive media coverage due to her celebrity ensued, and Stewart was indicted on June 4, 2003, on nine counts. In 2004, Stewart was found guilty of conspiracy, issuing false statements to federal investigators, and obstruction of justice. She served five months in a federal prison camp and paid a fine of $30,000. Afterward, she was assigned two years of supervised release, placed on home confinement, and electronically monitored for five months. In a related civil case, Stewart agreed to a five-year limitation on acting in any financial capacity for a public firm. Nevertheless, she made a business comeback by 2006.

Karla Faye Tucker (1959–1998)

An accomplice in a simple prank that turned deadly, Karla Faye Tucker was given the death penalty for her actions in the murder of Jerry Lynn Dean. Originally, she and Danny Garret, her boyfriend, sought to steal Dean's motorcycle while he was asleep. Dean had beaten his wife, Shawn, black and blue, and they sought revenge. While high on drugs, this plan was interrupted by Dean's awaking. Garret took a hammer and begin hitting him on the skull. Dean had been in bed with a woman other than his wife; Karla took a pick axe and murdered Deborah Thornton, later confessing to sexually climaxing three times during the act. In prison, during a series of appeals of the death penalty, Karla Faye Tucker read the Bible and found God. Her lawyers argued that she had changed and sought to at least have the sentence commuted to life. Her cause was taken up by the media, and even the pope wrote a letter on her behalf. George W. Bush, then governor of Texas, refused to stay execution, and she died on February 3, 1998, the first woman executed in Texas since the Civil War.

Christina S. Walters (1979–)

Christina S. Walters is a Native American who joined the Crips gang. In 1998, she and eight other teenagers took part in what the prosecution argues was an initiation ritual. The defense indicated it was a "wannabe gang." The group randomly kidnapped, robbed, and executed two strangers who were traveling and shot a woman, leaving her for dead. The tips of the bullets had been painted blue, the Crips' color, using nail polish found in Walters's home. Walters is the individual who took a gun, unjammed it, and shot the witness, Deborah Cheeseborough, who survived, eight times. Walters was given the death penalty for two murders in the first degree committed in 1998. She was also indicted and convicted on two counts for first-degree kidnapping and robbery with a dangerous weapon, and one count each of conspiracy to commit first-degree murder, conspiracy to commit first-degree kidnapping, and conspiracy to commit robbery with a dangerous weapon. A multi-count indictment was given for attempted first-degree murder, conspiracy to commit first-degree murder, assault with a deadly weapon with intent to kill inflicting serious injury, first-degree kidnapping, and robbery with a dangerous weapon. For the additional felony charges, she was sentenced to consecutive terms of imprisonment. She is an inmate in North Carolina.

Aileen Wuornos (1956–2002)

Sensationalized in the media as the United States' first woman serial killer, Aileen Wuornos is actually one among many women who have murdered on multiple occasions, but unusual in that she killed in a sequential fashion while acting as a prostitute. She was found guilty of killing six men in Florida between 1989 and 1990. In each case, she alleged that they had brutalized and raped her or attempted to rape her while she was selling services as a prostitute and that she had acted in self-defense. The Wuornos case provides insight into how disrupted family relations in which people move in and out of a child's life and alleged sexual victimization could have shaped the motivation to kill. She never knew her father, Leo Dale Pittman, a child molester, who was imprisoned for rape and attempted murder of an eight-year-old boy. Diane Pratt, her mother, had married Pittman at 15 years of age and abandoned Aileen and her older brother Keith in 1960, when Aileen was four years old. Her maternal grandparents, Lauri and Britta Wuornos, legally adopted them in 1960. Aileen Wuornos made the claim that her grandfather sexually and physically abused her. It is believed that she was sexually active at a young age, including with her brother. Raped and impregnated as a young teen by an unknown assailant, she gave birth at age 13 to a child who was put up for adoption. At age 15, her grandfather sent her away, and she began to survive as a prostitute. Afterward, Wuornos became established in a criminal career characterized by multiple charges: driving under the influence, disorderly conduct, disturbing the peace, prostitution, assault and battery, check forgery, grand theft auto, and armed robbery. She was sentenced to death for six of the seven murders she was implicated in, and she was executed using lethal injection on October 9, 2002.

Andrea Yates (1965–)

While enduring serious mental illness, Andrea Yates was the caretaker of four and then five children, whom she ultimately killed.

Recipient of a BA in nursing in 1986, Andrea worked until the birth of her first child. Rusty Yates, her husband, wanted her to be a stay-at-home mom and desired to have a large family. Ultimately, they had five children: Noah (seven years), John (five years), Paul (three years), Luke (two years), and Mary (six months). After the birth of Luke, Andrea Yates had experienced a condition known as postpartum depression and tried to commit suicide. She had been advised not to have any more children after her fourth birth. Yates was isolated as her children were home schooled; she was also taking care of her father, who was in his 80s and suffering from Alzheimer's disease. As the stress of her situation increased and with the death of her father, Yates developed postpartum psychosis, and she again tried to commit suicide several weeks before she snapped. She later explained that she killed her children to save them from damnation because she was a poor mother. On June 20, 2001, she drowned her children and called to report it to police. Yates pleaded not guilty by reason of insanity. The jury found her guilty and sentenced her to life. She would be eligible for parole in 2041, at age 77. Nevertheless, the testimony of Dr. Park Dietz, a prosecution psychiatrist, was overturned as falsified, and a retrial was ordered in 2005. On July 26, 2006, a jury found Andrea Yates not guilty by reason of insanity, and she was committed to a high-security mental health facility.

6

Data and Documents

The Dark Figure of Crime: Issues in Interpretation of Crime Data

The Uniform Crime Reports (UCR) reflects data reported to local, state, and federal policing agencies. Crimes which were *not* unreported will not be counted in the databases, which are used to determine the general crime rate and gendered crime rate. These unreported crimes are referred to as the "dark figure of crime." The National Crime Victimization Survey (NCVS) is based on all victimization, including crimes that may not be reported to the police. To estimate crime, both databases can be consulted, but an exact figure will remain elusive.

It is impossible to learn how crime rates are impacted by race-ethnicity, social class, and gender from current UCR statistics. The racial-ethnic categorization system used for the UCR has been criticized because the only racial breakdown is for "White" and "Black" or "Other." There is no breakdown by ethnicity including for Hispanic Whites and Asian Americans. Socioeconomic status, an important predictor of crime, is not included, either. Breakdown by sex of offender is supplied.

Uniform Crime Report Definitions

The Uniform Crime Report is the major source of information on the rate of crime commission in the United States. In the

Uniform Crime Report Handbook, each "index crime" is given a specific definition in the Uniform Crime Handbook. Selected definitions and examples of gender-related or gender neutral scenarios in which a woman could be the perpetrator are given below. The scenarios are all based on cases known to law enforcement. Additional illustrative scenarios to which categories apply are available in the Uniform Crime Report Handbook.

Source: Federal Bureau of Investigation (FBI), Department of Justice. *Uniform Crime Reporting* Handbook. Washington, DC: FBI. http://www.fbi.gov/about-us/cjis/ucr/additional-ucr -publications/ucr_handbook.pdf

Women and the Crime Rate

The crime rates of men and women vary greatly by offense and have fluctuated over time. The Uniform Crime Report (UCR), published by the Federal Bureau of Investigation (FBI), indicates a 1990s decline in arrests that has continued into the second decade of the 21st century. The decline has impacted women differently because small changes in their arrest rate impact their very low population base relative to men. The media makes big news out of statistical increases in women's arrest rate because it stimulates readership. They do not report how large percentage increases from a small population base are misleading. Instead, they represent women as more prone to commit crime because of the impact of the women's movement. Reporting which dramatizes crime occurs despite decline in the general arrest rate. The UCR (2010) indicates:

- Overall, the number of males arrested in 2009 declined 4.9 percent, but the number of females arrested rose 11.4 percent when compared with data for 2000.
- The number of male juveniles (persons under age 18) arrested dropped 22.9 percent and the number of female juveniles arrested decreased 13.1 percent when data for 2009 were compared with statistics for 2000.
- A comparison of data for 2009 and 2000 showed that the number of males arrested for violent crimes in 2009 decreased 8.1 percent from the number arrested in 2000, but the number of females arrested for violent crimes increased 0.1 percent.

- Arrests of juveniles for violent crimes declined in both genders in 2009 when compared with data for 2000. The number of arrests of male juveniles decreased 14.5 percent, and the number of arrests of female juveniles decreased 16.9 percent.
- A comparison of data for 2009 and 2000 showed that the number of males arrested for property crimes in 2009 declined 3.9 percent from the number arrested in 2000, but the number of females arrested for property crimes rose 33.2 percent.
- Arrests of male juveniles for property crimes decreased 29.2 percent, but arrests of female juveniles for property crimes increased 0.1 percent when data for 2009 were compared with data for 2000 (UCR, 2010).

Violent Crimes

Men commit 80% of violent crimes. The disparity in male and female rates is an aspect of what is called the gender gap in crime commission.

Women are far less likely to commit violent crimes than men. In 2009, the UCR (2010) reported 756 cases of murder and nonnegligent manslaughter in which women were arrested. This represents a decline of 10.4% from 844 arrests reported in 2000. In contrast, men were arrested in 6,473 cases of homicide and nonnegligent manslaughter. The men's rate had declined by 4.7% from 6,755 cases reported in 2000. When male and female rates of arrests are compared, women's rates are not only dramatically lower than men, but they declined at a faster rate. Among females under 18, the difference in rates is even more pronounced. In 1999, 80 arrests occurred for females, and in 2009, there were 53 arrests, representing a 33.8% decline. Males under 18 charged with homicide or nonnegligent manslaughter increased from 576 in 2000 to 599 in 2009, an increase of 4%. Clearly, juveniles are less likely to kill than adults, but the contrast between males and females is even more pronounced, with the female rate declining while the male rate increased.

Intimate partner homicide (IPH) involves killing a spouse, partner, boyfriend, or girlfriend. The social context of homicide committed by women is dramatically different from that of men because they are much more likely to kill in the intimate context of families and acquaintances, while men are more often involved in deaths of strangers while also committing intimate partner homicides. Following the inception of the women's movement and efforts to stop the violence, the rate of IPH has dropped for both women and men. Importantly, from 1993 to 2007, the rate of IPH of women declined 35%, from 1.66 to 1.07 per 100,000 females (Catalano, Smith, Snyder, and Rand, 2009: 4). In contrast, the rate of female-to-male IPH decreased 46% (from 0.87 to 0.47). The death rate for women victims of IPH is falling at a lower rate than for male victims.

Rape is recognized as a crime that men commit against women and other men. Less well known is female-to-male rape, a rare crime. There were 169 forcible rapes committed by women in 2000 and 148 in 2009, a decline of 12.4% (UCR, 2010). Among girls under 18, 22 forcible rapes occurred in 2000 and 28 in 2009. Forcible rape by females can be committed against males or females and may involve sexual abuse of children.

Robbery is recognized as a gender-typed, masculine crime. The circumstances vary from holdups of stores and banks or muggings on the street, to burglaries turned bad when household residents are home. In 2009, 67,906 robberies resulted in arrest of males as contrasted to 58,443 in 2000 (UCR, 2010). The male robbery rate increased by 16.2%. In contrast, 6,663 women's robbery arrests occurred in 2000 and 9,384 in 2009, a 40.8% increase. In 2000, 1,532 robberies resulted in arrest of girls under 18, and 1,994 in 2009, an increase of 30.2%. The increase in arrest of juvenile girls was paralleled by a smaller rate of increase in arrests of males. In 2009, 14,861 robbery-related arrests of male juveniles occurred as compared to 17,342 in 2009, a 16.2% increase. Arrest of female juveniles is increasing at a faster rate than for males, but there is a wide gender gap in robbery offending still.

Assault is still a primarily male-perpetrated crime. But mass media reports about violent girls have implied that it is a growing problem. In 2000, 240,528 males were arrested as compared to 209,078 in 2009, a 13.1% decline (UCR, 2010). The rate of female-perpetrated aggravated assault arrests decreased by 4.2%, but arrests of girls under 18 dropped by 24.4%. Altogether, 60,787 arrests of women for aggravated assault occurred in 2000 and 58,236 in 2009. Juvenile girls' arrests decreased from 9,583 to 7,247.

Assaults are reported in the UCR in two categories, aggravated assault and "other assaults," which may include simple assault. Males are arrested for the vast majority of assault crimes.

In 2000, 590,790 men were arrested, and 592,155 in 2009, a 0.2% rate of increase (UCR, 2010). In 2000, 179,874 females were arrested, as contrasted to 211,334 in 2009, a 17.5% increase. Girls under 18 arrested increased from 43,968 in 2000 to 46,494 in 2009, a 5.7% increase. Arrests of male juveniles declined from 98,731 n 2000 to 88,631 in 2009, a 10.2% drop. This differential has been the basis of media speculation that women and girls are becoming more violent despite the wide gender gap between male and female assault offending.

Offenses against the Family and Children

Since the 1960s, child abuse and neglect and family violence have been recognized as major and recurrent criminal offenses. Vigorous policing and prosecution is associated with a major decline in offenses committed. In 2009, 17,574 females were arrested, dropping from 18,828 in 2000, a decline of 6.7%. Men have consistently outnumbered women in arrests for offenses against the family and children. In 2009, 53,001 men were arrested, down from 67,421 in 2000, a drop of 21.4%.

Nonviolent Crimes

Since 1959, the number of women arrested for drug offenses has steadily increased and driven mass imprisonment trends for women (Bloom and Chesney-Lind, 2007). Again, there is a steep gender gap in offending because men are more frequently arrested for these crimes, which range from possession to sales to trafficking. In 2009, 189,039 women were arrested for drug offenses as compared to 167,968 in 2000, an increase of 12.5% (UCR, 2010). In contrast, 806,669 men were arrested in 2009 and 771,170 in 2000, an increase of 4.6%. Regardless of the gender gap in arrests, mandatory sentencing laws for drug violations has greatly increased state and federal imprisonment of women during this historical period of mass incarceration.

Despite imprisonment trends for women, the drug violation arrest rate for girls under 18 has dropped from 18,757 in 2000 to 16,800 in 2009, a decline of 10.4% (UCR, 2010). Boys under 18 arrested has declined from 102,909 in 2000 to 86,857 in 2009, a greater decrease than girls, down 15.6%. David Merolla (2008) considers that the War on Drugs made women and girls more vulnerable to arrest regardless of their offending patterns. Both the federally driven intensification of law enforcement efforts and legal penalties and the way that people think about drug use was subject to change. Drug users were socially constructed as criminals and, unlike images of dangerous criminals in the past, relatively "ungendered." Either men or women can be likely targets of drug arrests. In the mass media, women have been represented as more immoral than male drug users. This is partly due to the negative impact of drug use during pregnancy on the unborn fetus and attempts to criminalize it. Drug use is perceived as masculine behavior and violating traditional gender expectations. Merolla (2008) refers to women drug users as "double deviants": they have broken both the law and society's expectations for women. Conspiracy laws, combined with mandatory minimum sentencing law, has resulted in arrest of women who may know or be romantically involved with drug dealers (Merolla, 2008). The police place pressure on these women to provide information (Lusane, 1991). Women with boyfriends or sons who are drug dealers are at increased risk of arrest.

Women are more likely to commit crimes of shoplifting, bad-check writing, and embezzlement and are less likely to be involved in arson, auto theft, burglary, and acts of vandalism. Traditionally, women's involvement in property crime has been related to the degree of confrontation and likelihood of physical resistance involved in the crime. Burglary carries the need for physical action, a potential for armed confrontation with escalation to robbery and possibility of police chase. In contrast, larceny-theft, fraud, embezzlement, and similar crimes carry much less possibility for violent confrontation and physical capacity for breaking, entering, and the chase. Although penalties for property crime can be harsh, "safer" types attract women in need of money for survival, family needs, or personal want. Although national rates of property crime commission have declined since the 1970s, women's rate has increased, and the rate at which women are arrested for embezzlement now exceeds that for men.

Historically, obtaining resources through fraudulent means such as bouncing checks and welfare abuse has been a more frequently committed women's crime. Fraud is also a crime with a declining gender gap. In 2000, 100,219 women were arrested for fraud as compared to 116,447 men (UCR, 2010). Women's arrests dropped to 61,285 in 2009, a decrease of 38.7%; while 78,550 men were arrested, a decline of 32.5%.

Thieving is another prototypical crime committed by women. In 2009, 354,854 women were arrested as compared to 451,750 men. In 2000, 258,359 women and 454,947 men were arrested. The 2009 larceny-theft arrest rate represents a 37.3% increase for women and a 0.7% decrease for men. Clearly what has traditionally been a crime women are more likely to commit is also a crime in which the gender gap has greatly decreased.

Women's drug use is connected to larceny-theft. "Boosting" goods from stores can support a habit. The widespread availability of drugs and need for money to support a habit as well as women's increased involvement in public life, especially work, are likely to be factors impacting women's willingness to commit the crime and access to goods.

In order to embezzle, it is necessary to be in a position to handle finances. In 2009, 6,013 women were arrested for embezzlement as compared to 5,743 men (UCR, 2010). This is an unusual case in which women's crime rate has surpassed men, and it is presumably based in women's increased access to positions handling money in the labor market. This figure represented a decrease of 3.8% from 6,249 women arrested in 2000. There were 6,287 men arrested in 2000, when women were coming even with men in the rate of commission of this crime. By 2009, male rates of arrest for embezzlement had decreased 7.5%. Doubtless, this reversal of the gender gap is related to women's increased involvement in the labor market and even business ownership. Embezzlement is perceived as a crime of greed, but women's motivations may vary from those of men.

Despite the advent of computer crime and plastic card use in lieu of cash, arrests for forgery and counterfeiting are down. In 2009, 18,840 females were arrested for these crimes, dropping from 26,468 in 2000 (UCR, 2010). Reflecting the gender gap pattern, 31,152 males were arrested for forgery/counterfeiting in 2009, down from 40,765 in 2000, a decrease of 23.6%.

Burglary has been a masculinized crime involving greater risk of confrontation and resistance than larceny-theft, fraud, and embezzlement. In 2009, 159,017 men and 29,764 women were arrested for this crime (UCR, 2010). The men's rate increased 5.1% from 151,244 in 2000. Women's burglary arrests have increased by 26.7%. This was up from 23,497 arrests in 2000. There is still a wide gender gap in burglary offending, but women are increasingly more willing to try it.

Public Order Crimes

Crimes against public order violate standards of morality and norms for public view. In the case of driving while intoxicated, the viewer is not only irritated, but also endangered with loss of life. For women, a key public order crime is prostitution. Both men and women engage in the exchange of sex for money, but women are most often arrested for prostitution. Men engage in two types of prostitution activity: (1) purchase of sex as "johns," and (2) business managers as "pimps." The arrest of women for prostitution greatly outnumbers the arrest of men as customers, although there are periodic crackdowns on males. In 2009, 25,757 women were arrested as compared to 25,779 in 2000, a decline of 0.1% (UCR, 2010). In 2009, 11,639 men were arrested for various activities as customer or seller. This declined by 38.4% from 18,886 in 2000.

The rate at which women are arrested for driving under the influence has increased in the 21st century. In 2009, the Uniform Crime Report indicates that 190,455 women were arrested, a 31.5% increase since 2000 (FBI, 2010).

The crimes women commit can make them vulnerable to victimization. DeHart (2008) brings attention to physical assault against prostitutes, women dealing drugs being robbed or attacked by clients and the linkage between drug use or intoxication and being raped or robbed.

Sources: Catalano, Shannan, Erica Smith, Howard Snyder, and Erica Rand. 2009. "Female Victims of Violence." Washington, DC: Bureau of Justice Statistics. http://bjs.ojp.usdoj.gov/content/pub/pdf/fvv.pdf

DeHart, Diana. 2008. "Pathways to Prison: Impact of Victimization in the Lives of Incarcerated Women." *Violence against Women* 14(12): 1362–1381.

FBI (2010). http://www.fbi.gov.

Race and Sex of Homicide and Rape Offenders

The United States has a history of racial prejudice and discrimination based on skin color. The number of homicides committed by black males is disproportionate to their share of the population. On the other hand, white women are more likely to commit homicide than black women. Unfortunately, the FBI does not collect socioeconomic data, which would allow observers to consider the impact of poverty and other social class indicators such as living in public housing in a high crime minority neighborhood.

Increasing Women's Imprisonment Despite Crime Decline

Mandatory minimum sentencing for drug-related crimes is a major factor in women's increasing imprisonment. As can be seen in Table 6.1, women comprised 6.4% (85,044) of the state and federal prison population in the year 2000. By June 2009, women prisoners had increased to 6.9% (106,362), despite a drop in the crime rate. The lowering of mandatory minimums in federal level sentencing in 2011 is likely to decrease the number of women prisoners in federal penitentiaries.

TABLE 6.1

Number of Sentenced Female Prisoners under the Jurisdiction of State or Federal Correctional Authorities, December 31, 2000–2008, and June 30, 2008–2009

Year	Number of Sentenced Female Prisoners			Percent of All Sentenced Prisoners
	Total	Federal	State	
2000	85,044	8,397	76,647	6.4
2001	85,184	8,990	76,194	6.3
2002	89,066	9,308	79,758	6.5
2003	92,571	9,770	82,801	6.6
2004	95,998	10,207	85,791	6.7
2005	98,688	10,495	88,193	6.7
2006	103,343	11,116	92,227	6.9
2007	105,786	11,528	94,258	6.9
2008				
June 30	106,569	11,602	94,967	6.9
December 31	106,411	11,578	94,833	6.9
2009				
June 30	106,362	11,898	94,464	6.9
Annual Change				
Average Annual Change, 12/31/2000–12/31/2008	2.8%	4.1%	2.7%	:
Percent Change, 6/30/2008–6/30/2009	−0.2	2.6	−0.5	:

Note: Includes prisoners under the legal authority of state or federal correctional officials with sentences of more than 1 year, regardless of where they are held.: Not calculated
Source: Bureau of Justice Statistics. 2010. *Prison Inmates at Midyear 2009—Statistical Tables*. Washington, DC: U.S. Department of Justice. http://bjs.ojp.usdoj.gov/content/pub/pdf/pim09st.pdf

Gendered and Racial Disparities in Imprisonment

Although the number of women incarcerated in federal or state prisons and local jails has been increasing between 2000 and 2009, the racial and ethnic background of women prisoners has been changing. Table 6.2 details that the number of African American women has decreased somewhat from 69,500 to 64,800, but the number of Hispanic women prisoners considerably increased from 19,500 to 32,300. The most dramatic increase, however, is for a traditionally privileged group, white women. In 2000, 63,700 white women were in prison, and they were outnumbered by African American women. By 2009, this number increased to 92,100. Although the representation of African American and Hispanic women is still disproportionate to their frequency in the population, white women are increasingly being held.

TABLE 6.2
Estimated Number of Inmates Held in Custody in State or Federal Prison, or in Local Jails, by Sex, Race, and Hispanic Origin, June 30, 2000–2009

	Males				Females			
Year	Total[a]	White[b]	Black[b]	Hispanic	Total[a]	White[b]	Black[b]	Hispanic
2000	1,775,700	663,700	791,600	290,900	156,200	63,700	69,500	19,500
2001	1,800,300	684,800	803,400	283,000	161,200	67,700	69,500	19,900
2002	1,848,700	630,700	818,900	342,500	165,800	68,800	65,600	25,400
2003	1,902,300	665,100	832,400	363,900	176,300	76,100	66,800	28,300
2004	1,947,800	695,800	842,500	366,800	183,400	81,700	67,700	28,600
2005	1,992,600	688,700	806,200	403,500	193,600	88,600	65,700	29,300
2006	2,042,100	718,100	836,800	426,900	203,100	95,300	68,800	32,400
2007	2,090,800	755,500	814,700	410,900	208,300	96,600	67,600	32,100
2008	2,103,500	712,500	846,000	427,000	207,700	94,500	67,800	33,400
2009	2,096,300	693,800	841,000	442,000	201,200	92,100	64,800	32,300

Note: Detailed categories exclude persons who reported two or more races. All totals include persons under age 18.
[a]Includes American Indians, Alaska Natives, Asians, Native Hawaiians, and other Pacific Islanders, and persons identifying two or more races.
[b]Excludes persons of Hispanic or Latino origin.
Source: Bureau of Justice Statistics. 2010. *Prison Inmates at Midyear 2009—Statistical Tables*. Washington, DC: U.S. Department of Justice. http://bjs.ojp.usdoj.gov/content/pub/pdf/pim09st.pdf

Aging Out and Desistance

Crime is an activity of the young that is nuanced by gender and ethnicity. According to the FBI arrest statistics for 2009, young women and men suffered differing rates of arrests. Among women, 17 and 18 year olds were arrested for the highest percentage rates of property crimes. Women of 19 to 21 years tended to have the highest percentage arrest rates for violent crimes. Young men of 18 years of age were responsible for both the highest percentage rate of violent crime as well as the highest percentage of property crime among males.

Table 6.3 details statistics of the inmate population in the U.S. during 2009. The largest age categories of inmates are in the 25–29 year old category. This is consistent for men, but the largest category of women is older, at 35–39 years of age (with the exception of Hispanic women, who are younger). While there is

TABLE 6.3

Estimated Number of Inmates Held in Custody in State or Federal Prisons or in Local Jails, by Sex, Race, Hispanic Origin, and Age, June 30, 2009

	Male				Female			
Year	Total[a]	White[b]	Black[b]	Hispanic	Total[a]	White[b]	Black[b]	Hispanic
Total[c]	2,096,300	693,800	841,000	442,000	201,200	92,100	64,800	32,300
18–19	68,200	21,100	29,400	14,300	4,200	1,800	1,400	1,000
20–24	318,800	92,300	135,000	76,600	26,700	12,200	8,800	5,600
25–29	360,800	101,100	149,700	90,800	30,400	14,000	10,700	5,800
30–34	326,400	96,500	130,400	80,900	33,600	14,800	11,600	5,500
35–39	308,100	103,500	123,800	61,700	37,700	17,000	12,300	5,200
40–44	278,600	103,900	108,000	47,400	32,400	15,000	10,300	3,800
45–49	203,900	77,200	80,600	33,500	19,700	9,200	5,900	2,600
50–54	111,800	43,900	43,600	17,400	8,900	5,000	2,000	1,400
55–59	58,000	26,200	19,500	9,400	3,900	1,800	600	700
60–64	25,200	12,900	7,000	4,300	1,600	500	400	200
65 or older	21,000	11,500	5,600	2,800	1,100	500	100	100

Note: Detailed categories exclude persons who reported two or more races.
[a]Includes American Indians, Alaska Natives, Asians, Native Hawaiians, other Pacific Islanders, and persons identifying two or more races.
[b]Excludes persons of Hispanic or Latino origin.
[c]Includes persons under age 18.
Source: Bureau of Justice Statistics. 2010. *Prison Inmates at Midyear 2009—Statistical Tables.* Washington, DC: U.S. Department of Justice. http://bjs.ojp.usdoj.gov/content/pub/pdf/pim09st.pdf

a natural tendency for most women and men to desist from criminal activity with advancement of age (after the peak ages in
young adulthood), much remains to be learned about recidivism
reduction and desistance. In a time of continuous transition in
attitudes toward racial equality, gender equality, and structural
supports of equality, dynamics in desistance continue to change
as well. For instance, marriage was once thought to improve
desistance. More recent research shows that this tends to work
for men, in general. Marriage has less of a positive effect, however, on desistance in women (King et al. 2007).

Sources: FBI (2012) "Crime in the United States 2009," FBI,
http://www2.fbi.gov/ucr/cius2009/data/table_43_dd.html.

King, Ryan D., Michael Massoglia, and Ross Macmillan. 2007.
"The Context of Marriage and Crime: Gender, the Propensity to
Marry, and Offending in Early Adulthood." *Criminology* 45: 33–65.

Incarcerated Noncitizen Women

Because of a crackdown on undocumented immigration and,
additionally, crimes related to being a drug courier and
trafficking, the number of immigrant and visiting noncitizen
females has increased, as can be seen in Table 6.4.

TABLE 6.4
Reported Number of Non-U.S. Citizens Held in Custody in State or Federal Prisons, by
Sex, Region, and Jurisdiction, June 30, 2008 and 2009

Region and jurisdiction	2008			2009		
	Total	Male	Female	Total	Male	Female
U.S. total	93,682	86,971	3,936	94,458	90,567	3,931
Federal	28,995	26,908	2,087	30,445	28,404	2,041
State	64,687	60,063	1,849	64,053	62,163	1,890
Northeast	9,036	8,751	285	8,961	8,673	288
Connecticut[a]	742	710	32	802	767	35
Maine	16	16	0	21	20	1
Massachusetts	914	874	40	918	883	35
New Hampshire	/	/	/	82	79	3
New Jersey	/	/	/	/	/	/

(*continued*)

TABLE 6.4 (Continued)

Region and jurisdiction	2008			2009		
	Total	Male	Female	Total	Male	Female
New York[b]	6,334	6,148	186	6,111	5,922	189
Pennsylvania	1,008	985	23	1,008	985	23
Rhode Island[a]	/	/	/	/	/	/
Vermont[a]	22	18	4	19	17	2
Midwest	4,989	4,829	160	5,352	5,197	155
Illinois	1,746	1,698	48	1,946	1,900	46
Indiana	468	454	14	504	496	8
Iowa	186	183	3	151	148	3
Kansas	283	278	5	287	283	4
Michigan	615	608	7	680	670	10
Missouri[b]	440	411	29	452	428	24
Nebraska	187	184	3	204	200	4
North Dakota	12	11	1	14	13	1
Ohio	685	644	41	584	548	36
South Dakota	56	56	0	61	59	2
Wisconsin	/	/	/	/	/	/
South	23,291	22,633	658	23,137	22,487	650
Alabama	117	113	4	150	147	3
Arkansas	174	168	6	187	183	4
Delaware[a]	360	342	18	316	296	20
Florida	6,101	5,885	216	6,344	6,131	213
Georgia	1,766	1,738	28	1,777	1,754	23
Kentucky	134	131	3	168	164	4
Louisiana	106	103	3	105	102	3
Maryland[b]	686	663	23	430	408	22
Mississippi	/	/	/	/	/	/
North Carolina	1,687	1,641	46	1,785	1,742	43
Oklahoma[c]	363	348	15	340	331	9
South Carolina	376	371	5	462	449	13
Tennessee[b]	250	243	7	240	231	9
Texas	9,940	9,700	240	9,618	9,371	247
Virginia	1,223	1,179	44	1,209	1,172	37
West Virginia	8	8	0	6	6	0
West	27,371	23,850	746	26,603	25,806	797
Alaska[a]	14	13	1	11	11	0
Arizona	2,762	2,654	108	3,259	3,116	143
California[c]	17,010	16,575	435	18,705	18,225	480
Colorado[b]	1,112	1,082	30	1,250	1,207	43
Hawaii[a,d]	99	92	7	122	115	7
Idaho	324	312	12	288	275	13
Montana	13	13	0	15	15	0
Nevada[e]	2,775	/	/	/	/	/

(continued)

TABLE 6.4 (Continued)

Region and jurisdiction	2008			2009		
	Total	Male	Female	Total	Male	Female
New Mexico	120	120	0	105	102	3
Oregon	1,746	1,643	103	1,704	1,625	79
Utah	267	264	3	276	273	3
Washington	1,075	1,029	46	798	774	24
Wyoming	54	53	1	70	68	2

/ Not reported.
[a]Prisons and jails form one integrated system. Data include total jail and prison populations.
[b]Non-U.S. citizen defined as foreign-born.
[c]Non-U.S. citizen defined as inmates held by U.S. Immigration and Customs Enforcement (ICE).
[d]Number of U.S. citizens based only on inmates who reported their citizenship.
[e]Nevada was unable to provide sex breakouts for 2008.
Source: Bureau of Justice Statistics. 2010. *Prison Inmates at Midyear 2009—Statistical Tables*. Washington, DC: U.S. Department of Justice. http://bjs.ojp.usdoj.gov/content/pub/pdf/pim09st.pdf

Women and the Law

English Common Law Doctrine of Coverture

Prior to the second half of the 20th century, women's rights were greatly restricted. Women were more likely to be subsidiary to their husband or father than active agents in their own right. Women were also not considered for education, which did not become universalized until during modern time period. The major legal instrument impacting women in the North American English colonies and the United States was William Blackstone's commentaries, also known as the Doctrine of Coverture. The relevant text is below.

By marriage, the husband and wife are one person in law: that is, the very being or legal existence of the woman is suspended during the marriage, or at least is incorporated and consolidated into that of the husband; under whose wing, protection, and *cover*, she performs every thing; and is therefore called in our law-french a *feme-covert* . . . under the protection and influence of her husband, her *baron*, or lord; and her condition during her marriage is called her *coverture*. . . .

For this reason, a man cannot grant anything to his wife, or enter into covenant with her: for the grant would be to suppose her separate existence; and to covenant with her, would only to be to covenant with himself. . . .

The husband is bound to provide his wife with the necessaries by law, as much as himself; and, if she contracts debts for them, he is obliged to pay them. . . .

If the wife be injured in her person or her property, she can bring no action for redress without her husband's concurrence, and in his name, as well her own; neither can she be sued. . . . But in trials of any sort they are not allowed to be evidence for, or against, each other: partly because it is impossible their testimony should be indifferent, but principally because of the union of person. . . .

But though our law in general considers man and wife as one person, yet there are some instances in which she is separately considered; as inferior to him, and acting by his compulsion. And therefore all deeds executed, and acts done, by her, during her coverture, are void. . . .

She cannot by will devise lands to her husband, unless under special circumstances; for at the time of making it she is supposed to be under his coercion. . . .

These are the chief legal effects of marriage during the coverture; upon which we may observe, that even the disabilities which the wife lies under are for the most part intended for her protection and benefit; so great a favorite is the female sex of the laws of England (pp. 176–184 [421–433]).

Source: Blackstone, Sir William. (2006 [1765]). *Commentaries on the Laws of England Book the First*. Public Domain Books.

Mann Act of 1910

A product of the Progressive reform era, the Mann Act was referred to as the White Slave Traffic Act. Its primary purpose was to forbid the transportation of girls and women across state or national borderlines to engage in prostitution or "other immoral purposes." Excerpts from the act are below.

CHAP. 395 — An Act to further regulate interstate commerce and foreign commerce by prohibiting the transportation therein for immoral purposes of women and girls, and for other purposes. . . .

SEC. 2. That any person who shall knowingly transport or cause to be transported or aid or assist in obtaining transportation for, or in transporting in interstate or foreign commerce, or in any

Territory or the District of Columbia, any woman or girl for the purpose of prostitution or debauchery, or for any other immoral purpose, or with the intent and purpose to induce, entice, or compel such woman or girl to become a prostitute or give herself up to debauchery, or to engage in any other immoral practice ... shall be deemed guilty of a felony.

SEC. 3. That any person who shall knowingly persuade, induce, entice, or coerce, or cause to be persuaded, induced, enticed, or coerced, or aid or assist in persuading, inducing, enticing or coercing any woman or girl to go from one place to another in interstate or foreign commerce, or in any Territory or the District of Columbia, for the purpose of prostitution or debauchery, or for any other immoral purpose, or with the intent and purpose on the part of such person that such woman or girl shall engage in the practice of prostitution or debauchery, or any other immoral practice, whether with or without her consent, and who shall thereby knowingly cause or aid or assist in causing such woman or girl to go and be carried or transported as a passenger upon the line or route of any common carrier or carriers in interstate or foreign commerce, or any Territory or the District of Columbia, shall be deemed guilty of a felony. ...

SEC. 4. That any person who shall knowingly persuade, induce, entice or coerce any woman or girl under the age of eighteen years from any State or Territory or the District of Columbia to any other State or Territory or the District of Columbia, with the purpose and intent to induce or coerce her, or that she shall be induced or coerced to engage in prostitution or debauchery, or any other immoral practice, and shall in furtherance of such purpose knowingly induce or cause her to go and to be carried or transported as a passenger in interstate commerce upon the line or route of any common carrier or carriers, shall be deemed guilty of a felony. ...

SEC. 8. That this Act shall be known and referred to as the "White-slave traffic Act."

Source: The White-Slave Traffic Act, 1910 (ch. 395, 36 Stat. 825; codified as amended at 18 U.S.C. §§ 2421–2424).

United Nations Declaration of Human Rights (1948)

After World War II, the member nations of the United Nations adopted the auspicious task of guaranteeing all people, regardless of sex, race or ethnicity and nationality, a set of basic freedoms known as human rights. At this time, the United States had not yet conceived of the Civil Rights Act of 1964 or other legislation impacting the rights of American women. This document asserts the equality of all men and women, regardless of world conditions and a struggle to fully achieve these rights throughout world society is under way. The full text follows.

PREAMBLE

Whereas recognition of the inherent dignity and of the equal and inalienable rights of all members of the human family is the foundation of freedom, justice and peace in the world,

Whereas disregard and contempt for human rights have resulted in barbarous acts which have outraged the conscience of mankind, and the advent of a world in which human beings shall enjoy freedom of speech and belief and freedom from fear and want has been proclaimed as the highest aspiration of the common people,

Whereas it is essential, if man is not to be compelled to have recourse, as a last resort, to rebellion against tyranny and oppression, that human rights should be protected by the rule of law,

Whereas it is essential to promote the development of friendly relations between nations,

Whereas the peoples of the United Nations have in the Charter reaffirmed their faith in fundamental human rights, in the dignity and worth of the human person and in the equal rights of men and women and have determined to promote social progress and better standards of life in larger freedom,

Whereas Member States have pledged themselves to achieve, in co-operation with the United Nations, the promotion of universal respect for and observance of human rights and fundamental freedoms,

Whereas a common understanding of these rights and freedoms is of the greatest importance for the full realization of this pledge,

Now, Therefore THE GENERAL ASSEMBLY proclaims THIS UNIVERSAL DECLARATION OF HUMAN RIGHTS as a common standard of achievement for all peoples and all nations, to the end that every individual and every organ of society, keeping this Declaration constantly in mind, shall strive by teaching and education to promote respect for these rights and freedoms and by progressive measures, national and international, to secure their universal and effective recognition and observance, both among the peoples of Member States themselves and among the peoples of territories under their jurisdiction.

Article 1.

All human beings are born free and equal in dignity and rights. They are endowed with reason and conscience and should act towards one another in a spirit of brotherhood.

Article 2.

Everyone is entitled to all the rights and freedoms set forth in this Declaration, without distinction of any kind, such as race, colour, sex, language, religion, political or other opinion, national or social origin, property, birth or other status. Furthermore, no distinction shall be made on the basis of the political, jurisdictional or international status of the country or territory to which a person belongs, whether it be independent, trust, non-self-governing or under any other limitation of sovereignty.

Article 3.

Everyone has the right to life, liberty and security of person.

Article 4.

No one shall be held in slavery or servitude; slavery and the slave trade shall be prohibited in all their forms.

Article 5.

No one shall be subjected to torture or to cruel, inhuman or degrading treatment or punishment.

Article 6.

Everyone has the right to recognition everywhere as a person before the law.

Article 7.

All are equal before the law and are entitled without any discrimination to equal protection of the law. All are entitled to equal protection against any discrimination in violation of this Declaration and against any incitement to such discrimination.

Article 8.

Everyone has the right to an effective remedy by the competent national tribunals for acts violating the fundamental rights granted him by the constitution or by law.

Article 9.

No one shall be subjected to arbitrary arrest, detention or exile.

Article 10.

Everyone is entitled in full equality to a fair and public hearing by an independent and impartial tribunal, in the determination of his rights and obligations and of any criminal charge against him.

Article 11.

(1) Everyone charged with a penal offence has the right to be presumed innocent until proved guilty according to law in a public trial at which he has had all the guarantees necessary for his defence.

(2) No one shall be held guilty of any penal offence on account of any act or omission which did not constitute a penal offence, under national or international law, at the time when it was committed. Nor shall a heavier penalty be imposed than the one that was applicable at the time the penal offence was committed.

Article 12.

No one shall be subjected to arbitrary interference with his privacy, family, home or correspondence, nor to attacks upon his honour and reputation. Everyone has the right to the protection of the law against such interference or attacks.

Article 13.

(1) Everyone has the right to freedom of movement and residence within the borders of each state.

(2) Everyone has the right to leave any country, including his own, and to return to his country.

Article 14.

(1) Everyone has the right to seek and to enjoy in other countries asylum from persecution.

(2) This right may not be invoked in the case of prosecutions genuinely arising from non-political crimes or from acts contrary to the purposes and principles of the United Nations.

Article 15.

(1) Everyone has the right to a nationality.

(2) No one shall be arbitrarily deprived of his nationality nor denied the right to change his nationality.

Article 16.

(1) Men and women of full age, without any limitation due to race, nationality or religion, have the right to marry and to found a family. They are entitled to equal rights as to marriage, during marriage and at its dissolution.

(2) Marriage shall be entered into only with the free and full consent of the intending spouses.

(3) The family is the natural and fundamental group unit of society and is entitled to protection by society and the State.

Article 17.

(1) Everyone has the right to own property alone as well as in association with others.

(2) No one shall be arbitrarily deprived of his property.

Article 18.

Everyone has the right to freedom of thought, conscience and religion; this right includes freedom to change his religion or belief, and freedom, either alone or in community with others and in public or private, to manifest his religion or belief in teaching, practice, worship and observance.

Article 19.

Everyone has the right to freedom of opinion and expression; this right includes freedom to hold opinions without interference and to seek, receive and impart information and ideas through any media and regardless of frontiers.

Article 20.

(1) Everyone has the right to freedom of peaceful assembly and association.

(2) No one may be compelled to belong to an association.

Article 21.

(1) Everyone has the right to take part in the government of his country, directly or through freely chosen representatives.

(2) Everyone has the right of equal access to public service in his country.

(3) The will of the people shall be the basis of the authority of government; this will shall be expressed in periodic and genuine elections which shall be by universal and equal suffrage and shall be held by secret vote or by equivalent free voting procedures.

Article 22.

Everyone, as a member of society, has the right to social security and is entitled to realization, through national effort and international co-operation and in accordance with the organization and resources of each State, of the economic, social and cultural rights indispensable for his dignity and the free development of his personality.

Article 23.

(1) Everyone has the right to work, to free choice of employment, to just and favourable conditions of work and to protection against unemployment.

(2) Everyone, without any discrimination, has the right to equal pay for equal work.

(3) Everyone who works has the right to just and favourable remuneration ensuring for himself and his family an existence worthy of human dignity, and supplemented, if necessary, by other means of social protection.

(4) Everyone has the right to form and to join trade unions for the protection of his interests.

Article 24.

Everyone has the right to rest and leisure, including reasonable limitation of working hours and periodic holidays with pay.

Article 25.

(1) Everyone has the right to a standard of living adequate for the health and well-being of himself and of his family, including food, clothing, housing and medical care and necessary social services, and the right to security in the event of unemployment, sickness, disability, widowhood, old age or other lack of livelihood in circumstances beyond his control.

(2) Motherhood and childhood are entitled to special care and assistance. All children, whether born in or out of wedlock, shall enjoy the same social protection.

Article 26.

(1) Everyone has the right to education. Education shall be free, at least in the elementary and fundamental stages. Elementary education shall be compulsory. Technical and professional education shall be made generally available and higher education shall be equally accessible to all on the basis of merit.

(2) Education shall be directed to the full development of the human personality and to the strengthening of respect for human rights and fundamental freedoms. It shall promote understanding, tolerance and friendship among all nations, racial or religious groups, and shall further the activities of the United Nations for the maintenance of peace.

(3) Parents have a prior right to choose the kind of education that shall be given to their children.

Article 27.

(1) Everyone has the right freely to participate in the cultural life of the community, to enjoy the arts and to share in scientific advancement and its benefits.

(2) Everyone has the right to the protection of the moral and material interests resulting from any scientific, literary or artistic production of which he is the author.

Article 28.

Everyone is entitled to a social and international order in which the rights and freedoms set forth in this Declaration can be fully realized.

Article 29.

(1) Everyone has duties to the community in which alone the free and full development of his personality is possible.

(2) In the exercise of his rights and freedoms, everyone shall be subject only to such limitations as are determined by law solely for the purpose of securing due recognition and respect for the rights and freedoms of others and of meeting the just requirements of morality, public order and the general welfare in a democratic society.

(3) These rights and freedoms may in no case be exercised contrary to the purposes and principles of the United Nations.

Article 30.

Nothing in this Declaration may be interpreted as implying for any State, group or person any right to engage in any activity or to perform any act aimed at the destruction of any of the rights and freedoms set forth herein.

Source: United Nations, Universal Declaration of Human Rights. Adopted December 10, 1948 in General Assembly resolution 217 (A) III. Available at: http://www.un.org/en/documents/udhr/

The Civil Rights Act of 1964

This landmark antidiscrimination act was an impact of the African American and other minority civil rights movement. Originally, it was primarily directed toward ending discrimination against African Americans. The word "sex," to expand women's rights, was added in a later amendment. The outcome of this act and other related legislation was to expand educational and employment opportunity for women in the United States. Although women are increasingly represented in the judiciary and community corrections, they are still underrepresented in policing and have faced negative attitudes from male officers. Following are excerpts from the act.

To enforce the constitutional right to vote, to confer jurisdiction upon the district courts of the United States to provide injunctive relief against discrimination in public accommodations, to authorize the Attorney General to institute suits to protect constitutional rights in public facilities and public education, to extend the Commission on Civil Rights, to prevent discrimination in federally assisted programs, to establish a Commission on Equal Employment Opportunity, and for other purposes.

Title 7. Equal Employment Opportunity

DISCRIMINATION BECAUSE OF RACE, COLOR, RELI-
GION, SEX, OR NATIONAL ORIGIN

SEC. 703. (a) It shall be an unlawful employment practice for
an employer—

(1) to fail or refuse to hire or to discharge any individual, or
otherwise to discriminate against any individual with respect to
his compensation, terms, conditions, or privileges of employment, because of such individual's race, color, religion, sex, or
national origin; or

(2) to limit, segregate, or classify his employees in any way
which would deprive or tend to deprive any individual of
employment opportunities or otherwise adversely affect his status as an employee, because of such individual's race, color, religion, sex, or national origin.

(b) It shall be an unlawful employment practice for an
employment agency to fail or refuse to refer for employment, or
otherwise to discriminate against, any individual because of his
race, color, religion, sex, or national origin, or to classify or refer
for employment any individual on the basis of his race, color,
religion, sex, or national origin.

(c) It shall be an unlawful employment practice for a labor
organization—

(1) to exclude or to expel from its membership, or otherwise
to discriminate against, any individual because of his race, color,
religion, sex, or national origin;

(2) to limit, segregate, or classify its membership, or to classify
or fail or refuse to refer for employment any individual, in any
way which would deprive or tend to deprive any individual of
employment opportunities, or would limit such employment
opportunities or otherwise adversely affect his status as an
employee or as an applicant for employment, because of such
individual's race, color, religion, sex, or national origin; or

(3) to cause or attempt to cause an employer to discriminate
against an individual in violation of this section.

(d) It shall be an unlawful employment practice for any
employer, labor organization, or joint labor-management committee controlling apprenticeship or other training or retraining,
including on-the-job training programs to discriminate against
any individual because of his race, color, religion, sex, or national
origin in admission to, or employment in, any program established to provide apprenticeship or other training.

(e) Notwithstanding any other provision of this title, (1) it shall not be an unlawful employment practice for an employer to hire and employ employees, for an employment agency to classify, or refer for employment any individual, for a labor organization to classify its membership or to classify or refer for employment any individual, or for an employer, labor organization, or joint labor-management committee controlling apprenticeship or other training or retraining programs to admit or employ any individual in any such program, on the basis of his religion, sex, or national origin in those certain instances where religion, sex, or national origin is a bona fide occupational qualification reasonably necessary to the normal operation of that particular business or enterprise, and (2) it shall not be an unlawful employment practice for a school, college, university, or other educational institution or institution of learning to hire and employ employees of a particular religion if such school, college, university, or other educational institution or institution of learning is, in whole or in substantial part, owned, supported, controlled, or managed by a particular religion or by a particular religious corporation, association, or society, or if the curriculum of such school, college, university, or other educational institution or institution of learning is directed toward the propagation of a particular religion.

Source: Civil Rights Act of 1964 (Pub. L. 88-352, 78 Stat. 241, enacted July 2, 1964).

Women's Rate of Victimization in the United States

Detailed statistics on women's victimization, often a risk factor for criminal offending, is available from the National Crime Victimization Survey (NCVS) and is portrayed in Table 6.5. These statistics, illustrated in Table 6.6, establish that violent victimization including rape/sexual assault and aggravated and simple assault is often perpetrated by nonstrangers: an alarming fact, which suggests that many women are exposed. How do we know this?

The NCVS is an annual data collection conducted by the U.S. Census Bureau for the Bureau of Justice Statistics (BJS). The NCVS collects information on nonfatal crimes, reported and not reported, to the police, against persons age 12 or older from a

TABLE 6.5

Rates of Violent Crime, by Gender, Race, Hispanic Origin, and Age of Victim, 2008

Demographic Characteristic of Victim	Population	All	Rape/sexual assault	Robbery	All assault	Aggravated assault	Simple assault
					Violent Victimizations per 1,000 persons age 12 or older		
Gender							
Male	123,071,020	21.3	0.3^	2.7	18.3	3.9	14.5
Female	129,171,510	17.3	1.3	1.7	14.3	2.8	11.5
Race							
White	204,683,500	18.1	0.6	1.6	15.9	3.0	12.8
Black	30,709,860	25.9	1.9^	5.5	18.5	5.2	13.3
Other race*	13,952,240	15.2	0.9^	3.0^	11.3	2.8	8.5
Two or more races	2,896,930	51.6	1.9^	6.8	42.9	6.8	36.1
Hispanic origin							
Hispanic	34,506,680	16.4	0.6^	3.4	12.4	3.5	8.9
Non-Hispanic	217,351,750	19.7	0.8	2.0	16.9	3.3	13.6
Age							
12–15	16,414,550	42.2	1.6^	5.5	35.2	6.1	29.0
16–19	17,280,270	37.0	2.2	4.8	30.0	5.6	24.5
20–24	20,547,620	37.8	2.1	5.4	30.3	8.7	21.5
25–34	40,649,500	23.4	0.7	2.3	20.5	4.0	16.5
35–49	65,123,030	16.7	0.8	1.9	14.1	2.7	11.4
50–64	55,116,320	10.7	0.2^	0.8	9.7	2.0	7.7
65 or older	37,111,240	3.1	0.2^	0.2^	2.7	0.4^	2.3

Note: Violent crimes measured by the National Crime Victimization Survey include rape, sexual assault, robbery, and aggravated and simple assault. Because the NCVS interviews persons about their victimizations, murder and manslaughter cannot be included.

^Based on 10 or fewer sample cases.

*Includes American Indians, Alaska Natives, Asians, Native Hawaiians, and other Pacific Islanders.

Source: Rand, Michael R. 2009. "National Criminal Victimization Survey: Criminal Victimization, 2008." *Bureau of Justice Statistics Bulletin,* September. Washington, DC: Bureau of Justice Statistics. http://bjs.ojp.usdoj.gov/content/pub/pdf/cv08.pdf

TABLE 6.6
Relationship between Victim and Offender, by Gender of Victim, 2008

Relationship to victim	Violent crime		Rape/sexual assault		Robbery		Aggravated assault		Simple assault	
	Number	Percent	Number	Percent	Number	Percent	Number	Percent	Number	Percent
Male victims										
Total	2,626,000	100%	39,590	100%	328,690	100%	476,390	100%	1,781,330	100%
Nonstranger	1,286,170	49%	39,590	100%^	112,230	34%	241,900	51%	892,440	50%
Intimate partner	88,120	3	8,310	21^	0	0^	37,430	8^	42,380	2
Other relative	83,630	3	0	0^	0	0^	25,560	5^	58,070	3
Friend/acquaintance	1,114,410	42	31,280	79^	112,230	34	178,910	38	791,990	44
Stranger	1,163,410	44%	0	0%^	200,150	61%	206,300	43%	756,970	42%
Relationship unknown	176,420	7%	0	0%^	16,310	5%	28,190	6%^	131,920	7%
Female victims										
Total	2,230,500	100%	164,240	100%	223,140	100%	363,550	100%	1,479,580	100%
Nonstranger	1,556,790	70%	102,950	63%	118,220	53%	250,190	69%	1,085,430	73%
Intimate partner	504,980	23	29,060	18	34,830	16	61,170	17	379,920	26
Other relative	196,070	9	5,220	3^	33,210	15^	28,150	8^	129,490	9
Friend/acquaintance	855,740	38	68,680	42	50,180	22	160,860	44	576,010	39
Stranger	592,570	27%	52,890	32%	99,450	45%	104,410	29%	335,810	23%
Relationship unknown	81,150	4%	8,390	5%^	5,470	2%^	8,950	2%^	58,340	4%^

Note: Percentages may not total to 100% because of rounding.

^Based on 10 or fewer sample cases.

*Defined as current or former spouses, boyfriends, or girlfriends.

Source: Rand, Michael R. 2009. "National Crime Victimization Survey: Criminal Victimization, 2008." Bureau of Justice Statistics Bulletin, September. Washington, DC: Bureau of Justice Statistics. http://bjs.ojp.usdoj.gov/content/pub/pdf/cv08.pdf

nationally representative sample of U.S. households. Table 6.7 details victims of crimes reported to police in 2008, differentiating between violent crimes and property crimes. Violent crimes measured by the NCVS include rape or sexual assault, robbery, aggravated assault, and simple assault. Property crimes include household burglary, motor vehicle theft, and theft. Survey results are based on the data gathered from residents living throughout the United States, including persons living in group quarters, such as dormitories, rooming houses, and religious group dwellings. The scope of the survey excluded armed forces personnel living in military barracks and persons living in an institutional setting, such as a correctional facility.

In 2008, women are more likely than men to report rape or sexual assault. Men outnumber women as victims of other violent victimization: robbery, and aggravated and simple assault. Seventy percent of violent victimizations of women are perpetrated by intimates—partners, other relatives, or friends/acquaintances—as compared to 49% of violent victimization reported by men.

TABLE 6.7
Crime Reported to the Police, by Gender, Race, and Hispanic Origin, 2008

Victim Gender, Race, and Hispanic Origin	Percent of Crime Reported to Police, 2008	
	Violent	Property
Total	47.1%	40.3%
Male	44.2%	41.6%
White	44.1	42.1
Black	50.4	39.4
Other race*	30.7	36.8
Hispanic	44.0%	36.7%
Non-Hispanic	44.3	42.6
Female	50.4%	39.0%
White	47.9	37.1
Black	68.5	48.7
Other race*	46.7	33.7
Hispanic	54.1%	35.4%
Non-Hispanic	50.0	39.7

Note: Total includes estimates for persons identifying with two or more races, not shown separately. Racial categories displayed are for persons who identified with one race.
*Includes American Indians, Alaska Natives, Asians, Native Hawaiians, and other Pacific Islanders.
Source: Rand, Michael R. 2009. "National Criminal Victimization Survey: Criminal Victimization, 2008." *Bureau of Justice Statistics Bulletin*, September. Washington, DC: Bureau of Justice Statistics. http://bjs.ojp.usdoj.gov/content/pub/pdf/cv08.pdf

Sixty-three percent of sexual assault and rape of women was committed by nonstrangers, 53% of robberies, 69% of aggravated assaults, and 73% of simple assaults. In contrast, men are more likely to experience stranger-perpetrated violence than women, although they experience intimate assault as well. African American and non-Hispanic white women were more likely to report criminal victimization than Hispanic women.

Rape

Rape is a crime that leaves women in fear and causes self-regulation of behavior to try to avoid danger. Although most men do not live with a fear of rape, they are also susceptible, and crimes against men would be included in the FBI forcible rape statistics. The vast majority of rapes are committed by men against women victims. Rape is considered an extensively underreported crime, but the reported incidence has been increasing. In 1960, there were 17,190 rapes reported: a rate of 9.6 per 1,000 inhabitants. Over the years, attempts have been made to strengthen the rights of rape victims and make the process of crime reporting less traumatic, such as during the physical examination with a "rape kit." In 1998, there were 93,144 reported rapes, a rate of 34.5 per 1,000 inhabitants. This had dropped to 29.3 per 1,000 in 2008, as can be seen in Table 6.8.

TABLE 6.8
Estimated Number and Rate (per 100,000 inhabitants) of Forcible Rape Offenses Known to Police, United States, 1998–2008

	Number	Rate per 1,000 Inhabitants
1998	93,144	34.5
1999	89,411	32.8
2000	90,178	32.0
2001	90,863	31.8
2002	95,235	33.1
2003	93,883	31.8
2004	95,089	32.3
2005	94,347	31.8
2006	92,757	32.0
2007	90,427	30.0
2008	89,000	29.3

Source: U.S. Department of Justice, Federal Bureau of Investigation. *Crime in the United States, 1975* (p. 49, Table 2; 1995, p. 58). Washington, DC: USGPO. 2008, Table 1 (Online). http://www2.fbi.gov/ucr/cius2008/data/table_01.html. Table adapted by Sourcebook Staff.

Violence against Women and Department of Justice Reauthorization Act of 2005

The Violence against Women Act was first passed in 1994 and renewed in 2005. It is again up for authorization in 2012.

TITLE I—ENHANCING JUDICIAL AND LAW ENFORCEMENT TOOLS TO COMBAT VIOLENCE AGAINST WOMEN

Sec. 101. Stop grants improvements.

Sec. 102. Grants to encourage arrest and enforce protection orders improvements.

Sec. 103. Legal Assistance for Victims improvements.

Sec. 104. Ensuring crime victim access to legal services.

Sec. 105. The Violence Against Women Act court training and improvements.

Sec. 106. Full faith and credit improvements.

Sec. 107. Privacy protections for victims of domestic violence, dating violence, sexual violence, and stalking.

Sec. 108. Sex offender management.

Sec. 109. Stalker database.

Sec. 110. Federal victim assistants reauthorization.

Sec. 111. Grants for law enforcement training programs.

Sec. 112. Reauthorization of the court-appointed special advocate program.

Sec. 113. Preventing cyberstalking.

Sec. 114. Criminal provision relating to stalking.

Sec. 115. Repeat offender provision.

Sec. 116. Prohibiting dating violence.

Sec. 117. Prohibiting violence in special maritime and territorial jurisdiction.

Sec. 118. Updating protection order definition.

Sec. 119. GAO study and report.

Sec. 120. Grants for outreach to underserved populations.

Sec. 121. Enhancing culturally and linguistically specific services for victims of domestic violence, dating violence, sexual assault, and stalking.

TITLE II—IMPROVING SERVICES FOR VICTIMS OF DOMESTIC VIOLENCE, DATING VIOLENCE, SEXUAL ASSAULT, AND STALKING

Sec. 201. Findings.

Sec. 202. Sexual assault services program.

Sec. 203. Amendments to the Rural Domestic Violence and Child Abuse Enforcement Assistance Program.

Sec. 204. Training and services to end violence against women with disabilities.

Sec. 205. Training and services to end violence against women in later life.

Sec. 206. Strengthening the National Domestic Violence Hotline.

TITLE III—SERVICES, PROTECTION, AND JUSTICE FOR YOUNG VICTIMS OF VIOLENCE

Sec. 301. Findings.

Sec. 302. Rape prevention and education.

Sec. 303. Services, education, protection, and justice for young victims of violence.

Sec. 304. Grants to combat violent crimes on campuses.

Sec. 305. Juvenile justice.

Sec. 306. Safe havens.

TITLE IV—STRENGTHENING AMERICA'S FAMILIES BY PREVENTING VIOLENCE

Sec. 401. Preventing violence against women and children.

Sec. 402. Study conducted by the Centers for Disease Control and Prevention.

Sec. 403. Public Awareness Campaign.

TITLE V—STRENGTHENING THE HEALTHCARE SYSTEM'S RESPONSE TO DOMESTIC VIOLENCE, DATING VIOLENCE, SEXUAL ASSAULT, AND STALKING

TITLE VI—HOUSING OPPORTUNITIES AND SAFETY FOR BATTERED WOMEN AND CHILDREN

TITLE VII—PROVIDING ECONOMIC SECURITY FOR VICTIMS OF VIOLENCE

TITLE VIII—PROTECTION OF BATTERED AND TRAFFICKED IMMIGRANTS

Subtitle A—Victims of Crime

Sec. 801. Treatment of spouse and children of victims.

Sec. 802. Presence of victims of a severe form of trafficking in persons.

Sec. 803. Adjustment of status.

Sec. 804. Protection and assistance for victims of trafficking.

Sec. 805. Protecting victims of child abuse.

Subtitle B—VAWA Self-Petitioners

Sec. 811. Definition of VAWA self-petitioner.

Sec. 812. Application in case of voluntary departure.

Sec. 813. Removal proceedings.

Sec. 814. Eliminating abusers' control over applications and limitation on petitioning for abusers.

Sec. 815. Application for VAWA-related relief.

Sec. 816. Self-petitioning parents.

Sec. 817. VAWA confidentiality nondisclosure.

Subtitle C—Miscellaneous Amendments

Sec. 821. Duration of T and U visas.

Sec. 822. Technical correction to references in application of special physical presence and good moral character rules.

Sec. 823. Petitioning rights of certain former spouses under Cuban adjustment.

Sec. 824. Self-petitioning rights of HRIFA applicants.

Sec. 825. Motions to reopen. Sec. 826. Protecting abused juveniles.

Sec. 827. Protection of domestic violence and crime victims from certain disclosures of information.

Sec. 828. Rulemaking.

Subtitle D—International Marriage Broker Regulation

Sec. 831. Short title.

Sec. 832. Access to VAWA protection regardless of manner of entry.

Sec. 833. Domestic violence information and resources for immigrants and regulation of international marriage brokers.

Sec. 834. Sharing of certain information.

TITLE IX—SAFETY FOR INDIAN WOMEN

Sec. 901. Findings.

Sec. 902. Purposes.

Sec. 903. Consultation.

Sec. 904. Analysis and research on violence against Indian women.

Sec. 905. Tracking of violence against Indian women.

Sec. 906. Grants to Indian tribal governments.

Sec. 907. Tribal deputy in the Office on Violence Against Women.

Sec. 908. Enhanced criminal law resources.

Sec. 909. Domestic assault by an habitual offender.

SEC. 3. UNIVERSAL DEFINITIONS AND GRANT PROVISIONS.

(a) IN GENERAL—The Violence Against Women Act of 1994 (108 Stat. 1902 et seq.) is amended by adding after section 40001 the following:

'SEC. 40002. DEFINITIONS AND GRANT PROVISIONS.

'(a) DEFINITIONS—In this title:

'(1) COURTS—The term 'courts' means any civil or criminal, tribal, and Alaskan Village, Federal, State, local or territorial court having jurisdiction to address domestic violence, dating violence, sexual assault or stalking, including immigration, family, juvenile, and dependency courts, and the judicial officers serving in those courts, including judges, magistrate judges, commissioners, justices of the peace, or any other person with decisionmaking authority.

'(2) CHILD ABUSE AND NEGLECT—The term 'child abuse and neglect' means any recent act or failure to act on the part of a parent or caregiver with intent to cause death, serious physical or emotional harm, sexual abuse, or exploitation, or an act or failure to act which presents an imminent risk of serious harm. This definition shall not be construed to mean that failure to leave an abusive relationship, in the absence of other action constituting abuse or neglect, is itself abuse or neglect.

'(3) COMMUNITY-BASED ORGANIZATION—The term 'community- based organization' means an organization that—

'(A) focuses primarily on domestic violence, dating violence, sexual assault, or stalking;

'(B) has established a specialized culturally specificprogram that addresses domestic violence, dating violence, sexual assault, or stalking;

'(C) has a primary focus on underserved populations (and includes representatives of these populations) and domestic violence, dating violence, sexual assault, or stalking; or

'(D) obtains expertise, or shows demonstrated capacity to work effectively, on domestic violence, dating violence, sexual assault, and stalking through collaboration.

'(4) CHILD MALTREATMENT—The term 'child maltreatment' means the physical or psychological abuse or neglect of a child or youth, including sexual assault and abuse.

'(5) COURT-BASED AND COURT-RELATED PERSONNEL—The term 'court-based' and 'court-related personnel' mean persons working in the court, whether paid or volunteer, including—

'(A) clerks, special masters, domestic relations officers, administrators, mediators, custody evaluators, guardians ad litem, lawyers, negotiators, probation, parole, interpreters, victim assistants, victim advocates, and judicial, administrative, or any other professionals or personnel similarly involved in the legal process;

'(B) court security personnel;

'(C) personnel working in related, supplementary offices or programs (such as child support enforcement); and 42 USC 13925.

'(D) any other court-based or community-based personnel having responsibilities or authority to address domestic violence, dating violence, sexual assault, or stalking in the court system.

'(6) DOMESTIC VIOLENCE—The term 'domestic violence' includes felony or misdemeanor crimes of violence committed by a current or former spouse of the victim, by a person with whom the victim shares a child in common, by a person who is cohabitating with or has cohabitated with the victim as a spouse, by a person similarly situated to a spouse of the victim under the domestic or family violence laws of the jurisdiction receiving grant monies, or by any other person against an adult or youth victim who is protected from that person's acts under the domestic or family violence laws of the jurisdiction.

'(7) DATING PARTNER—The term 'dating partner' refers to a person who is or has been in a social relationship of a romantic or intimate nature with the abuser, and where the existence of such a relationship shall be determined based on a consideration of—

'(A) the length of the relationship;

'(B) the type of relationship; and

'(C) the frequency of interaction between the persons involved in the relationship.

'(8) DATING VIOLENCE—The term 'dating violence' means violence committed by a person—

'(A) who is or has been in a social relationship of a romantic or intimate nature with the victim; and

'(B) where the existence of such a relationship shall be determined based on a consideration of the following factors:

'(i) The length of the relationship.

'(ii) The type of relationship.

'(iii) The frequency of interaction between the persons involved in the relationship.

'(9) ELDER ABUSE—The term 'elder abuse' means any action against a person who is 50 years of age or older that constitutes the willful—

'(A) infliction of injury, unreasonable confinement, intimidation, or cruel punishment with resulting physical harm, pain, or mental anguish; or

'(B) deprivation by a person, including a caregiver, of goods or services with intent to cause physical harm, mental anguish, or mental illness.

'(10) INDIAN—The term 'Indian' means a member of an Indian tribe.

'(11) INDIAN COUNTRY—The term 'Indian country' has the same meaning given such term in section 1151 of title 18, United States Code.

'(12) INDIAN HOUSING—The term 'Indian housing' means housing assistance described in the Native American Housing

Assistance and Self-Determination Act of 1996 (25 U.S.C. 4101 et seq., as amended).

'(13) INDIAN TRIBE—The term 'Indian tribe' means a tribe, band, pueblo, nation, or other organized group or community of Indians, including any Alaska Native village or regional or village corporation (as defined in, or established pursuant to, the Alaska Native Claims Settlement Act (43 U.S.C. 1601 et seq.), that is recognized as eligible for the special programs and services provided by the United States to Indians because of their status as Indians.

'(14) INDIAN LAW ENFORCEMENT— The term 'Indian law enforcement' means the departments or individuals under the direction of the Indian tribe that maintain public order.

'(15) LAW ENFORCEMENT—The term 'law enforcement' means a public agency charged with policing functions, including any of its component bureaus (such as governmental victim services programs), including those referred to in section 3 of the Indian Enforcement Reform Act (25 U.S.C. 2802).

'(16) LEGAL ASSISTANCE—The term 'legal assistance' includes assistance to adult and youth victims of domestic violence, dating violence, sexual assault, and stalking in—

'(A) family, tribal, territorial, immigration, employment, administrative agency, housing matters, campus administrative or protection or stay away order proceedings, and other similar matters; and

'(B) criminal justice investigations, prosecutions and post-trial matters (including sentencing, parole, and probation) that impact the victim's safety and privacy.

'(17) LINGUISTICALLY AND CULTURALLY SPECIFIC SERVICES—

The term 'linguistically and culturally specific services' means community-based services that offer full linguistic access and culturally specific services and resources, including outreach, collaboration, and support mechanisms primarily directed toward underserved communities.

'(18) PERSONALLY IDENTIFYING INFORMATION OR PERSONAL

INFORMATION—The term 'personally identifying information' or 'personal information' means individually identifying information for or about an individual including information likely to disclose the location of a victim of domestic violence, dating violence, sexual assault, or stalking, including—

'(A) a first and last name;

'(B) a home or other physical address;

'(C) contact information (including a postal, e-mail or Internet protocol address, or telephone or facsimile number);

'(D) a social security number; and

'(E) any other information, including date of birth, racial or ethnic background, or religious affiliation, that, in combination with any of subparagraphs (A) through (D), would serve to identify any individual.

'(19) PROSECUTION—The term 'prosecution' means any public agency charged with direct responsibility for prosecuting criminal offenders, including such agency's component bureaus (such as governmental victim services programs).

'(20) PROTECTION ORDER OR RESTRAINING ORDER—The term 'protection order' or 'restraining order' includes—

'(A) any injunction, restraining order, or any other order issued by a civil or criminal court for the purpose of preventing violent or threatening acts or harassment against, sexual violence or contact or communication with or physical proximity to, another person, including any temporary or final orders issued by civil or criminal courts whether obtained by filing an independent action or as VerDate a pendente lite order in another proceeding so long as any civil order was issued in response to a complaint, petition, or motion filed by or on behalf of a person seeking protection; and

'(B) any support, child custody or visitation provisions, orders, remedies, or relief issued as part of a protection order, restraining order, or stay away injunction pursuant to State, tribal, territorial, or local law authorizing the issuance of protection orders, restraining orders, or injunctions for the protection of victims of domestic violence, dating violence, sexual assault, or stalking.

'(21) RURAL AREA AND RURAL COMMUNITY—The term 'rural area' and 'rural community' mean—

'(A) any area or community, respectively, no part of which is within an area designated as a standard metropolitan statistical area by the Office of Management and Budget; or

'(B) any area or community, respectively, that is—

'(i) within an area designated as a metropolitan statistical area or considered as part of a metropolitan statistical area; and

'(ii) located in a rural census tract.

'(22) RURAL STATE—The term 'rural State' means a State that has a population density of 52 or fewer persons per square mile or a State in which the largest county has fewer than 150,000 people, based on the most recent decennial census.

'(23) SEXUAL ASSAULT—The term 'sexual assault' means any conduct prescribed by chapter 109A of title 18, United States Code, whether or not the conduct occurs in the special maritime and territorial jurisdiction of the United States or in a Federal prison and includes both assaults committed by offenders who are strangers to the victim and assaults committed by offenders who are known or related by blood or marriage to the victim.

'(24) STALKING—The term 'stalking' means engaging in a course of conduct directed at a specific person that would cause a reasonable person to—

'(A) fear for his or her safety or the safety of others; or

'(B) suffer substantial emotional distress.

'(25) STATE—The term 'State' means each of the several States and the District of Columbia, and except as otherwise provided, the Commonwealth of Puerto Rico, Guam, American Samoa, the Virgin Islands, and the Northern Mariana Islands.

'(26) STATE DOMESTIC VIOLENCE COALITION—The term 'State domestic violence coalition' means a program determined by the Administration for Children and Families under the Family Violence Prevention and Services Act (42 U.S.C. 10410[b]).

'(27) STATE SEXUAL ASSAULT COALITION—The term 'State sexual assault coalition' means a program determined by the Center for Injury Prevention and Control of the Centers for Disease Control and Prevention under the Public Health Service Act (42 U.S.C. 280b et seq.).

'(28) TERRITORIAL DOMESTIC VIOLENCE OR SEXUAL ASSAULT

COALITION—The term 'territorial domestic violence or sexual or dating violence under the auspices or supervision of a court or a law enforcement or prosecution agency.

'(35) VICTIM SERVICES OR VICTIM SERVICE PROVIDER—The term 'victim services' or 'victim service provider' means a nonprofit, nongovernmental organization that assists domestic violence, dating violence, sexual assault, or stalking victims, including rape crisis centers, domestic violence shelters, faith based organizations, and other organizations, with a documented history of effective work concerning domestic violence, dating violence, sexual assault, or stalking.

'(36) YOUTH—The term 'youth' means teen and young adult victims of domestic violence, dating violence, sexual assault, or stalking.

SEC. 106. FULL FAITH AND CREDIT IMPROVEMENTS.

(a) ENFORCEMENT OF PROTECTION ORDERS ISSUED BY TERRITORIES—

(c) LIMITS ON INTERNET PUBLICATION OF PROTECTION ORDER

INFORMATION—Section 2265(d) of title 18, United States Code, is amended by adding at the end the following:

'(3) LIMITS ON INTERNET PUBLICATION OF REGISTRATION INFORMATION—A State, Indian tribe, or territory shall not make available publicly on the Internet any information regarding the registration or filing of a protection order, restraining order, or injunction in either the issuing or enforcing State, tribal or territorial jurisdiction, if such publication would be likely to publicly reveal the identity or location of the party protected under such order. A State, Indian tribe, or territory may share court-generated and law enforcement-generated information contained in secure, governmental registries for protection order enforcement purposes.''

(d) DEFINITIONS—Section 2266 of title 18, United States Code, is amended—

(1) by striking paragraph (5) and inserting the following:

'(5) PROTECTION ORDER—The term 'protection order' includes—

'(A) any injunction, restraining order, or any other order issued by a civil or criminal court for the purpose of preventing violent or threatening acts or harassment against, sexual violence, or contact or communication with or physical proximity to, another person, including any temporary or final order issued by a civil or criminal court whether obtained by filing an independent action or as a pendente lite order in another proceeding so long as any civil or criminal order was issued in response to a complaint, petition, or motion filed by or on behalf of a person seeking protection; and

'(B) any support, child custody or visitation provisions, orders, remedies or relief issued as part of a protection order, restraining order, or injunction pursuant to State, tribal, territorial, or local law authorizing the issuance of protection orders, restraining orders, or injunctions for the protection of victims of domestic violence, sexual assault, dating violence, or stalking.''; and

(2) in clauses (i) and (ii) of paragraph (7)(A), by striking "2261A, a spouse or former spouse of the abuser, a person who shares a child in common with the abuser, and a person who cohabits or has cohabited as a spouse with the abuser" and inserting "2261A—

'(I) a spouse or former spouse of the abuser, a person who shares a child in common with the abuser, and a person who cohabits or has cohabited as a spouse with the abuser; or

'(II) a person who is or has been in a social relationship of a romantic or intimate nature with the abuser, as determined by the length of the relationship, the type of relationship, and the frequency of interaction between the persons involved in the relationship.'

Source: Violence against Women and Department of Justice Reauthorization Act of 2005. 109th Congress, HR 3402. Available at: http://www.govtrack.us/congress/bill.xpd?bill=h109-3402.

Sex Trafficking

Torture Definition and Prostitution

Torture is "any act by which severe pain or suffering, whether physical or mental, is intentionally inflicted on a person for such purposes as punishing him ... or intimidating or coercing him or a third person, or for any reason based on discrimination of any kind, when such pain or suffering is inflicted by or at the instigation of or with the consent or acquiescence of a public official or other person acting in an official capacity" (United Nations, 1984).

Source: United Nations Convention against Torture and Other Cruel, Inhuman or Degrading Treatment or Punishment, 1465 U.N.T.S. 85, Dec. 10, 1984.

Prostitution activities that overlap with torture techniques (Farley, 2006):

- Deprivation of hygiene
- Sexualized verbal abuse and mockery
- Coerced nudity
- Physical sexual harassment (groping)
- Sexual assault

Source: Farley, Melissa. 2006. "Prostitution, Trafficking and Cultural Amnesia: What We Must Not Know in Order to Keep the Business of Sexual Exploitation Running Smoothly." *Yale Journal of Law and Feminism* 18: 101–136.

Trafficking Victims Protection Act of 2000 (TVPA)

Although the Mann Act addressed both internal and international transport of women for prostitution or other "debauchery," it did not address the globalization and transnational organization of crime of the 21st century. This act further criminalizes trafficking in persons within the United States and provides protection and immigrant status for those willing to testify against traffickers and/or individuals holding them in slavery. Of great importance, it includes other types of slavery applying to both women and men, and not just sex trafficking offenses Reflecting internationalization, it includes a three-tier measurement scheme to rate the progress of other countries. Those nations that fail to make progress in fighting trafficking can be placed in the third tier and denied foreign aid. After listing the basic sections of the act, excerpts are provided below.

PUBLIC LAW 106–386—OCT. 28, 2000

DIVISION A—TRAFFICKING VICTIMS PROTECTION ACT OF 2000

Sec.101. Short title.

Sec.102. Purposes and findings.

Sec.103. Definitions.

Sec.104. Annual Country Reports on Human Rights Practices.

Sec.105. Interagency Task Force To Monitor and Combat Trafficking.

Sec.106. Prevention of trafficking.

Sec.107. Protection and assistance for victims of trafficking.

Sec.108. Minimum standards for the elimination of trafficking.

Sec.109. Assistance to foreign countries to meet minimum standards.

Sec.110. Actions against governments failing to meet minimum standards.

Sec.111. Actions against significant traffickers in persons.

Sec.112. Strengthening prosecution and punishment of traffickers.

Sec.113. Authorizations of appropriations.

DIVISION A—TRAFFICKING VICTIMS PROTECTION ACT OF 2000
SEC. 101. SHORT TITLE.
This division may be cited as the "Trafficking Victims Protection Act of 2000."
SEC. 102. PURPOSES AND FINDINGS.

(a) PURPOSES.—The purposes of this division are to combat trafficking in persons, a contemporary manifestation of slavery whose victims are predominantly women and children, to ensure just and effective punishment of traffickers, and to protect their victims.

(b) FINDINGS.—Congress finds that:

   (1) As the 21st century begins, the degrading institution of slavery continues throughout the world. Trafficking in persons is a modern form of slavery, and it is the largest manifestation of slavery today. At least 700,000 persons annually, primarily women and children, are trafficked within or across international borders. Approximately 50,000 women and children are trafficked into the United States each year.

   (2) Many of these persons are trafficked into the international sex trade, often by force, fraud, or coercion. The sex industry has rapidly expanded over the past several decades. It involves sexual exploitation of persons, predominantly women and girls, involving activities related to prostitution, pornography, sex tourism, and other commercial sexual services. The low status of women in many parts of the world has contributed to a burgeoning of the trafficking industry.

   (3) Trafficking in persons is not limited to the sex industry. This growing transnational crime also includes forced labor and involves significant violations of labor, public health, and human rights standards worldwide.

(4) Traffickers primarily target women and girls, who are disproportionately affected by poverty, the lack of access to education, chronic unemployment, discrimination, and the lack of economic opportunities in countries of origin. Traffickers lure women and girls into their networks through false promises of decent working conditions at relatively good pay as nannies, maids, dancers, factory workers, restaurant workers, sales clerks, or models. Traffickers also buy children from poor families and sell them into prostitution or into various types of forced or bonded labor.

(5) Traffickers often transport victims from their home communities to unfamiliar destinations, including foreign countries away from family and friends, religious institutions, and other sources of protection and support, leaving the victims defenseless and vulnerable.

(6) Victims are often forced through physical violence to engage in sex acts or perform slavery-like labor. Such force includes rape and other forms of sexual abuse, torture, starvation, imprisonment, threats, psychological abuse, and coercion.

(7) Traffickers often make representations to their victims that physical harm may occur to them or others should the victim escape or attempt to escape. Such representations can have the same coercive effects on victims as direct threats to inflict such harm.

(8) Trafficking in persons is increasingly perpetrated by organized, sophisticated criminal enterprises. Such trafficking is the fastest growing source of profits for organized criminal enterprises worldwide. Profits from the trafficking industry contribute to the expansion of organized crime in the United States and worldwide. Trafficking in persons is often aided by official corruption in countries of origin, transit, and destination, thereby threatening the rule of law.

(9) Trafficking includes all the elements of the crime of forcible rape when it involves the involuntary participation of another person in sex acts by means of fraud, force, or coercion.

(10)   Trafficking also involves violations of other laws, including labor and immigration codes and laws against kidnapping, slavery, false imprisonment, assault, battery, pandering, fraud, and extortion.

(11)   Trafficking exposes victims to serious health risks. Women and children trafficked in the sex industry are exposed to deadly diseases, including HIV and AIDS. Trafficking victims are sometimes worked or physically brutalized to death.

(12)   Trafficking in persons substantially affects interstate and foreign commerce. Trafficking for such purposes as involuntary servitude, peonage, and other forms of forced labor has an impact on the nationwide employment network and labor market. Within the context of slavery, servitude, and labor or services which are obtained or maintained through coercive conduct that amounts to a condition of servitude, victims are subjected to a range of violations.

(13)   Involuntary servitude statutes are intended to reach cases in which persons are held in a condition of servitude through nonviolent coercion. In United States v. Kozminski, 487 U.S. 931 (1988), the Supreme Court found that section 1584 of title 18, United States Code, should be narrowly interpreted, absent a definition of involuntary servitude by Congress. As a result, that section was interpreted to criminalize only servitude that is brought about through use or threatened use of physical or legal coercion, and to exclude other conduct that can have the same purpose and effect.

(14)   Existing legislation and law enforcement in the United States and other countries are inadequate to deter trafficking and bring traffickers to justice, failing to reflect the gravity of the offenses involved. No comprehensive law exists in the United States that penalizes the range of offenses involved in the trafficking scheme. Instead, even the most brutal instances of trafficking in the sex industry are often punished under laws that also apply to lesser offenses, so that traffickers typically escape deserved punishment.

(15) In the United States, the seriousness of this crime and its components is not reflected in current sentencing guidelines, resulting in weak penalties for convicted traffickers.

(16) In some countries, enforcement against traffickers is also hindered by official indifference, by corruption, and sometimes even by official participation in trafficking.

(17) Existing laws often fail to protect victims of trafficking, and because victims are often illegal immigrants in the destination country, they are repeatedly punished more harshly than the traffickers themselves.

(18) Additionally, adequate services and facilities do not exist to meet victims' needs regarding health care, housing, education, and legal assistance, which safely reintegrate trafficking victims into their home countries.

(19) Victims of severe forms of trafficking should not be inappropriately incarcerated, fined, or otherwise penalized solely for unlawful acts committed as a direct result of being trafficked, such as using false documents, entering the country without documentation, or working without documentation.

(20) Because victims of trafficking are frequently unfamiliar with the laws, cultures, and languages of the countries into which they have been trafficked, because they are often subjected to coercion and intimidation including physical detention and debt bondage, and because they often fear retribution and forcible removal to countries in which they will face retribution or other hardship, these victims often find it difficult or impossible to report the crimes committed against them or to assist in the investigation and prosecution of such crimes.

(21) Trafficking of persons is an evil requiring concerted and vigorous action by countries of origin, transit or destination, and by international organizations.

(22) One of the founding documents of the United States, the Declaration of Independence, recognizes the inherent dignity and worth of all people. It states that

all men are created equal and that they are endowed by their Creator with certain unalienable rights. The right to be free from slavery and involuntary servitude is among those unalienable rights. Acknowledging this fact, the United States outlawed slavery and involuntary servitude in 1865, recognizing them as evil institutions that must be abolished. Current practices of sexual slavery and trafficking of women and children are similarly abhorrent to the principles upon which the United States was founded.

(23) The United States and the international community agree that trafficking in persons involves grave violations of human rights and is a matter of pressing international concern. The international community has repeatedly condemned slavery and involuntary servitude, violence against women, and other elements of trafficking, through declarations, treaties, and United Nations resolutions and reports, including the Universal Declaration of Human Rights; the 1956 Supplementary Convention on the Abolition of Slavery, the Slave Trade, and Institutions and Practices Similar to Slavery; the 1948 American Declaration on the Rights and Duties of Man; the 1957 Abolition of Forced Labor Convention; the International Covenant on Civil and Political Rights; the Convention Against Torture and Other Cruel, Inhuman or Degrading Treatment or Punishment; United Nations General Assembly Resolutions 50/167, 51/66, and 52/98; the Final Report of the World Congress against Sexual Exploitation of Children (Stockholm, 1996); the Fourth World Conference on Women (Beijing, 1995); and the 1991 Moscow Document of the Organization for Security and Cooperation in Europe.

(24) Trafficking in persons is a transnational crime with national implications. To deter international trafficking and bring its perpetrators to justice, nations including the United States must recognize that trafficking is a serious offense. This is done by prescribing appropriate punishment, giving priority to the prosecution of trafficking offenses, and protecting rather than punishing the victims of such offenses.

The United States must work bilaterally and multi-laterally to abolish the trafficking industry by taking steps to promote cooperation among countries linked together by international trafficking routes. The United States must also urge the international community to take strong action in multilateral form to engage recalcitrant countries in serious and sustained efforts to eliminate trafficking and protect trafficking victims.

SEC. 103. DEFINITIONS.

In this division:

(1) APPROPRIATE CONGRESSIONAL COMMITTEES.—The term "appropriate congressional committees" means the Committee on Foreign Relations and the Committee on the Judiciary of the Senate and the Committee on International Relations and the Committee on the Judiciary of the House of Representatives.

(2) COERCION.—The term "coercion" means—

(A) threats of serious harm to or physical restraint against any person;

(B) any scheme, plan, or pattern intended to cause a person to believe that failure to perform an act would result in serious harm to or physical restraint against any person; or

(C) the abuse or threatened abuse of the legal process.

(3) COMMERCIAL SEX ACT.—The term "commercial sex act" means any sex act on account of which anything of value is given to or received by any person.

(4) DEBT BONDAGE.—The term "debt bondage" means the status or condition of a debtor arising from a pledge by the debtor of his or her personal services or of those of a person under his or her control as a security for debt, if the value of those services as reasonably assessed is not applied toward the liquidation of the debt or the length and nature of those services are not respectively limited and defined.

(5) INVOLUNTARY SERVITUDE.—The term "involuntary servitude" includes a condition of servitude induced by means of—

(A) any scheme, plan, or pattern intended to cause a person to believe that, if the person did not enter into or continue in such condition, that person or another person would suffer serious harm or physical restraint; or

(B) the abuse or threatened abuse of the legal process.

(6) MINIMUM STANDARDS FOR THE ELIMINATION OF TRAFFICKING.—

The term "minimum standards for the elimination of trafficking" means the standards set forth in section 108.

(7) NONHUMANITARIAN, NONTRADE-RELATED FOREIGN ASSISTANCE.—The term "nonhumanitarian, nontrade-related foreign assistance" means—

(A) any assistance under the Foreign Assistance Act of 1961, other than—

i. assistance under chapter 4 of part II of that Act that is made available for any program, project, or activity eligible for assistance under chapter 1 of part I of that Act;

ii. assistance under chapter 8 of part I of that Act;

iii. any other narcotics-related assistance under part I of that Act or under chapter 4 or 5 part II of that Act, but any such assistance provided under this clause shall be subject to the prior notification procedures applicable to reprogrammings pursuant to section 634A of that Act;

iv. disaster relief assistance, including any assistance under chapter 9 of part I of that Act;

v. antiterrorism assistance under chapter 8 of part II of that Act;

vi. assistance for refugees;

vii. humanitarian and other development assistance in support of programs of nongovernmental organizations under Chapters 1 and 10 of that Act;

viii. programs under title IV of chapter 2 of part I of that Act, relating to the Overseas Private Investment Corporation; and

ix. other programs involving trade-related or humanitarian assistance; and

(B) sales, or financing on any terms, under the Arms Export Control Act, other than sales or financing provided for narcotics-related purposes following notification in accordance with the prior notification procedures applicable to reprogrammings pursuant to section 634A of the Foreign Assistance Act of 1961.

(8) SEVERE FORMS OF TRAFFICKING IN PERSONS.—The term "severe forms of trafficking in persons" means—

(A) sex trafficking in which a commercial sex act is induced by force, fraud, or coercion, or in which the person induced to perform such act has not attained 18 years of age; or

(B) the recruitment, harboring, transportation, provision, or obtaining of a person for labor or services, through the use of force, fraud, or coercion for the purpose of subjection to involuntary servitude, peonage, debt bondage, or slavery.

(9) SEX TRAFFICKING.—The term "sex trafficking" means the recruitment, harboring, transportation, provision, or obtaining of a person for the purpose of a commercial sex act.

(10) STATE.—The term "State" means each of the several States of the United States, the District of Columbia, the Commonwealth of Puerto Rico, the United States Virgin Islands, Guam, American Samoa, the Commonwealth of the Northern Mariana Islands, and territories and possessions of the United States.

(11) TASK FORCE.—The term "Task Force" means the Inter-agency Task Force to Monitor and Combat Trafficking established under section 105.

(12) UNITED STATES.—The term "United States" means the fifty States of the United States, the District of Columbia, Samoa, Guam, the Commonwealth of the Northern Mariana Islands, and the territories and possessions of the United States.

(13) VICTIM OF A SEVERE FORM OF TRAFFICKING.—The term "victim of a severe form of trafficking" means a person subject to an act or practice described in paragraph (8).

(14) VICTIM OF TRAFFICKING.—The term "victim of trafficking" means a person subjected to an act or practice described in paragraph (8) or (9).

SEC. 106. PREVENTION OF TRAFFICKING.

(a) ECONOMIC ALTERNATIVES TO PREVENT AND DETER TRAFFICKING.—

   The President shall establish and carry out international initiatives to enhance economic opportunity for potential victims of trafficking as a method to deter trafficking. Such initiatives may include—

   (1) microcredit lending programs, training in business development, skills training, and job counseling;

   (2) programs to promote women's participation in economic decisionmaking;

   (3) programs to keep children, especially girls, in elementary and secondary schools, and to educate persons who have been victims of trafficking;

   (4) development of educational curricula regarding the dangers of trafficking; and

   (5) grants to nongovernmental organizations to accelerate and advance the political, economic, social, and educational roles and capacities of women in their countries.

(b) PUBLIC AWARENESS AND INFORMATION.—The President, acting through the Secretary of Labor, the Secretary of Health and Human Services, the Attorney General, and the Secretary of State, shall establish and carry out programs to increase public awareness, particularly among potential victims of trafficking, of the dangers of trafficking and the protections that are available for victims of trafficking.

(c) CONSULTATION REQUIREMENT.—The President shall consult with appropriate nongovernmental organizations with respect to the establishment and conduct of initiatives described in subsections (a) and (b).

SEC. 107. PROTECTION AND ASSISTANCE FOR VICTIMS OF TRAFFICKING.

(a) ASSISTANCE FOR VICTIMS IN OTHER COUNTRIES.—

   (1) IN GENERAL.—The Secretary of State and the Administrator of the United States Agency for

International Development, in consultation with appropriate nongovernmental organizations, shall establish and carry out programs and initiatives in foreign countries to assist in the safe integration trafficking. Such programs and initiatives shall be designed to meet the appropriate assistance needs of such persons and their children, as identified by the Task Force.

(2) ADDITIONAL REQUIREMENT.—In establishing and conducting programs and initiatives described in paragraph (1), the Secretary of State and the Administrator of the United States Agency for International Development shall take all appropriate steps to enhance cooperative efforts among foreign countries, including countries of origin of victims of trafficking, to assist in the integration, reintegration, or resettlement, as appropriate, of victims of trafficking, including stateless victims.

(b) VICTIMS IN THE UNITED STATES.— (1) ASSISTANCE.—

(A) ELIGIBILITY FOR BENEFITS AND SERVICES.— Notwithstanding title IV of the Personal Responsibility and Work Opportunity Reconciliation Act of 1996, an alien who is a victim of a severe form of trafficking in persons shall be eligible for benefits and services under any Federal or State program or activity funded or administered by any official or agency described in subparagraph (B) to the same extent as an alien who is admitted to the United States as a refugee under section 207 of the Immigration and Nationality Act.

(B) REQUIREMENT TO EXPAND BENEFITS AND SERVICES.— Subject to subparagraph (C) and, in the case of nonentitlement programs, to the availability of appropriations, the Secretary of Health and Human Services, the Secretary of Labor, the Board of Directors of the Legal Services Corporation, and the heads of other Federal agencies shall expand benefits and services to victims of severe forms of trafficking in persons in the United States, without regard to the immigration status of such victims.

(C) DEFINITION OF VICTIM OF A SEVERE FORM OF TRAFFICKING IN PERSONS.—For the purposes of this paragraph, the term "victim of a severe form of trafficking in persons" means only a person—

x. who has been subjected to an act or practice described in section 103(8) as in effect on the date of the enactment of this Act; and (ii)(I) who has not attained 18 years of age; or

xi. who is the subject of a certification under subparagraph (E).

Source: U.S. Pub. L. No. 106-386. October 28, 2000, Victims of Trafficking and Violence Protection Act. http://www.state.gov/documents/organization/10492.pdf

TABLE 6.9

List of Countries Practicing FGM with Year of Law Passage and Legal Conviction Status

Country	Prevalence	Type of FGC Practiced	Year Law Passed	Convictions
Burkina Faso	71%	Type II		Yes
Central African Republic	43.4%	Type I and II		No
Côte d'Ivoire	44.5%	Type I and II	1998	Unknown
Dijibouti	90%–98%	Type II	1995	Unknown
Egypt	78%–97%	Type I, II, III	2007	Yes
Eritrea	90%–95%	Type I, II, III	2007	No
Ghana	9%–15%	Type I, II, III	1998*	Unknown
Guinea	98.6%	Type I, II, III	Yes	No
Indonesia	Not available	Not available	In Progress**	No
Nigeria	25.1%	Type I, II, III	No***	No
Senegal	5%–20%	Type II, III	1999	No
Somalia	90%–98%	Type I, III	1999	No
Sudan	91%	Type I, II, III	No****	Yes
Tanzania	17.6%	Type I, II, III	1998	Yes
Togo	12%	Type II	1998	Unknown
Uganda	<5%	Type I, II	No*****	Yes

*Presidential Declaration; Constitutional Article.
**Decree to be released banning doctors and paramedics from performing operations.
***Section 34(1) of the 1999 Constitution of the Federal Republic of Nigeria against "torture or inhumane or degrading treatment" is cited against the practice. Bill drafted.
****1925 Penal Code prohibits Type III; Anglo-Sudan prohibitory law in 1946 not in effect.
*****In 1996, Section 8 of the Children Statute was utilized by a court to prevent FGC.
Sources: FGM Education and Networking Project at http://www.fgmnetwork.org/intro/world.php. Department of State. Bureau of Democracy, Human Rights, and Labor. Country Reports for Human Rights Practices for 2011 at http://www.state.gov/j/drl/rls/hrrpt/humanrightsreport/index.htm#wrapper. Stop Violence Against Women at http://www.stopvaw.org/law_and_policy_2.html. UK Border Agency. Country of Origin Information Report. Female Genital Mutilation (FGM) at http://www.unhcr.org/refworld/pdfid/48776e342.pdf.

Female Genital Circumcision in U.S. Criminal Law

Title 18 Crimes and Criminal Procedure refers directly to FGM. The law has been in effect since January 3, 2007 and reads:

Sec. 116. Female Genital Mutilation

(b) whoever knowingly circumcises, excises, or infibulates the whole or any part of the labia majora labia minora or clitoris of another person who has not attained the age of 18 years shall be fined under this title or imprisoned not more than 5 years, or both (From the U.S. Code Online via GPO Access; 18USC116, page 32–33).

The Congressional Findings were as follows:

Section 645 (a) of div. C of Pub. L. 104-208 provided that: "The Congress finds that—

"(1) the practice of female genital mutilation is carried out by members of certain cultural and religious groups within the United States;

"(2) the practice of female genital mutilation often results in the occurrence of physical and psychological health effects that harm the women involved;

"(3) such mutilation infringes upon the guarantees of rights secured by Federal and State law, both statutory and constitutional;

"(4) the unique circumstances surrounding the practice of female genital mutilation place it beyond the ability of any single State or local jurisdiction to control:

"(5) the practice of female genital mutilation can be prohibited without abridging the exercise of any rights guaranteed under the first amendment to the Constitution or under any other law; and

"(6) Congress has the affirmative power under section 8 of article I, the necessary and proper clause, section 5 of the fourteenth Amendment, as well as under the treaty clause, to the Constitution to enact such legislation."

Source: 18 U.S.C. Sec. 116

7

Directory of Organizations and Government Agencies

U.S. Agencies and Organizations

Center for Sex Offender Management (CSOM)
http://www.csom.org

CSOM is a national clearinghouse and technical assistance center that supports state and local jurisdictions in the effective management of sex offenders. CSOM aims to provide those responsible for managing sex offenders with ready access to the most current knowledge by synthesizing and disseminating research and effective practices to the field; and by offering specialized training and technical assistance on a wide variety of issues related to sex offender management.

Department of Justice (DOJ)
950 Pennsylvania Avenue NW
Washington, DC 20530-0001
202-514-2000
http://www.justice.gov

The Department of Justice seeks to enforce the nation's laws and administer justice. Its strategic goals include to: (1) Prevent terrorism and Promote the nation's security; (2) Prevent crime, Enforce Federal Laws, and represent the Rights and Interests of the American People; and (3) Ensure the Fair and Efficient

Administration of Justice. The Department of Justice includes the U.S. Office on Violence Against Women.

Department of State
2201 C Street NW
Washington, DC 20520
202-647-4000
http://www.state.gov

The Department of State's mission is to advance freedom for the benefit of the American people and the international community by helping to build and sustain a more democratic, secure, and prosperous world composed of well-governed states that respond to the needs of their people, reduce widespread poverty, and act responsibly within the international system. A chief concern is human trafficking. The Department of State contains the Office to Monitor and Combat Trafficking in Persons, which conducts bilateral and multilateral diplomacy, provides targeted foreign assistance, and engages with foreign governments on the issue of modern slavery to develop effective counter-trafficking strategies. The *Trafficking in Persons Report* on 175 countries is issued annually and available online.

The State Department's Office of Global Women's Issues promotes political, economic and social empowerment of women. It administers the Secretary of State's International Fund for Women and Girls for the support of nongovernmental organizations working on women's issues. It issues an Innovation Award for the Empowerment of Women and Girls and an International Women of Courage Award.

Federal Bureau of Investigation (FBI)
J. Edgar Hoover Building
935 Pennsylvania Avenue
NW Washington, DC 20535-0001
(202) 324-3000
http://www.fbi.gov

The FBI has jurisdiction over more than 200 categories of federal law. Since 9/11, it has become a global intelligence and security agency. The FBI's priorities are to: (1) protect the United States from terrorist attack; (2) protect the United States against foreign intelligence operations and espionage; (3) protect the United States against cyber-based attacks and high technology crime; (4) combat public corruption at all levels; (5) protect civil rights; (6) combat transnational/national criminal organizations and enterprises; (7) combat white collar crime; (8) combat significant violent crime; (9) support federal, state, local, and international partners; and (10) upgrade technology to successfully perform the FBI's mission. One focus of the civil rights initiative is involuntary servitude/slavery and human trafficking. Its investigative programs include Crimes against Children, including online child pornography, which seeks to identify and rescue the victims, and to identify child sex abusers through online interactions and arrest them. This program also targets child prostitution under the 2003 Innocence Lost Initiative. The FBI has 35,437 employees. As of March 2010, the FBI employed 15,135 women and 8,110 minority members, including 2,580 women as special agents. The Criminal Justice Information Services division (CJIS) includes the National Crime Information Center (NCIC), the National Instant Criminal Background Check System (NICS), Law Enforcement Online (LEO), and the Uniform Crime Reporting (UCR) program

Federal Bureau of Prisons (BOP)
320 First Street NW
Washington, DC 20534
202-307-3198
http://www.bop.gov

The Federal Bureau of Prisons contains a central office (headquarters), six regional offices, 116 institutions, and 22 community corrections offices. The central office and regional offices provide oversight and support for federal prisons and community corrections offices. Community corrections offices oversee residential reentry programs and programs for home confinement. In 2010, BOP was responsible for 210,000 federal offenders and 82% were confined to facilities. The remainder were in private or community-managed facilities and jails. More than 38,000 employees provide services for prisoners serving time in secure facilities.

BOP has recognized that female offenders are more likely than men to be nonviolent and has increased low- and minimum-security bed space. Their Web site indicates that they provide educational and recreational programs similar to those of male inmates. Services for pregnant inmates include the postnatal Mothers and Infants Nurturing Together (MINT) program, a residential-reentry based program in which a mother can participate for three months to bond with her baby before returning to prison to complete her sentence. Federal funds cannot be used for abortions except in cases where the mother's life is endangered or the pregnancy is a result of rape. BOP publishes the *Federal Prisons Journal* and provides links to statistics and research on women prisoners.

Government Accountability Office (GAO)
441 G Street NW
Washington, DC 20548
http://www.gao.gov

The GAO is an independent, nonpartisan agency that works for Congress. Among its general activities, it has primary responsibility for evaluating the various federal administrative and law-enforcement efforts. Congressional committees and subcommittees can request a report on how tax dollars are spent. GAO has carried out studies of how federal prisons are managing an increasing prisoner population and alternatives to incarceration and of the cybertipline for reporting child pornography. GAO provides information for Congress and the federal government on how to be more efficient, ethical, and responsive to the public.

National Center for the Analysis of Violent Crime (NCAVC)
Federal Bureau of Investigation Critical Incidents Response Group
http://www.fbi.gov/about-us/cirg/investigations-and-operations
-support/investigations-operations-support#cirg_ncavc

NCAVC's primary mission is to provide "behavioral-based operational support to federal, state, local, and international law enforcement agencies involved in the investigation of unusual or repetitive violent crimes, communicated threats, terrorism, and other matters of interest to law enforcement and national security agencies." The NCAVC consists of Behavioral Analysis Unit 1 (counterterrorism/threat assessment); Behavioral Analysis Unit 2 (crimes against adults); Behavioral Analysis Unit 3 (crimes against children); and Violent Criminal Apprehension Program

(ViCAP). The special agents and other professionals provide advice and support to law enforcement professionals for a range of cases, including child abduction or mysterious disappearance of children; serial, spree, mass, and other murder; serial rape; threats; and kidnapping.

National Crime Information Center (NCIC)
Federal Bureau of Investigation
http://www.fbi.gov/about-us/cjis/ncic

NCIC is an online clearinghouse of crime that local and state criminal justice agencies can tap into 24 hours a day, 365 days a year. It handles 7.5 million transactions a day. The NCIC database contains 19 files. There are seven property record files: stolen articles, boats, guns, license plates, parts, securities, and vehicles. Seven persons files contain names of those with Supervised Release, the National Sex Offender Registry, foreign fugitives, immigration violators, missing persons, individuals under a protection order, unidentified persons, U.S. Secret Service Protective, gang members (known or appropriately suspected), terrorists, wanted persons, and identify theft files. It contains images to help identify people and property items. The Interstate Identification Index contains criminal history record information and is accessible through this network.

National Criminal Justice Reference Service
P.O. Box 6000
Rockville, MD 20849–6000
http://www.ncjrs.gov/spotlight/wgcjs/Summary.html

This federal information service contains information on women and girls in the criminal justice system including nonfederal sites. This topical resource contains information on facts and figures, legislation, publications, programs, training and technical assistance, and grants and funding.

National GAINS Center
Department of Health and Human Services, Substance Abuse and Mental Health Services Administration (SAMHSA)
http://www.gainscenter.samhsa.gov/html/default.asp

GAINS stands for Gathering information, Assessing what works, Interpreting/integrating the facts, Networking, and Stimulating change. The SAMSHA National GAINS Center distributes information about effective mental health and substance abuse services for people with co-occurring disorders within the criminal justice system. The GAINS office contains the TAPA Center for Jail Diversion and the Center for Evidence-Based Programs in the Justice System. This organization seeks to expand access to community-based services for women and men with co-occurring mental illness and substance abuse disorders. It seeks to promote collaboration between the criminal justice, mental health, and substance abuse treatment systems. Information is provided on co-occurring disorders, a condition more likely to impact women in jail and prison.

National Institute of Corrections (NIC)
320 First Street
Washington, DC 20534
800-995-6423
http://nicic.gov

The National Institute of Corrections is an agency within the Department of Justice, Federal Bureau of Prisons. Its strategic outcomes include: (1) effectively managed prisons, jails, and community correction programs and facilities; (2) enhanced professional and organizational performance in corrections; (3) community, staff, and offender safety; (4) improved correctional practices through the exploration of trends and public policy issues; and (5) enhanced services through improved organizational and staff effectiveness. NIC provides training and technical assistance. NIC, in partnership with the Women's Prison Association, has developed the *National Directory of Programs for Women with Criminal Justice Involvement*, which is available online. A recent publication is *Employment and Female Offenders: An Update of the Empirical Research* by Shawn N. Flower (2010).

National Institute on Drug Abuse (NIDA)
National Institute of Health
6001 Executive Boulevard, Suite 5213
Bethesda, MD 20892-95461
http://www.nida.nih.gov/nidahome.html

NIDA's mission is to advance scientific research on drug abuse and addiction. It provides strategic support across many disciplines and provides rapid and effective access to the results. NIDA seeks to improve prevention and treatment and to shape policy.

Office of Justice Programs, National Institute of Justice (NIJ)
810 Seventh Street NW
Washington, DC 20531
202-307-2942
http://nij.gov

The NIJ is the research, development, and evaluation agency of the Department of Justice. It provides objective evidence-based information on crime and justice issues, particularly at the state and local level. Its research priorities include women and crime, violence against women and child neglect/abuse. It provides current crime statistics and publications on human trafficking and other issues.

Office of Juvenile Justice and Delinquency Prevention
(OJJDP)
810 Seventh Street NW
Washington, DC 20531
202–307–5911
http://www.ojjdp.gov

The Office of Juvenile Justice and Delinquency Prevention is charged by Congress to deal with serious, violent, and chronic offenders and victims of abuse and neglect. It is a component of the Office of Justice Programs in the U.S. Department of Justice. Its mission is to support states, local communities, and tribal jurisdictions in developing and implementing effective programs for juveniles. OJJDP's research and programs are meant to hold offenders accountable, protect public safety, and enable services for youth and their families. It is active in research, training, and program development; develops goals and priorities regarding federal juvenile justice issues; provides funds for states to support local programs; and makes information available through the Juvenile Justice Clearinghouse. Its projects include the Amber Alert for missing children, a National Sex Offender Public Web site, and a reentry initiative. Its information on girls' delinquency is based on Girls Study Group research and available online.

Office of Justice, Bureau of Justice Statistics (BJS)
810 Seventh Street, NW
Washington, DC 20531
http://bjs.ojp.usdoj.gov/index.cfm

The Bureau of Justice Statistics is responsible for crime data collection, analysis and publication of crime information, including
statistics specific to women's criminal offending. Federal, state
and local governments and policy makers use the data to fight
crime and help the process of justice to run smoothly.

Office of Violence against Women (OVW)
950 Pennsylvania Avenue NW
Washington, DC 20530-001
202-513-2000
http://www.ovw.usdoj.gov

The mission of the OVW is as the federal agency responsible for
reduction in violence against women and administration of
justice for domestic violence, dating violence, sexual assault, and
stalking victims. The OVW, a component of the U.S. Department
of Justice, facilitates the operation of the National Advisory Committee on Violence against Women (NAC), which was rechartered
by the attorney general in 2010. This federal advisory committee
gives advice and recommendations on improving response to
violence against women with a particular focus on developing
interventions for children and teens who witness or are victims
of domestic violence, dating violence, and sexual assault.

Substance Abuse and Mental Health Services Administration
(SAMHSA)
1 Choke Cherry Road
Rockville, MD 20857
http://www.samhsa.gov

Many women entering the criminal justice system have used illegal substances. SAMHSA's mission is to "reduce the impact of
substance abuse and mental illness on America's communities."
To this end, it is pursuing eight strategic initiatives including: (1)
to prevent substance abuse and mental illness; (2) to reduce the
harmful and costly impact of trauma by addressing the needs of
individuals at risk for entering the juvenile justice or criminal

justice systems; (3) providing support for recovery and increasing social inclusion of those impacted; (4) broadening health coverage for substance abuse, mental illness, and HIV/AIDS; and (5) providing data on behavioral health care. One of their publications is a *Guide to Substance Abuse Treatment for Women Offenders*.

U.S. Sentencing Commission
Office of Public Affairs
One Columbus Circle, NE
Suite 2-500
Washington, DC 20002-8002
202-502-4500
http://www.ussc.gov

The U.S. Sentencing Commission is an independent agency in the judicial branch of government. It creates federal court sentencing policies, including guidelines for the form and severity of punishment for federal offenders. The Sentencing Commission gives advice and assistance to Congress, the Executive Branch, and law enforcement agencies for development of crime policy. It collects statistics and information on federal crime and sentencing, which is public. Each year, the U.S. Sentencing Commission publishes an annual report on sentencing trends and policy issues, and the *Sourcebook of Sentencing Statistics*, including information on gender and race. It also publishes special reports and makes all materials and data available online.

National Information Organizations

Brookings Institution
1775 Massachusetts Avenue NW
Washington, DC 20036
202-797-6000
http://www.brookings.edu

A nonprofit public policy organization, the Brookings Institution mission is to conduct independent research to develop innovative, practical recommendations that (1) strengthen American democracy; (2) foster the economic and social welfare, security, and opportunity of all Americans; and (3) secure a more open, safe, prosperous, and cooperative international system. In

January 2009, *Foreign Policy* magazine's Think Tank Index ranked Brookings as number 1 think tank and number 1 in the following categories: impact on public policy debates, international and security affairs, international development, international economic policy, health policy, domestic economic policy, and social policy. Topics researched include globalization and human trafficking. Recently, the paper *From Prison to Work: A National Reentry Program* by Bruce Western (2008) advocated the reduction in recidivism and cost-effectiveness that would be fostered by advanced work and educational programs in prison, transitional jobs, substance abuse treatment, housing assistance, and repeal of the revocation of eligibility for federal benefits for felony offenders.

Center for Strategic and International Studies (CSIS)
1800 K Street, NW
Washington, DC 20006
202-887-0200
http://csis.org

A provider of strategic insights and policy solutions, CSIS is a bipartisan nonprofit organization. It assists government, business, and citizens with foreign policy and national security issues. Among its activities is the Human Rights and Security Initiative that includes a Human Trafficking and Peacekeeping Operations component, which indicates how use of trafficked women for sex harms security and undermines missions.

Criminal Justice Mental Health Consensus Project
The Council of State Governments Justice Center
100 Wall Street, 20th Floor
New York, NY 10005
http://consensusproject.org

The Criminal Justice Mental Health Consensus Project, coordinated by the Council of State Governments Justice Center, assists local, state, and federal policy makers and criminal justice and mental health professionals to improve the response to people with mental illnesses who come into contact with the criminal justice system. They provide on-site technical assistance; information about programs, research, and policy developments in the field; and educational presentations. Their site has information on women prisoners with mental illness and violence against women with mental illness.

Criminal Justice Policy Foundation (CJPF)
8730 Georgia Ave,, Suite 400
Silver Spring, MD 20910
http://www.cjpf.org

CJPF is a nonprofit organization working to change the laws associated with the War on Drugs. Its mission is to "educate the public about the impact of drug policy and the problems of policing on the criminal justice system." They provide information and advice to policy makers, criminal justice professionals, and the public through consultation, education programs, conferences, publications, the news media, and the Internet. CJPF assists drug policy reform organizations with advice on legal organization, management, outreach, research, media relations, and coalition building.

International Organization for Migration (IOM)
17, Route de Morillons
CH-1211 geneva 19
Switzerland
Tel: +41.22.717 9111
http://www.iom.int/jahia/Jahia/lang/en/pid/1

The IOM is an intergovernmental migration organization that assists governmental, nongovernmental, and intergovernmental partners. It has 127 member states, including the United States, 17 states with observer status, and over 100 offices in different countries. Seventy-six global and regional international governmental organizations (IGOs) and nongovernmental organizations (NGOs) are members. Over 6,000 staff work on over 2,000 projects with more than $1 billion in expenditures. The IOM has a counter-trafficking effort to protect and empower trafficked women, girls, and boys and promote justice for trafficking victims. The organization facilitates prevention through information campaigns, provides direct assistance to victims of trafficking and maintains a standardized Counter Trafficking (CT) data management tool, the Counter-Trafficking Module (CTM), which is the largest global database on trafficking victims.

National Center on Crime Victims (NCVC)
2000 M Street NW, Suite 480
Washington, DC 20036
http://www.ncvc.org/ncvc/Main.aspx

NCVC is a resource and advocacy organization for crime victims
and those who serve them. It works with grassroots organizations
and criminal justice agencies serving millions of crime victims
over time. Its mission "is to forge a national commitment to help
victims of crime rebuild their lives." NCVC is involved in devis-
ing new federal and state laws and in mobilizing public support
for their passage. It contains a Dating Violence Resource Center
and a Stalking Center, among its subsites.

National Council on Crime and Delinquency (NCCD)
NCDD Center for Girls and Young Women
1022 Park Street, Suite 207
Jacksonville, FL 32204
http://www.justiceforallgirls.org

The NCCD Center for Girls and Young Women is "guided by the
courageous life experiences of girls and young women in the
juvenile and child welfare systems." The center is involved in
activism to "ensure equitable, humane, and gender-appropriate
responses to improve outcomes for girls and young women." A
key issue is promoting gender equity for girls in the juvenile
justice system. It provides a center newsletter and *Getting the Facts
Straight about Girls in the Juvenile Justice System*. The center supports girl-only juvenile justice environments. It also has a section
on girls' voices, parents' voices, and community voices.

National Crime Prevention Council
2001 Jefferson Davis Highway, Suite 901
Arlington, VA 22202
http://www.ncpc.org

The originator of McGruff, the Crime Dog, the National Crime
Prevention Council has as its mission to "be the nation's leader
in helping people keep themselves, their families, and their communities safe from crime." NCPC produces tools that communities can use to learn crime prevention strategies, engage
community members, and coordinate with local agencies,

including publications and teaching materials on a variety of topics; programs that can be implemented in communities and schools; local, regional, and national trainings; and support for a national coalition of crime prevention practitioners. NCPC provides resources that cover the issues of bullying, cyberbullying, girls and drug abuse, fraud and identity theft, gang violence prevention, hate crime, home and neighborhood safety, Internet safety, violent crime, and personal safety and reentry. One Web page it hosts is *Prenatal Care and Drug Abuse Treatment for Pregnant Women.*

National Gang Crime Research Center (NGCRC)
P.O. Box 990
Peotone, IL 60468-0990
http://www.ngcrc.com

The NGCRC is a nonprofit independent agency with the mission statement to: "(1) Promote research on gangs, gang members, and gang problems in cooperation with federal, state, and local government agencies; (2) To disseminate up-to-date valid and reliable information about gangs and gang problems through the official publication of the NGCRC, the Journal of Gang Research, and, (3) To provide training and consulting services about gangs to federal, state and local government agencies." Its publications include *Female Gang Members and the Rights of Children* and *Females and Gangs: Sexual Violence, Prostitution and Exploitation.*

National Human Trafficking Resource Center (NHTRC, the Polaris Project)
P.O. Box 53315
Washington, DC 20009
http://www.polarisproject.org/human-trafficking/overview

The Polaris Project operates the NHTRC Center hotline for reporting tips about trafficking victims. They work with survivors and advocate for stronger federal and state legislation on human trafficking and slavery. This Web site offers a broad range of resources on human trafficking, sex trafficking, labor trafficking, and anti-trafficking initiatives, both national and international. Tools for law enforcement, service providers, and community assessment are available.

National Juvenile Justice Education Data Clearinghouse
Center for Criminology and Public Policy Research
Florida State University
Hecht House, 634 W. Call Street
Tallahassee, FL 32306-1127
http://www.criminologycenter.fsu.edu/p/jje-national-data-clearinghouse.php

The FSU Center for Criminology and Public Policy Research maintains this National Juvenile Justice Education Clearinghouse. To address the lack of research and information available in the field of juvenile justice education, the Juvenile Justice NCLB Collaboration Project collected information and data from states in 2008 and built this resource. It enables individuals to search, view, and print state documents that can provide data that will inform policy recommendations, government and research reports, and program planning. It provides state documents including juvenile justice education annual reports and/or educational outcome reports; juvenile justice annual reports, which include recidivism results; special reports and/or studies conducted in juvenile justice education; and states' educational monitoring standards for juvenile justice education.

National Resource Center on Justice Involved Women (NRCJIW)

NRCJIW provides assistance to professionals working with adult women involved with the justice system. This clearinghouse provides model policies, tools, and research reports with a focus on a gender-sensitive response.

National White Collar Crime Center (NW3C)
10900 Nuckols Road, Suite 325
Glen Allen, VA 23060
http://www.nw3c.org

The mission of NW3C is "to provide training, investigative support and research to agencies and entities involved in the prevention, investigation and prosecution of economic and high tech crime." Their reports include Women and White Collar Crime.

Rand Corporation
http://www.rand.org

The Rand Corporation is a global institution dedicated to research. One of their initiatives has been to track the correctional capacity of the California prison system.

The Sentencing Project
514 10th Street NW, Suite 1000
Washington, DC 20014
http://www.sentencingproject.org

This site provides the online document *Gender and Justice: Women, Drugs and Sentencing Policy.*

Urban Institute
2100 M Street
Washington, DC 20037
202-833-7200
http://www.urban.org

The Urban Institute gathers and analyzes research data on economic and social policy issues, including human trafficking and domestic violence. Recent research includes an analysis of the STOP block grants to deal with violence against women.

Woodrow Wilson International Center for Scholars
Online Contact: sharonmccarter@wilson.org
http://www.wilsoncenter.org

The Woodrow Wilson Center was established by an act of Congress in 1968. It supports linkage of knowledge to the policy process. Scholars are brought to Washington, D.C., to conduct research and interact with policy makers. The center has been very active in international research on human trafficking.

International Organizations

CEDAW Task Force of The Leadership Conference on Human and Civil Rights
CEDAW Education Project

The Leadership Conference
202-263-2852
http://www.cedaw2011.org

This task force is part of a coalition to provide education and outreach about the U.S. ratification of CEDAW. Members engaged in key activities include Citizens for Global Solutions and Amnesty International (advocacy); Communications Consortium Media Center and the Leadership Conference (communications); the Leadership Conference and Citizens for Global Solutions (outreach) and the National Women's Law Center and ACLU (legal issues). One focus is violence against women and girls.

DrugText Foundation
Koninginneweg 189
1075 CP Amsterdam
The Netherlands

This international substance use library contains medical, treatment, and international legal information. A search will locate special materials on gender and drug use and sex, work, and prostitution. It contains a series of reports that are both historical and worldwide on substance use.

International Women's Rights Project (IWRP)
Center for Global Studies, University of Victoria
P.O. 1700 STN CSC
Victoria, BC V8W 2Y2
Canada
1-250-721-8800
http://iwrp.org
infor@iwrp.org

In 1999, IWRP began its efforts to strengthen women's nongovernmental organizations (NGOs) in Canada and globally. It acts to implement world human rights standards through participatory research, evidence-based advocacy, and collaboration. Its projects include a CEDAW impact study. A current project involves assessment of Canadian and International recognition of women's centrality in the implementation of the United Nations' Responsibility to Protect Doctrine (R2P), especially in the social environment of failed states.

United Nations
1775 K Street
Suite 400
Washington, DC 20006
http://www.un.org

The United Nations Universal Declaration of Human Rights was issued by the General Assembly on December 10, 1948. The United Nations contains the Office of the High Commissioner for Human Rights.

United Nations Global Initiative to Stop Human Trafficking (UN.GIFT)
http://ungift.org/knowledgehub/en/about/steering
-committee.html

UN.GIFT combats human trafficking on the basis of UN international agreements. One hundred forty nations have signed the Protocol to Prevent, Suppress and Punish Trafficking in Persons especially Women and Children, which supplements the Palermo Convention against transnational organized crime. Its goals are to make governments, nongovernmental organizations, media and the international community aware of global policies and efforts to combat human trafficking. Assistance is given to countries establishing support structures for trafficking victims. Its publications include *Recommended Principles and Guidelines on Human Rights and Human Trafficking*.

UNWOMEN: United Nations Entity for Gender Inequality and the Empowerment of Women
304 East 45th Street
15th Floor
New York, NY 10017
http://www.unwomen.org

The focus areas of this office within the United Nations include violence against women, peace and security concerns involving the use of rape as a weapon in war, and implementation of the Convention on the Elimination of All Forms of Discrimination against Women (CEDAW). Programs include Say No: UNITE to End Violence against Women. It administers the UN Development Fund for Women and provides technical assistance.

World Health Organization (WHO)
Avenue Appia 20
1211 Geneva 27
Switzerland
Telephone: + 41 22 791 21 11
http://www.who.int

WHO directs and coordinates United Nations health initiatives, including research, setting health standards and norms, presenting evidence-based policy options, giving technical support, and the monitoring and assessment of health trends. They provide an annual *World Health Statistics Report* and have published a World Report on Violence and Health for the 193 member nations. They provide data on women's health including reproductive issues. Female genital mutilation is a major prevention concern.

The World Bank
1818 H Street, NW
Washington, DC 20433
202-473-1000
http://www.worldbank.org

Established in 1944, the World Bank contains two development institutions: the International Bank for Reconstruction and Development (IBRD), and the International Development Association (IDA). The IRBD promotes inclusive and sustainable globalization through reduction of poverty in middle-income and "creditworthy poorer countries." The IDA targets the poorest nations. These institutions are connected to the International Finance Corporation (IFC), the Multilateral Investment Guarantee Agency (MIGA), and the International Center for the Settlement of Investment Disputes (ICSID). Together, these institutions work to provide low-interest loans, interest-free credits, and grants to developing countries for agriculture, natural resources, environmental, education, infrastructure, financial, and private-sector development. Headquartered in Washington, DC, the World Bank has more than 10,000 employees and offices in over 100 countries. Their mission is to fight poverty through encouraging self-help and building capacity including women's projects. An initiative of great import to women is the World Banks effort to prevent HIV/AIDS transmission among prostitutes/sex workers.

International Advocacy Organizations

American Friends Service Committee (AFSC)
1501 Cherry Street
Philadelphia, PA 19102
215-241-7000
http://afsc.org/project/immigrants-rights

The American Friends Service Committee believes in the "worth and inherent dignity of every human being." This organization has a Women's Program. This staff works to recognize and create programs to eliminate sexism and gender inequality, which they consider a root cause of violence. They have recently done research on the solitary confinement of women in detention in Arizona as part of its STOPMAX campaign. It conducts projects in various areas of the country, including a U.S.-Mexico border program that monitors the actions of law enforcement toward migrants.

Amnesty International USA (AIUSA)
5 Penn Plaza
New York, NY 10001
212-807-8400
http://www.amnestyusa.org

Amnesty International is a Nobel Prize–winning grassroots activist organization with branches in over 150 nations and a worldwide membership of over 2 million supporters, activists, and volunteers. Amnesty International USA is one of its branches. They advocate that all peoples should receive the rights in the United Nations' Universal Declaration of Human Rights and other international standards. They seek to have governments stop violations and to change law and practice. It supports research and action on all human rights. In regards to women's rights, AIUSA has been active internationally in efforts to free women political prisoners and nationally in regard to immigrant women in detention and ending violence against girls and women.

Equality Now
P.O. Box 20646
Columbus Circle Station
New York, NY 10023
USA

+1-212-586-1611
info@equalitynow.org
http://www.equalitynow.org/english/index.html

Equality Now is an international organization dedicated to the promotion and protection of girls and women's rights. It works with national human rights organizations and activists to document discrimination and violence against women and mobilize support to end human rights abuses. Its Women's Action Network provides information about women's rights violations to bring attention to these issues and takes action. Issues considered urgent include rape, domestic violence, trafficking of women, and female genital mutilation. They have taken action about the conditions of women's imprisonment in Colombia.

Human Rights Watch
350 Fifth Avenue, 34th floor
New York, NY 10118-3299
212-290-4700
http://www.hrw.org

Human Rights Watch is an independent nongovernmental organization (NGO) that seeks to defend and protect human rights. They investigate ongoing situations in which human rights may be violated and publicize their findings. Their work is international in scope and includes investigations and targeted advocacy for a wide range of human rights, including those of women. Their international work in protecting the rights of women migrants and immigrants includes research on the exploitation of unauthorized immigrants in the workplace. Their research has covered women in U.S. prisons, honor killings and violence against women, and segregation of women prisoners with HIV/AIDS. Human Rights Watch has been critical of the failure to prevent sexual assault of women in prison and is actively lobbying for reform. They publish numerous reports on human rights in many nations, including the United States.

Witness
80 Hansen Place, Fifth Floor
New York, New York 11217
718-783-2000
http://www.witness.org

Witness records human rights violations on video to change stories of abuse into tools for justice. They envision a just and equitable world in which all individuals' and communities' human rights are upheld. Their core partner program works with 12–15 human rights organizations for a period of 1–3 years to train and support it to use video as a tool for human rights campaigns with high visibility and impact. These videos have been used as evidence in domestic and international courts, in reports on human rights abuses and the media.

National Advocacy Organizations

American Civil Liberties Union (ACLU)
125 Broad Street
18th Floor
New York, NY 10004
http://www.aclu.org

The ACLU monitors the increase in imprisonment of women and detention of girls due to the War on Drugs and harsh sentencing policies for nonviolent offenders. Imprisoned women struggle with substance abuse, mental illness, and the impact of past histories of extensive physical or sexual abuse in an environment poorly equipped to provide services. They believe that substance abuse should be treated as a public health issue rather than a crime. The ACLU has taken steps to document abusive practices such as strip searches and solitary confinement and the lack of quality women's health care. In 2008, a class-action suit was filed against the Brownwood State School Youth Prison in central Texas, challenging strip searches, solitary confinement, and lack of female physical and mental health care. They are opposed to government and private post-conviction penalties for women and girls that hamper their reentry in obtaining education and employment and deny access to public housing. In 2009, the ACLU filed a lawsuit against the Housing Authority of the City of Annapolis, challenging a policy denying convicted offenders the right to be on or near public housing, even if attempting to visit their families. In addition, the assist in employment discrimination cases against convicted individuals.

The ACLU is active in protecting women and girls who are victims of domestic violence, dating violence, and sexual assault from discrimination in education, employment, and housing.

Justice Policy Institute
1012 14th St. NW, Suite 400
Washington, DC 20005
202-558-7974
http://www.justicepolicy.org/index.html

Justice Policy Institute is a nonprofit organization oriented toward developing new policies for justice reform. They provide research and analysis of effective programs, training, and technical assistance support. Their mission is to limit the use of imprisonment and the criminal justice system and to develop policies for improving the lives of individuals and communities. They have issued reports on overcrowding of women in Alabama's prisons.

National Association of Women Lawyers (NAWL)
American Bar Center MS 15.2
321 North Clark Street
Chicago, IL 60654
312-988-6186

NAWL is a nonprofit legal professional organization that supports women's networking and provides resources, research, and programming for women's rights, including the concerns of women working in the law. It seeks to increase diversity for women in all activities and at all levels of the legal profession.

National Organization for Women (NOW)
1100 H Street NW, 3rd Floor
Washington, DC 20005
202 628-8669
http://www.now.org

NOW is the largest feminist nonprofit organization in the United States, with 500,000 contributors and 550 chapters in all states and Washington, D.C. It combats discrimination and harassment in the justice system, workplace, and schools. A specific goal is ending violence against women. It has taken action against sexual assault on campus and in the military, provides an anti-shackling kit to end chaining women to beds as they give birth and lobbies to expand funding for shelters.

Southern Poverty Law Center (SPLC)
400 Washington Avenue
Montgomery, AL 36104
http://www.splcenter.org

Since 1971, the nonprofit SPLC has taken legal action against hate groups and discrimination. The SPLC legal department has taken civil suits against individuals suspected of hate crimes and hate groups, including to the Supreme Court. Its SPLC Intelligence project monitors the activities of hate groups and extremists, including their actions against immigrant girls and women, and publishes information on its research available at its Web site. Recently, SPLC has taken up the causes of school and teacher dropout and extensive use of detention in such states as Florida. It offers the Teaching Tolerance program for K–12 teachers to generate respect and offers antibias resources. Recently, its Immigrant Justice project has taken and began an antidiscrimination and sexual harassment educational project for immigrant women to notify them of their rights.

Prison Advocacy Organizations

Prison Activist Resource Center (PARC)
P.O. Box 70447
Oakland, CA 94612
510-893-4648
http://www.prisonactivist.org

PARC is a radical nonprofit organization that seeks to abolish prisons and challenges discrimination against all groups particularly within the prison industrial complex. PARC believes that communities can be safe without police or prisons. PARC works with prisoners, their families, and friends. They work with and provide materials for teachers and activists.

Prison Policy Initiative
P.O. Box 127

Northampton, MA 01061
http://www.prisonpolicy.org

Prison Policy Initiative is a nonpartisan, nonprofit organization that researches the impact of mass incarceration. It is famous for documenting the manner in which the U.S. census has counted imprisoned individuals where they are confined rather than their site of residence when arrested. This practice is considered to have resulted in gerrymandering the size of legislative districts, and the U.S. Court of Appeals has suggested that the way New York State uses census data violates the Voting Rights Act. It provides links to research on women in the criminal justice system.

Prison Watch for Imprisoned Women (Blog)
http://imprisonedwomenprisonwatch.blogspot.com/2010/11/resisting-gender-violence-and-prison.html

This blog provides information for women prisoners and postings by them to help them and their families achieve recognition of their rights. Its goal is a world in which people are not imprisoned as punishment. The blog provides the names of many women prisoners and discusses issues relating to women in the criminal justice system from a partisan viewpoint.

Women and Prison: A Site for Resistance
Beyondmedia Education
4001 N. Ravenswood, #204 B
Chicago, IL 60613
773-857-7300
http://www.womenandprison.org

Women and Prison: A Site for Resistance documents women's stories about their experiences in the criminal justice system. This Web site tries to correct for the invisibility of women's viewpoint in the debate about the prison industrial complex, especially in light of women's increasing incarceration. They use women's ideas and perspective to challenge the design of the prison system. The site provides links to organizations, reports, and other information on women in prison.

Women's Prison Association
Institute on Women and Criminal Justice

110 Second Avenue
New York, NY 10003
646-292-7740
http://www.wpaonline.org/index.html

WPA provides services and advocates for women with criminal justice histories in order that they realize new self and family possibilities. Women are assisted in finding work, housing, and health care to rebuild their families. Its Institute on Women and criminal justice does research for policy development and advocacy. WPA considers that women's imprisonment is growing at an "alarming" rate and that their incarceration has a disproportionately negative effect on children and communities. The site provides links to reports and other resources.

Domestic Violence Advocacy Organizations

American Coalition for Fathers and Children (ACFC)
1718 M. Street NW, #187
Washington, DC 20036
800-978-3237

The members of ACFC consider that: "Children Need Both Parents." They are opposed to the current family law and policy and promote equal rights for "ALL parties affected by issues of the modern family." They support equally shared parenting by biological parents or joint custody. They are against certain impacts of the domestic violence shelter system and related custody arrangements that negatively impact fathers. Certain sections of the site are for members only.

Break the Cycle
Los Angeles Office
5777 W. Century Boulevard, Suite 1150
Los Angeles, CA 90045
310-286-3383

Break the Cycle is a national nonprofit organization concerned with teen dating violence. It promotes safe and healthy relationships and seeks to engage and educate youth to realize communities free from domestic violence. Their programs include in school prevention education, youth leader activism, training and support help, and legal services and public information programs. Their Web site provides state law report cards.

National Coalition against Domestic Violence (NCADV)
One Broadway, Suite B210
Denver, CO 80203
303-839-1852
http://www.ncadv.org

NCADV's mission is to transform society by linking individuals and communities to create collective power to end violence. Their efforts are directed toward local, state, regional, and national coalition building to establish community-based, nonviolent alternatives including safe homes and shelters for battered women and children. They engage in provision of public education, technical assistance, policy development, and creation of related legislation. They target diverse underrepresented groups in both urban and rural areas and try to change social conditions that foster violence against women and children. They support relationship equality and seek to help women take control of their life situations.

National Network to End Domestic Violence (NNEDV)
2001 S Street NW, Suite 400
Washington, DC 20009
202-543-5566
http://nnedv.org

Seeking to end domestic violence, NNEDV is an advocacy organization comprised of state domestic violence organizations, coalitions, and individuals that seek to address the complex causes of domestic violence and empower survivors. It provides training, technical assistance, innovative programming, and funding. Since 2006, NNEDV's *Domestic Violence Counts: National Census of Domestic Violence Services* has provided an unduplicated and noninvasive count of adults and children asking for services at U.S. domestic violence shelters during a single 24-hour survey period. The confidentiality and safety of victims are protected.

Prostitution/Sex Work Advocacy Organizations

Children of the Night
14530 Sylvan Street
Van Nuys, California 91411
Hotline: 800-551-1300
Main: 818-908-4474
http://www.childrenofthenight.org

Children of the Night is the only nonprofit organization that focuses solely on child prostitutes. It offers a 24-hour hotline seven days a week. Staff are knowledgeable about street life and bring in law enforcement if a child's life is endangered. In Van Nuys, California, it operates a 24-bed home for child prostitutes. Children from other states are also counseled and directed to shelters.

COYOTE (Call Off Your Tired Old Ethics)
P. O. Box 210256
San Francisco, CA 94121
415-751-1659
http://coyotela.org

This sex worker organization advocates the repeal of laws criminalizing prostitution, pandering, and pimping. COYOTE seeks to end the stigmatization of prostitution, which it refers to as sex work. Additional sex work categories it advocates for include phone sex, stripping, and adult film performers. COYOTE provides sex worker counseling and assistance in leaving this line of work. It provides advice and sensitivity training for law enforcement and social services and offers education about safe sex, HIV/AIDS, and sexually transmitted diseases. COYOTE members have testified at government hearings, acted as expert trial witnesses, and assisted police investigating crimes against sex workers. COYOTE has offices in both Los Angeles and San Francisco. The Los Angeles office has a detailed Web site.

Desiree Alliance
P.O. Box 470597

Brookline Village, MA 02447
866-525-7967
http://www.desireealliance.org

This nonprofit coalition unites sex workers, health professionals, social scientists, and their networks to provide a better understanding of the sex industry and to advocate for sex workers' human rights. Their research on sex work includes best practice policies, an End Demand fact sheet connected to opposition of this provision of the 2005 reauthorization of the Trafficking Victims Protection Act, and model decriminalization legislation passed in Australia. This site contains some adult content relevant for sex workers.

North American Task Force on Prostitution (NTFP)
2785 Broadway, 4L
New York, NY 10025-2834
http://www.bayswan.org/NTFP.html

NTFP is a nonprofit umbrella organization for prostitutes and other sex workers and prostitute's rights organizations. It has five goals. First is the repeal of prostitution laws. Second is to establish rights of prostitutes and other sex workers to bargain with employers who manage their work with third parties and working condition betterment. Third is to inform the public about prostitution and sex work issues. Fourth is development of HIV/AIDS/STD and other support services and violence prevention projects for sex workers. Fifth is to end the stigmatization of sex work. It distributes position papers, manuals for program development, biographies, and other publications. By 2012, it is expected to become an online information resource with a newsgroup. One of its activities is to encourage sex workers to attain academic degrees for the purpose of research based on their own experiences.

Our Voices Matter
P.O. Box 674
Northampton, MA 01061
http://voicesmatter.org/home.html

Our Voices Matter is a nonprofit grassroots organization that offers testimonials by women who have been hurt by prostitution, trafficking, and pornography. The stories of survivors are meant to remove blame from victims and to examine the system and individuals that perpetrate harm. OVM aims to shatter silence, invisibility, marginalization, and shame; provide a safe space for survivors to share their stories in ways that may lead to healing and help others; raise awareness on the hidden realities and injuries of prostitution, pornography, and trafficking; challenge dominant ideology and beliefs that prostitution is a "victimless crime" and that pornography is mere "fantasy" and harmless fun; interrupt people's compliance and defense of these systems of harm; and incite community awareness, response, and action.

Prostitution ProCon.org
233 Wilshire Blvd., Suite 200
Santa Monica, CA 90401
310-451-9596
http://prostitution.procon.org

ProCon.org is an Internet issues site with a mission of developing critical thinking skills and informing the public about many controversial issues in a nonpartisan pro-con format. Among the 41 issues it researches is prostitution. Its core question is "Should prostitution be legal?" It provides a definition of terms, key concepts, and demographics, and it issues questions related to brothels, crime, decriminalization versus legalization, demeaning of women, economics, health, marriage, morality, personal freedom and liberty, pornography, red light districts, and opposing viewpoints of key players. Its projects include a compilation of 100 countries and their prostitution policies; U.S federal and state prostitution laws and punishments; prostitution-related arrest data, opinion polls, and surveys; and "The Johns Chart," the percentage of men who have paid for sex at least once.

Prostitution Research and Education (PRE)
http://www.prostitutionresearch.com
A nonprofit organization, PRE researches prostitution, pornography, and trafficking. It provides education and other services for survivors, researchers, policy makers, and the public. PRI strives to abolish and advocate for alternatives to prostitution and trafficking, including provision of health and emotional care for prostitutes. Their Internet site provides extensive information on prostitution research, prostitution laws, trafficking, escaping

prostitution, men who purchase sex, and the writings of survivors.

Sage Project, Inc.
1275 Mission Street
San Francisco, CA 94103
415-905-5050
http://www.sagesf.org

The Standing against Global Exploitation Project (SAGE Project) is a nonprofit organization that seeks to end the commercial sexual exploitation of children and adults. SAGE raises awareness about child sexual abuse including commercial exploitation and offers outreach and services for child survivors of sexual exploitation. This project is a collaboration between social services, law enforcement, public health, and private agencies oriented toward restorative justice. They offer services to several hundred women and girls per week with a survivor based perspective. A key issue for the Sage Project is language. They believe that child prostitutes should be viewed as sexual abuse victims who are commercially exploited and that those who exploit them should be criminalized, not the victims.

Sex Workers' Outreach Project-USA (SWOP)
309 Cedar Street, #200
Santa Cruz, CA 95060
877-776-2004
http://www.swopusa.org

SWOP is a social justice network with nationwide activity. It advocates for the rights of sex workers and their communities with a focus on ending stigmatization and violence through education and action. It seeks to address violence against sex workers; violence considered to be related to their criminal status. SWOP-USA seeks to educate the public about institutional practices that harm sex workers and render them vulnerable to violent assault. SWOP has taken a position against the Trafficking Victims Protection Act (TVPA) of 2000 and its 2005 reauthorization with provisions to end demand for increased criminal punishment because it believes it increased stigma for sex workers and associated harm. SWOP has chapters in Arizona, Michigan, Chicago, Minnesota, North Carolina, Las Vegas,

New York, Los Angeles (UCLA), and the Northwest (states not specified).

Human/Sex Trafficking Advocacy Organizations

American Anti-Slavery Group
198 Tremont Street, #421
Boston, MA 02116
http://www.iabolish.org

American Anti-Slavery Group is a nonprofit organization "dedicated to eradicating modern-day human bondage and to promoting a non-politicized, bias-free human rights community." This group works with Christian Solidarity International to free slaves in the Sudan. Their focus is primarily upon Sudan and Mauritania. Their Web site provides news and commentary.

Anti-Slavery International
Thomas Clarkson House
The Stableyard
Broomgrove Road
London SW 9TL
+44 (0)20 7738 4110
http://www.antislavery.org/english/default.aspx

Founded in 1787, Anti-Slavery International is the world's oldest international human rights organization. This nonprofit works locally, nationally, and internationally to end all forms of slavery. Through research, lobbying, and the raising of awareness, they seek to end human trafficking, forced labor, child labor, and child domestic work. They stress the connection between what people buy and the use of forced labor in its production. The organization has conducted many successful campaigns and works with the new Special Rapporteur on Slavery in the United Nations, the first new UN special mechanism on slavery in 30 years. They have lobbied to pass a new anti-trafficking law in the European Union and have organized the Home Alone campaign to protect domestic workers.

Coalition against Trafficking in Women (CATW)
P.O. Box 7427
Jaf Station
New York, NY 10116
http://www.catwinternational.org

Founded in 1988, CATW is a nongovernmental organization that promotes human rights by working internationally to prevent sexual exploitation of women and girls. It was the first international organization to focus on human trafficking, particularly sex trafficking. In 1989, it received Category II Consultative status with the United Nations Economic and Social Council. CATW considers women and girls have a "right to sexual integrity and autonomy."

Free the Slaves
1320 19th Street NW
Suite 600
Washington, DC 20036
202-775-7480
http://www.freetheslaves.net

Free the Slaves is an international nongovernmental organization with a mission of ending slavery worldwide. They work with grassroots organizations in countries with endemic slavery. They record the stories of slaves and share them with people with power in order to promote working for their freedom. They ask business to remove slave labor from their product chains and advise consumers on products that involved slave labor in order to boycott them. Free the Slaves is very involved with government to develop antislavery laws and engages in research on successful antislavery actions. Their publications include *Hidden Slaves: Forced Labor in the United States* which is coauthored with UC-Berkeley.

Polaris Project
P.O. Box 53315
Washington, DC 20009
Hotline: 888-373-7888
Main: 202-745-1001
http://www.polarisproject.org

This nonprofit organization focuses on combating all forms of human trafficking and assists both U.S. citizens and foreign national victims. They have worked with slavery survivors to structure policy and advocate improving federal and state laws regarding slavery. They operate the National Human Trafficking Resource Center hotline. In addition, they offer client services, training, and technical assistance, and run campaigns against criminal trafficking networks.

The Protection Project
The Paul H. Nitze School of Advanced International Studies
The Johns Hopkins University
1717 Massachusetts Avenue, NW
Washington, DC 20036
202-663-5896
http://www.protectionproject.org

This human rights institute is contained within the Foreign Policy Institute at the Johns Hopkins University School of Advanced International Studies. It was founded to deal with trafficking in humans as a legal issue and human rights violation. It focuses on the promotion of human rights values and the protection of human security, especially the rights of women and children. It seeks to foster nongovernmental organization (NGO) development through coalition and capacity building, bringing citizens into the political and legal process, advancing education about human rights, and ending the trafficking in persons. The Protection Project contributed to the drafting of the Trafficking Victims Protection Act of 2000, assists in drafting model anti-trafficking legislation, identifies trafficking victims through field research and data collection, provides training and services to professionals working with victims of human trafficking, and maintains an online database on human trafficking.

Sex Offenders and Missing/Exploited Children Advocacy

Association for the Treatment of Sexual Abusers (ATSA)
4900 S.W. Griffith Drive, Suite 274
Beaverton, OR 97005
503-643-1023
http://atsa.com

ATSA is a nonprofit association of clinicians and researchers who seek to develop treatment for sexual abusers. They believe sexual abuse is a public health problem and seek to research effective treatments, some of which are controversial. Their policy papers include *Anti-Androgen Therapy and Surgical Castration, Sexual Offender Residence Restrictions* and *Civil Commitment of Sexually Violent Offenders*. They do not consider residence restriction of sex offenders to be effective for deterrence of reoffending.

National Office of Missing and Exploited Children
Charles B. Wang International Children's Building
699 Prince Street
Alexandria, VA 22314-3175
Hotline: 800-THE-LOST (800-843-5678)
Main: 703-224-2150
http://www.ncmec.org/missingkids/servlet/
PublicHomeServlet?LanguageCountry=en_US&

The National Center for Missing and Exploited Children (NCMEC) is a nonprofit organization with the mission to serve as the nation's resource on the issues of missing and sexually exploited children. It provides resources for law enforcement, parents, children including child victims, law enforcement, and other professionals. It offers information and data on the Amber Alert child abduction program.

Stop Child Predators
1419 37th Street NW, #108
Washington, DC 20007
202-248-7052
http://www.stopchildpredators.org

Stop Child Predators is a nonprofit organization of policy experts and community leaders who share the goal of protecting children and holding their victimizers accountable. Stop Child Predators helps the parents of child victims to tell their stories, assists law enforcement in program development, and helps major players to develop more effective policies. It provides education, out-reach, and advocacy. It seeks penalty enhancements for federal and some state laws which may not imprison sex offenders who abuse and assault or commercially exploit children and are found guilty. Stop Child Predators is working on improving the nationwide sex offender registry in order that all offenders be constantly registered and not lost. In addition, they believe that victims and their families should speak during the sentencing of sex offenders and notified if and when these individuals are released into the community.

Nonprofit Organizations

Brennan Center for Justice
NYC School of Law
161 Sixth Avenue, 12th Floor
New York, NY 10013
http://www.brennancenter.org

The Brennan Center for Justice focuses on achieving justice in a democracy and covers a broad range of issues. The center is part think tank and part law firm. In recent years, they have examined the trend for increasing imprisonment of women and the progress of women lawyers.

Center for Gender and Justice (CGJ)
7946 Ivanhoe Avenue, Suite 201B
La Jolla, CA 92037
http://www.centerforgenderandjustice.org

The Center for Gender and Justice (CGJ) "seeks to develop gender-responsive policies and practices for women and girls who are under criminal justice supervision." It focuses on research and the implementation of policies and programs that will encourage positive outcomes for women, an under-served population. They stress being gender responsive, which they define as "creating an environment through site selection, staff selection, program development, content, and material that reflects an understanding of the realities of the lives of women and girls and that addresses and responds to their strengths and challenges." Their site provides a gender-responsive program assessment tool, research papers, and on-line articles.

Chicago Legal Advocacy for Incarcerated Mothers (CLAIM)
70 East Lake Street, Suite 1120

Chicago, IL 60601
http://www.claim-il.org

CLAIM provides legal and educational services to maintain the bond between imprisoned mothers and their children. CLAIM advocates for policies and programs that benefit families of imprisoned mothers and reduce incarceration of women and girls. CLAIM reports on Illinois legislation to end shackling of pregnant women while giving birth.

Division on Women and Crime (DWC)
American Society of Criminology (ASC)
http://ascdwc.com

The DWC is a section of the American Society of Criminology, which is focused on theory development and research on women and crime. They strive to improve college and high school pedagogy and curriculum. Their journal, *Feminist Criminology*, highlights some of their work.

Families against Mandatory Minimums (FAMM)
1612 K Street NW, Suite 700
Washington, DC 20006
http://famm.org

Families against Mandatory Minimums is a national organization promoting "fair and proportionate sentencing laws." They advocate for state and federal sentencing reform by repeal of mandatory minimum sentences and mobilize individuals and families whose lives are adversely affected by unjust sentences. Their site contains information on women's success stories after release.

Family Justice
Carnegie Mellon University
http://www.cmu.edu/homepage/innovation/2007/fall/familyjustice.org.shtml

Family Justice is a new initiative developed at a support center called *La Bodega de la familia* in New York City. The Bodega model is a strengths-based approach developed at this site, which partners families with government agencies and community organizations. This nonprofit uses family mapping tools to strength individual and community social networks. Instead of focusing solely on substance abuse and criminal behavior, it maps family strengths, productive behaviors, and coping mechanisms.

Justice Policy Institute (JPI)
1012 14th Street NW, Suite 400
Washington, DC 20005
http://www.justicepolicy.org/index.html

Justice Policy Institute is a national nonprofit organization concerned with justice reform. Its research and analyses identify effective programs and policies, and they provide training and technical assistance. Their mission is to "reduce the use of incarceration and the justice system and promote policies that improve the well-being of all people and communities." They "envision a society with safe, equitable and healthy communities, just and effective solutions to social problems, and alternatives to incarceration that promote positive life outcomes." Their Web site contains information on efforts to reduce women's jail and prison populations.

National Resource Center on Children and Families of the Incarcerated (NRCCFI)
Family and Corrections Network
93 Old York Road, Suite 1 #510
Jenkintown, PA 19046
http://fcnetwork.org

The mission of NRCCFI is to raise awareness about the needs and concerns of the children of the incarcerated and their families by providing information based on academic research and the experiences of the families and practitioners in the field. This is "to promote the creation of effective and relevant policies and practices in public and private systems." They "work to connect program providers, policy makers, researchers, educators, correctional personnel and the public with the families of the incarcerated for dialogue, advocacy, action and planning and do this by: (1) convening local, regional and national meetings; (2) distributing information through our publications, our Web site, and our speakers' bureau; (3) providing training and technical assistance; and (4) advocating for family strengthening policies that uphold the values and needs of children of the incarcerated and their families."

Vera Institute for Justice
1330 Connecticut Avenue NW, Suite B
Washington, DC 20036
http://www.vera.org

The Vera Institute of Justice conducts research, develops demonstration projects, and provides technical assistance to help government and civil society "improve the systems people rely on for justice and safety." "Vera is an independent, nonpartisan, nonprofit center for justice policy and practice." Vera has programs or centers covering: (1) substance use and mental health; (2) prosecution and racial justice; (3) family justice; (4) cost-benefit analysis of the criminal justice system; (5) youth justice; (6) victimization and safety; and (7) sentencing and corrections. A Vera publication is *Domestic Violence and Prisoner Reentry: Experiences of African American Women and Men*.

Women in Prison and Sentencing Law Reform

American Civil Liberties Union (ACLU) Women in Prison Project
http://www.aclu.org/prisoners-rights/women-prison

The ACLU Women in Prison Project provides news on legal and government actions, blogs, legal documents, and multimedia resources. They have taken lawsuits regarding the condition of women's prisons and have an initiative to prevent the shackling of women while giving birth. The ACLU supports breaking the link between poverty and prison and improving reentry alternatives for women prisoners.

Women's Prison Association
110 Second Avenue
New York, NY 10003
http://www.wpaonline.org/index.html

This service and advocacy organization works to help "women with a criminal justice history to find a new future for themselves and their families." They support women's efforts to find work, housing, and health care while bringing their family together again and complying with the criminal justice system. They help approximately 2,500 women per year. They provide the *Focus on Women* series of fact sheets and the publication *Women, Reentry and Everyday Life: Time to Work?* Their online publications service is highly recommended.

Human Rights

Human Rights Watch: Women's Rights News
http://www.hrw.org/en/by-issue/news-filter/681

The Women's Rights Division of Human Rights Watch provides a biannual newsletter that provides an overview of their work on women's rights in the United States and internationally as well as information on advocacy and opportunities to volunteer. Issues include gendered criminalization such as depriving women of the right to drive in Saudi Arabia; domestic violence, rape, and other forms of victimization of women; and issues regarding treatment of immigrant women in detention or women prisoners. This site also provides links to reports, commentaries, and multimedia.

Human Rights Today
http://humanrights.einnews.com/category/women-s-rights
This site offers a free trial.

This information service for global professionals has information on domestic violence, femicide, honor killing, and trafficking of women among other women's rights issues.

Global Issues: Women's Rights
http://www.globalissues.org/article/166/womens-rights

This women's rights Web page offers information on the progress or lack thereof of women's rights treaties and law. The legislation and enforcement of rights for women is critical for global well-being. Women's rights are an issue in both Islamic and Western countries. In addition, there is a special news section entitled "Women, Militarism and Violence."

United Nations Women's Watch
http://www.un.org/womenwatch

Women Watch is an Internet initiative of the United Nations' Inter-agency Network on Women and Gender Equality

(IANWGE) which is led by UNWomen. It provides news, information, and resources on the empowerment of women and gender equality from throughout the United Nations system, which includes the UN Secretariat, regional commissions, special agencies, funds, programs, and academic and research institutions.

Domestic Violence

MINCAVA

http://www.mincava.umn.edu. Minnesota Center Against Violence and Abuse (MINCAVA) began as a legislative effort to provide resources that would improve the quality of programs in higher education addressing issues of violence. The website is an electronic clearing house which provides current, relevant, and effective resources. MINCAVA addresses the issues of child abuse, domestic violence, sexual violence, stalking, trafficking, workplace violence, youth violence, gendered violence, systemic violence, peacemaking, and more.

National Resource Center on Domestic Violence
3605 Vartan Way, Suite 101
Harrisburg, PA 17112
http://www.nrcdv.org

The NRCDV mission is "to improve societal and community responses to domestic violence and, ultimately, prevent its occurrence." The U.S. Department of Health and Human Services funds the Pennsylvania Coalition against Domestic Violence (PCADV); and the Centers for Disease Control, with other sources, funds VaW-net, an online resource center. Free resources include comprehensive and individualized training and technical assistance as well as specialized materials and projects to enhance intervention and prevention strategies. The NRCDV provides information on emergent issues in policy and practice and publishes innovative and model intervention and prevention practices, protocols, and policies.

National Sexual Violence Resource Center (NSVRC)
123 North Enola Drive
Enola, PA 17025
http://www.nsvrc.org

NSVRC distributes information and resources on all aspects of sexual violence. Recent resources include a Rape Prevention and Education Program (RPE) Factsheet, a Child Sexual Abuse

Prevention Information Packet, the publication *Strengthening Military-Civilian Community Partnerships to Respond to Sexual Assault*, and the SART Toolkit: Resources for Sexual Assault Response Teams. NSVRC provides leadership, consultation, and technical assistance while developing sexual violence intervention and prevention strategies. It tackles the causes and impact of sexual violence and works to prevent it.

The Battered Women's Justice Project (BWJP)
1801 Nicolette Ave South, Suite 102
Minneapolis, MN 55403
http://www.bwjp.org/bwjp_home.aspx

This organization contains a Criminal and Civil Justice Office and a Defense Office for women subject to domestic abuse. Each office provides training, technical assistance, and other resources on domestic violence concerning women's access and representation in civil court, the criminal justice system's response and self-defense issues for battered women. This organization does not accept individual cases. The Criminal and Civil Justice Office provides analysis of effective policing, prosecution, sentencing, and tracking of domestic violence offenders. It also covers protection orders, confidentiality issues, divorce and custody issues, and violence after separation.

Health Resource Center on Domestic Violence
Futures without Violence
100 Montgomery Street, The Presidio
San Francisco, CA 94129

This program operated by Futures without Violence (formerly the Family Violence Prevention Fund) provides technical assistance and tools and materials related to health and educational and clinical tools for patients and providers. They offer a free online journal, *Family Violence Prevention and Health Practice*. Online webinars with expert presenters on current topics can be accessed.

National Center On Protection Orders and Full Faith and Credit (NCPOFFC)
1901 North Fort Myer Drive, Suite 1011
Arlington, VA 22209
http://www.bwjp.org/ncffc_home.aspx

NCPOFFC is a suborganization of the Battered Women's Justice Project. Its mission is to facilitate the implementation of the Full Faith and Credit clause of the Violence against Women Act in all territories, tribes, and states through increasing public knowledge of its statutory requirements and giving problem-solving technical assistance or support to jurisdictions and individuals. Assistance and training are provided regarding: (1) full faith and credit; (2) federal prohibition of firearm ownership in cases of domestic violence; (3) federal domestic violence and stalking crimes; and inter-jurisdictional child custody cases impacted by domestic violence.

National Clearinghouse for the Defense of Battered Women
125 South 9th Street, Suite 302
Philadelphia, PA 19107
http://www.ncdbw.org

This nonprofit is a resource and advocacy center for battered women facing criminal charges related to their battering. The organization seeks to provide information for arrested, convicted, and/or incarcerated battered women to reduce further victimization. It assists women who were defending themselves against physical or sexual assault and were charged with assault or homicide. They provide assistance for women coerced into crime by abusive partners, accused of failing to protect their children from abusers' violence, or charged with "parental kidnapping" when seeking to protect themselves and children from the abuser. Custom technical assistance is provided for women and their defense teams. They do not legally represent the women but provide assistance in conducting a defense.

National Immigrant Family Violence Institute (NIFVI)
NIFVI—International Institute of Saint Louis
3654 South Grand Boulevard
St. Louis, MO 63118
http://www.nifvi.org/index.html

Dedicated to elimination of domestic violence in immigrant communities, the National Immigrant Family Violence Institute provides technical assistance, training seminars, and culturally appropriate resource materials relevant to address immigrant specific issues. Their work involves linguistic and cultural minorities, and their vision is for "a society in which cultural norms support non-violent relationships." NIFVI comprises six immigrant serving agencies across the country, which are part of the U.S. Committee for Refugees and Immigrants. NIFVI seeks to enhance intervention and prevention strategies for immigrant domestic violence and serves domestic violence agencies, immigrant serving agencies, law enforcement, and legal practitioners.

National Training and Technical Assistance Center on Domestic Violence, Trauma and Mental Health (NTTAC)
29 E. Madison, Suite 1750
Chicago, IL 60602
http://www.dvmhpi.org

NTTAC is a new national center that will provide resources, tools, and consensus building to fill a gap in services for survivors with unmet mental health and advocacy needs and develop culturally appropriate responses to trauma-related issues faced by domestic violence survivors and their children. It seeks to develop strategies to deal with social and psychological conditions that promote intergenerational violence and abuse. It provides online resources relating to trauma and mental health related to domestic violence.

National Stalking Resource Center
National Center for Victims of Crime
2000 M Street NW, Suite 480
Washington, DC 20036
http://www.ncvc.org/src/Main.aspx

The Stalking Resource Center is a part of the National Center for Victims of Crime. Its mission is to "enhance the ability of professionals, organizations and systems to respond to stalking." It "envisions a future in which the criminal justice system and its many allied community partners will have the best tools to effectively collaborate and respond to stalking, improve victim safety and well-being, and hold offenders accountable." The Web site provides a list of state and federal legislation on stalking and protection order statutes, statistical overviews, multidisciplinary curricula , model protocols, forms and procedures, and other information. Services provided include training, technical assistance, an information clearinghouse, and a Web site. It provides local, state, and national training on: (1) stalking,

prevalence, lethality, and impact; (2) stalking and intimate partner violence; (3) stalking and sexual assault; (4) using technology to stalk; (5) stalking on campus; (6) teens and stalking; (7)
analyzing stalking laws; (8) investigating stalking; (9) prosecuting stalking; (10) threat assessment; (11) safety planning; (12)
working with stalking victims; and (13) developing a coordinated community response to stalking. Technical assistance
related to a coordinated community response to stalking
include development and implementation of stalking protocols
and policies, accessing civil and criminal remedies for stalking
victims, and developing and enhancing services for stalking
victims.

Culturally Competent Responses to Domestic Violence

There are four national institutes to address domestic violence
needs and concerns of underserved populations.

Asian and Pacific Islanders Institute on Domestic Violence (API
Institute)
450 Sutter Street, Suite 600
San Francisco, CA 94108
http://www.apiidv.org

The API Institute is a national resource center and clearinghouse
on Asian, Native Hawaiian, and Pacific Islander gender violence.
It serves a national network of community-based organizations,
advocates, and professionals in social services, mental health,
health and legal matters. It is involved in: (1) "increasing awareness about the extent and depth of the problem"; (2) "making
culturally-and linguistically-specific issues visible"; (3) "strengthening community models of prevention and intervention"; (4)
"identifying and expanding resources"; (5) "informing and promoting research and policy"; and (6) "deepening understanding
and analyses of the issues surrounding violence against women."
This organization analyzes critical issues and conducts ethnic
specific research regarding policies that impact Asian and Pacific
Islander victims/survivors of domestic violence and has a technical assistance and resource center. It is involved in policy advocacy and start-up programs.

Institute on Domestic Violence in the African American Community (IDVAAC)
290 Peters Hall
1404 Gortner Avenue
St. Paul, MN 55108-6142
http://www.dvinstitute.org

IDVAAC focuses on the impact of family violence on African
American communities including intimate partner violence, child
abuse, elder maltreatment, and community violence. It works
with individuals, families, and communities to build knowledge
on how to end violence in the African American community. It
provides information and technical assistance for legal and criminal justice system professionals, family and community violence
practitioners, researchers, and policy makers. Some issues it is
examining include culturally competent strategies for ending
domestic violence in the African American community, father-
hood and domestic violence, the impact of prisoner reentry on
domestic violence, safe haven visitation and safe exchange, and
safe return initiatives.

National Latino Alliance for the Elimination of Domestic Violence
(ALIANZA)
P.O. Box 7886
Albuquerque, NM 87194
http://www.dvalianza.org

Alianza is a network of Latina and Latino advocates, practitioners, and researchers working to eliminate domestic violence
in Latino/a families and communities. Alianza's mission is: "to
promote understanding, initiate and sustain dialogue, and generate solutions that move toward the elimination of domestic violence affecting Latino communities, with an understanding of
the sacredness of all relations and communities." Training and
technical assistance provided include the organization of national
conferences and training forums for advocates and service providers working with Latinas/os. They provide culturally and linguistically appropriate resource materials and make agency
referrals. They organize media and community events about the
negative impact of domestic violence on Latino families and communities. Some of this information was obtained by conducting
national surveys and community focus assessments with

survivors. Informational and research resources are used to formulate public policy,

Sacred Circle: National Resource Center to End Violence Against Native Women
777 Deadwood Avenue
Rapid City, SD 57702
http://www.sacred-circle.com

Native Americans have been an underserved population. The Sacred Circle organization is a member of a comprehensive national domestic violence resource center network. It provides policy development and technical assistance and resource information to develop tribal strategies to end violence against native women.

Sacred Circle provides technical assistance, policy development, training, materials, and resource information regarding violence against Native women and assists in developing tribal strategies and responses to end the violence. Their services include: (1) "Enhance tribes' and tribal organizations' creation of coordinated community response efforts, including advocacy and shelter programs, criminal justice, law enforcement, and other related systems"; (2) "Increase Indian Nations' capacity to provide direct services and advocacy to women and their children victimized by battering and sexual assault through technical assistance, model programming, training, and information consistent with the Indigenous worldview"; (3) "Enhance the infrastructure of the tribal justice system's capacity to provide for victim safety and batterer accountability through analysis and development of statutes, policies, procedures and protocols"; (4) "Increase community awareness and grassroots support to stop violence against native women"; (5) "Provide tribal service providers with training and programming regarding the development and facilitation of batterers' programs"; (6) "Expand tribal law enforcement's capacity to respond to domestic violence and sexual assault by providing specific training, information, model policy, procedure, and protocols"; (7) "Enhance the potential for change and continuity by strengthening the infrastructure of tribal organizations responding to violence against women"; and (8) "Analyze national policies and practices that impact violence against women initiatives in tribal communities."

Think Tanks

Center for Women Policy Studies (CWPS)
1776 Massachusetts Avenue, Suite 450
Washington, DC 20036
http://www.centerwomenpolicy.org/default.asp

The Center for Women Policy Studies' mission is to shape public policy to improve women's lives and preserve women's human rights. Their research and advocacy includes issues of violence against women and girls and combatting human trafficking. The institute's programs consider the combined impact of gender, race, ethnicity, class, age, disability, and sexual orientation. Their Contract with Women of the USA sets out 12 key principles of women's rights. U.S. Policy Advocacy to Combat Trafficking (US PACT) provides a clearinghouse for trafficking research information, and model provisions for state trafficking laws.

The Urban Institute
2100 M Street NW
Washington, DC 20037
http://www.urban.org/index.cfm

The Urban Institute "gathers data, conducts research, evaluates programs, offers technical assistance overseas, and educates Americans on social and economic issues—to foster sound public policy and effective government." It contains a Justice Policy Center, whose projects include a human trafficking research portfolio and a reentry portfolio.

8

Print and Nonprint Resources

Books and Articles

General Works

Alarid, Leanne Fiftal, and Paul Cromwell (Eds.). 2006. *In Her Own Words: Women Offender's Views on Crime and Victimization.* **New York: Oxford University Press.**

This collection of qualitative studies provides an insightful analysis of women's views and comments about crime and victimization. The sections include: (1) "Women's Pathways to Crime: Linking Victimization and Criminalization"; (2) "The Nexus between Criminal Behavior and Family"; (3) "Crime Partnerships, Networks, and Gangs"; (4) "Economic Marginality and Survival Crimes"; and (5) "Women's Crime as Rational Choice." The quotations and descriptions of women's criminal activities and victimization trauma are very useful. Of special note is the essay by Ira Summers, Deborah B. Baskin, and Jeffrey Fagan, "Pathways Out of Crime: Crime Desistance by Female Street Offenders," which isolates factors in women's decision to quit crime, including the impact on their children, health effects of drug use, and the effect of repeated imprisonment.

Britton, Dana M. 2011. *The Gender of Crime.* **Lanham, MD: Rowman & Littlefield.**

This book explores the gendered origins of criminology, which focused on men, and gender patterns in inequality, victimization, and offending. As a study of gender, it compares both men and

291

women. Separate chapters focus on offending, the criminal justice system, victimization, and work in the criminal justice system. It offers information on how criminalization has restructured patterns of offending and imprisonment. The gendered focus provides a different perspective from that of works that concentrate solely on women and compliments them.

Chesney-Lind, Meda, and Lisa Pasko. 2012. *The Female Offender, Girls, Women and Crime* **(3rd ed.). Thousand Oaks, CA: Sage.**

Chesney-Lind and Pasko focus on girls and their pathways toward adult criminality. Despite a movement toward community sanctions for delinquent girls, minority adolescents are still channeled into detention by many judges. In contrast, white girls are placed in institutions for social and medical intervention. Among adult women, they indicate that the War on Drugs has become a "War on Women," sending women addicts to prison due to mandatory sentencing but having reduced success in arrest of dealers and those higher up in drug organizations. Sentencing reform is seen as a major cause of increased women's imprisonment. They chart how both race-ethnicity and gender shape entrance into the criminal justice system.

Davies, Pamela. 2011. *Gender, Crime and Victimization.* **Thousand Oaks, CA: Sage.**

Pamela Davies takes a feminist approach to explanation of women's patterns of crime and victimization. She examines both levels and correlates of crime and victimization. This conceptually advanced book is based on research in the United Kingdom and the United States. At the center of the analysis is the author's case study research on women who commit economic crimes. Davies asks important questions about media exaggeration of women's crimes and gender neutrality in examination of crimes committed by men. The central question of the relationship between female victimization and crime is also challenged in examining women as "real offenders" who are not always motivated by victimization.

History of Women and Crime

Dodge, Mary. 2002. *"Whores and Thieves of the Worst Kind": A Study of Women, Crime and Prisons, 1835–2000.* **DeKalb, IL: Northern Illinois University Press.**

Mary Dodge's work on corrections in Illinois is based on historical records and staff and inmate interviews. It chronicles the legal reasons for female imprisonment and prison conditions at the start of the women's prison movement. The social characteristics of women prisoners are covered from 1890 to 1960. This analysis includes race, ethnicity, social class, and marital status. Trends in women's imprisonment are shown to be impacted by both moral concerns and position in social hierarchies. Stereotypical attitudes about women's depravity and the hopelessness of rehabilitation are documented.

Gross, Kali N. 2006. *Colored Amazons: Crime, Justice and Black Women in the City of Brotherly Love, 1880–1910.* **Durham, NC: Duke University Press.**

This cultural, social, and political history covers African American women's experiences with the criminal justice system in Philadelphia in the late 19th century and first decade of the 20th century. Criminal records establish that black women and state criminal justice policies shaped their offending. Kali Gross finds that violent victimization and racial hostility toward them shaped their experience. Her study documents African American women's experience with economic marginality and criminal justice in this era.

Women's Patterned Offending

Bailey, Frankie Y., and Donna C. Hale. 2004. *Blood on Her Hands: Women Who Murder.* **Belmont, CA: Wadsworth.**

Bailey and Hale's history of women and murder begins with an introduction to the Greek mythology and the status of women in Greece and Rome. It proceeds to medieval, Renaissance, and Victorian women, developing a focus on the American colonies and the United States as it emerges. Three chapters are devoted to the early 20th century, pre–World War II, and post–World War II. Especially fascinating are sections on women's homicide and true crime as well as its coverage in literature, music, and film.

Dodge, Mary. 2009. *Women and White Collar Crime.* **Upper Saddle River, NJ: Prentice-Hall.**

Mary Dodge's book is the first work devoted to women and white collar crime. It covers theories of white collar crime and gendered patterns of offending. Chapters are devoted to embezzlement, corporate crime committed by women, state crimes committed by and against women, occupational crimes committed by and against women, women as whistle-blowers, and future expectations for women and white collar crime. At issue is whether gender equality and women's increasing representation as white collar workers and professionals will lead to an equalization of criminal offending. Dodge considers whether women who transcend traditional gender roles may display the same human traits that lead to offending in men similarly employed.

Heimer, Karen, Stacey Wittrock, and Halime Unal. 2006. "The Crimes of Poverty: Economic Marginalization and the Gender Gap in Crime." In Karen Heimer and Candace Kruttschnitt (Eds.), *Gender and Crime: Patterns in Victimization and Offending.* New York: New York University Press.

This essay explores the role of economic inequality in generating a gender gap in violent and property criminal offending. It examines the supporting literature on the economic marginalization hypothesis and tests it using data from 100 U.S. cities. Their findings include that in larger cities and in times when economic disadvantage increases for women relative to men, the gender gap in criminal offending decreases.

Jensen, Vickie. 2001. *Why Women Kill: Homicide and Gender Equality.* Boulder, CO: Lynn Reiner.

This work uses the concept of gender equality to examine social change in the rate at which women commit homicide. The *FBI Supplemental Homicide Report* provides data on gender and social relationships which is analyzed in relation to social and economic census data. The author hypothesizes that gendered social and economic equality is indirectly related to women's commission of intimate partner and familial homicides. Women's inability to flee abusive relationships due to lack of resources under conditions of gender inequality is viewed as the underlying reason that increased women's equality would reduce their homicide rate. Although the study is confined to data from large cities and the measurement of gender equality could be improved, this research provides insight into how the changing social status of women impacts their violent offending patterns. Suggestions are offered for dealing with the raced and gendered environment of troubled girls.

Raphael, Jody. 2004. *Listening to Olivia: Violence, Poverty and Prostitution*. Boston, MA: Northeastern University Press.

This qualitative research documents the life trajectory of Olivia, a low-income minority woman who engages in prostitution. Various perspectives, ranging from the individual to the social-structural, are used to examine how Olivia's life has been shaped. Raphael studies how one woman tries to negotiate a life of independence while dealing with men and constantly being exposed to violence and sexually objectified. She situates Olivia's experience within a context of entrapment and victimization and examines various types of sex work that Olivia engages in, ranging from stripping, accepting money for sex, and street prostitution. This research monograph is organized in a chronology. The chapter titles are "Groomed," "Reeled In," "Stripping," "Shooting Up," "Doped Up," "Entrapped," "Escape," and "What Is to Be Done?" Raphael begins by describing Olivia being groomed for sex work in a dysfunctional family marked by addiction and then running away and engaging in sex work to keep her independence. Each chapter places Olivia's life in the context of theory and research, making Olivia's life resonate with important questions about how victimization is connected to women's criminality and the role of domestic violence in shaping a girl's mistaken view of sex work as empowering. In conclusion, Jody Raphael offers some insight into how to change this process.

Minority Women's Criminal Offending

Diaz-Cotto, Juanita. 2006. *Chicana Lives and Criminal Justice*. Austin: University of Texas Press.

This path-breaking qualitative research analysis situates Latina adolescent's pre-incarceration experiences and later incarceration at the Sybil Brand Institute for Women in the context of criminal justice policy. Juanita Diaz-Cotto connects early experience of abuse with youth arrests and placements related to survival sex, addiction, and juvenile gangs.

Adolescent Girl's Offending

Schaffner, Laurie. 2006. *Girls in Trouble with the Law*. New Brunswick, NJ: Rutgers University Press.

In this outstanding study of 191 female juvenile offenders, Laurie Schaffner provides information based on interviews, observation of girls in correctional facilities, focus groups, and study of neighborhood and school settings. Interviews and observations of correctional workers and settings illuminate outdated and stereotypical adult views of how girls should be handled. The theme of blurred boundaries between victimization and offending is highlighted by an examination of how family violence and community violence (gendered abuse and harassment in homes, neighborhoods, and schools) produces a girl's violent reactions. Schaffner explores how girls' reaction to traumatic and unrelieved feelings, victimization, and gender inequality condition a violent response to their environment. In reaction, corrections offers "gender specific" responses which are not in tune with girls' social environment and do not address the social conditions that may lead to adult offending.

History of Women's Victimization

Block, Sharon. 2006. *Rape and Sexual Power in Early America.* Chapel Hill: University of North Carolina Press.

This monograph involves a qualitative and quantitative study of historical records on rape and sexually coercive relationships in early America (1700–1820). Block provides insight into how raced and gendered hierarchies made women vulnerable and allowed men to go unpunished in the British colonies and the early republic. An examination of the legal issue of consent finds that forced sexual relations with a stranger against a woman's will was recognized as rape, while coerced sex facilitated by use of force or a man's authority over children, servants, or slaves was not because of the public belief that women had consented. Sharon Block documents how colonial law increasingly racialized black and white rape and sexual coercion cases by providing harsh punishment for black men convicted of raping a white woman and lesser penalties for a white male who raped a black woman, whether she was enslaved or free.

Women's Victimization

Ferraro, Kathleen J. 2006. *Neither Angels nor Demons: Women, Crime and Victimization.* Boston, MA: Northeastern University Press.

Kathleen J. Ferraro's ethnography provides insight into the life history of battered women and her own experience in working with women victims and defendants in 45 criminal cases as an expert witness. This monograph illustrates how women have been stereotyped as victims or offenders without realization of the connection of victimization and offending. The meaning and social context of the victimization-offending linkage is illuminated through quotations and vignettes from women's lived experience. The inclusion of seven cases in which women victims of domestic violence were accused of criminal abuse or murder of their children actually committed by a spouse/partner is illustrative of flaws in how the criminal justice system deals with women victims. Ferraro refers to this as "law as enemy" and documents how the criminal justice system and social services failed to assist women domestic violence victims. She provides insight into how women have been stereotyped as having the ability to end violent relationships rather than facing barriers to exit. Women's biographies illustrate how they survived the pain as neither "angels (victims without agency)" or "demons (monsters)" dealing with social structural constraints such as economic marginality and discrimination and male privilege.

Journals

Feminist Criminology

http://www.sagepub.com/journals/Journal201772

Feminist Criminology presents research related to women, girls, and crime that provides a feminist critique of criminology. An international publication, it focuses on research and theory that highlights the gendered nature of crime. Its perspective emphasizes that the paths to crime differ for males and females. Mainstream research that uses sex as a control variable often leaves undiscovered the factors that predict female criminality. *Feminist Criminology* features research utilizing both quantitative and qualitative methodology and includes the topics or perspectives of race, ethnicity, and gender diversity, cross-cultural/international issues, treatment of women offenders in the criminal justice system, girls and women as victims, feminist theory of crime, and girls, women, and the justice system.

Women and Criminal Justice

Taylor and Frances Online

http://www.tandfonline.com/loi/wwcj20

Women and Criminal Justice is an interdisciplinary and international scholarly research and criminal justice practice journal. It presents peer-reviewed articles on cross-cultural studies on gender, race, ethnicity, and criminal justice, socio-legal and historical studies on gender and crime and victimization, gender studies on women professionals, theory pertaining to women and criminal justice, women and the law, women in crime and punishment literature, women as victims of rape, incest, battering, stalking and sexual harassment, women and human trafficking, implications of legally mandated change for professionals, victims, and offenders, juvenile females in the criminal justice system, women in criminal justice professions, including academia, incarcerated women (legal rights, programs, pregnancy, AIDS, children of incarcerated women, aged and infirm, women on death row), legal restraints on improving the conditions for women in the criminal justice system, international efforts to respond to the needs of women in the criminal justice system. It includes commentaries for authors to exchange ideas, discuss methodological issues and present reports of ongoing research and research findings.

Victimization Hotlines

National Domestic Violence Hotline: 1-800-799-SAFE (7233) or 1-800-787-3224 (TTY) available 24 hours a day/7 days a week.

National Sexual Assault Hotline: 1-800-656-HOPE (4673) available 24/7 for the nearest rape crisis center.

National Stalking Resource Center: 1-800-FYI-CALL (1-800-394-2255) M–F 8:30 a.m.–8:30 p.m. EST or e-mail at gethelp@ncvc.org.

National Teen Dating Abuse Helpline: 1-866-331-9474 (1-866-331-8453 TTY) available 24/7 or connect with a trained peer advocate online at http://www.loveisrespect.org from 4:00 p.m. to 2:00 a.m. daily (CST).

Internet Resources

Sourcebook of Criminal Justice Statistics
http://www.albany.edu/sourcebook

Statistical information about crime and criminal justice in the United States is published by hundreds of public and private agencies, academic institutions, research organizations, public opinion polling firms, and other groups. All levels of government collect and disseminate such data. The objective of the sourcebook is to compile information from a variety of sources, which meet certain standards, and to make it accessible to a wide audience. Nearly all data presented are national in scope and, where possible, are also displayed by regions, states, and cities to increase their value for local decision makers and for comparative analyses. Second, all data presented must be methodologically sound with respect to sampling procedures, data collection methods, estimation procedures, and reliability of information. The book is divided into six major sections:

(1) Characteristics of criminal justice systems
(2) Public attitudes toward crime and criminal justice–related topics
(3) Nature and distribution of known offenses
(4) Characteristics and distribution of persons arrested
(5) Judicial processing of defendants
(6) Persons under correctional supervision

The book also features an annotated list of reference sources, both public and private, from which tables are collected.

Sourcebook of Federal Sentencing Statistics. 2010 Edition. http://www.ussc.gov/Data_and_Statistics/Annual_Reports_and_Sourcebooks/2010/SBTOC10.htm

State and Local Law Enforcement Statistics
http://bjs.ojp.usdoj.gov/index.cfm?ty=tp&tid=7
Provides summary findings, links to BJS publications, and links to related Web sites.

Uniform Crime Reports
Crime in the United States
http://www.fbi.gov/ucr/ucr.htm
Also available as paper report at the Main Library Reference Desk under the call number J1.14/7. Previous volumes available in the Government Documents Library Stacks.

Since 1929, the UCR program has provided crime counts for the nation as a whole as well as for regions, states, counties, cities, and towns. In addition to crime counts and trends, this report includes data on crimes cleared; persons arrested; law-enforcement personnel, including the number of sworn officers killed and assaulted; and the characteristics of homicides, including age, sex, and race of victims and offenders, victim-offender relationships, weapons used, and circumstances surrounding the homicides. The Web site provides the full text and tables from 1995 to date.

Victim Characteristics (BJS)
http://bjs.ojp.usdoj.gov/index.cfm?ty=tp&tid=9
Provides summary statistics, links to various reports on female victims, elderly victims, teenage victims, etc. generated from the National Crime Victimization Surveys, and information about data collection procedures. (Last checked March 4, 2009.)

International Organizations and Internet Resources

Bureau of Justice Statistics
http://bjs.ojp.usdoj.gov

Crime and Society: A Comparative Criminology Tour of the World
http://www-rohan.sdsu.edu/faculty/rwinslow/index.html
Provides user-friendly access to crime and justice information via a world map upon which you click your continent or country of interest.

European Institute for Crime Prevention and Control
http://www.unodc.org/unodc/en/commissions/CCPCJ/institutes-HEUNI.html

European Sourcebook of Crime and Criminal Justice Statistics
http://www.europeansourcebook.org
The third or 2006 edition includes statistics on police (including "crimes known to"), prosecution, conviction, and corrections, available for more than 30 European countries. The fourth edition was released in 2010.

Home Office Research Development Statistics
http://www.homeoffice.gov.uk/rds
This site from the United Kingdom provides a description of the
statistical collections available as well as links to publications
with data in certain areas.

National Human Trafficking Resource Center (State and
Federal Law)
http://www.polarisproject.org/resources/state-and-federal
-laws

National Human Trafficking Resource Center State Map
(Local Information and Resources)
http://www.polarisproject.org/state-map

ProCon.org: Prostitution
http://prostitution.procon.org

Public Insecurity in Mexico: Statistics and Analysis
http://www.seguridadpublicaenmexico.org.mx/red/
public_in.htm

Transactional Records Access Clearinghouse
http://trac.syr.edu
This site provides crime statistics from the Department of
Homeland Security, the Federal Bureau of Investigation,
and the Drug Enforcement Administration and issues TRAC
statistical reports in many areas of law enforcement.

United Nations Surveys of Crime Trends and Operations of
Criminal Justice Systems
http://www.uncjin.org/Statistics/WCTS/wcts.html
The data sets of the First through Sixth United Nations
Surveys of Crime Trends and Operations of Criminal Justice
Systems are available from this site.

VAWnet
National Resource Center on Domestic Violence/ Pennsylvania
Coalition Against Domestic Violence
3605 Vartan Way, Suite 101
Harrisburg, PA 17110
http://www.vawnet.org

A comprehensive online collection of full-text, searchable materials and resources on domestic violence, sexual violence, and related issues is available at VAWnet. This information supports local, state, and national intervention and prevention strategies and the needs of victims and survivors. They emphasize: (1) innovative approaches for underserved communities; (2) the interconnection of sexual and domestic violence with racism and homophobia; and (3) researching the impact of citizenship status, poverty, and physical or mental disability in the lives of citizens and survivors. The National Resource Center on Domestic Violence (NRCDV) and the Pennsylvania Coalition against Domestic Violence (PCADV) facilitate VAWnet.

Virtual Knowledge Center to End Violence against Women and Girls
http://www.endvawnow.org
This UNWOMEN-hosted Web site provides international information in six ways: (1) programming essentials, monitoring, and evaluation; (2) tools in the form of downloadable sources for implementation; (3) a sources-of-expertise section on organizations; (4) a calendar of events and trainings; (5) a leading initiatives section on programs in action; and (6) an FAQ section where individuals can ask for programming help.

World Factbook of Criminal Justice Systems
http://www.bjs.gov/content/pub/html/wfcj.cfm
Provides basic information about crime and criminal justice in various countries, including statistics. Courtesy of the U.S. Department of Justice. (Last checked March 4, 2009.)

World Prison Population List (7th ed., 2007)
http://www.kcl.ac.uk/depsta/law/research/icps/downloads/world-prison-pop-seventh.pdf
Roy Walmsley, Kings College London International Centre for Prison Studies. (Last checked March 4, 2009.)

Documentaries

History of Women and the Law

Blind Justice: Women and the Law

Length: 30 minutes total (4 DVDs)
Date: 1990
Cost: $129.00
Source: Insight Media
http://www.insight-media.com

This set of animated programs traces the legal history of women in Western law back to ancient Greece. It profiles gender inequity in the courts and covers an actual case. Information is presented on the impact of detention on young girls. It contains strong language.

Women Offenders

Ending the Cycle
Length: 37 minutes
Date: 2005
Source: Insight Media
http://insight-media.com/IMShop.aspx?ShopID=14&ShopName=Criminal Justice

Criminology professor Barbara Owen discusses reasons why women become involved in the criminal justice system and offers potential solutions. Topics covered include criminal lifestyle, substance abuse, dysfunctional and abusive family patterns, intergenerational patterns and problems, prison life, and the prison system's failure to provide adequate treatments for offenders.

Homicide

Snapped: The Killer Collection
Length: 9.5 hours/ 273 minutes
Date: 2004 and 2005
Cost: $34.98
Source: Timeless Video
http://www.timelessvideo.com/dvds/snapped.html
This Oxygen network "true crime" format deals with the cases of 26 women who committed murder. The 26 women profiled include Carolyn (Aileen) Warmus and Pamela Smart.

Drug Trafficking and Use

A&E Investigative Reports: The Junkie Next Door: Women and Heroin
Length: 50 minutes
Date: 2008
Cost: $24.99
Source: Arts & Entertainment Network
http://shop.history.com/detail.php?p=67424&v=aetv
Heroin is associated with inner-city drug use, but its use has spread to the suburbs, where women have become addicts. This criminal justice program focuses on the cases of women users, how they obtain the drug through contacts and even transit to the inner city, and the effects upon a family when the mother needs her fix.

Prostitution

Madams of the Barbary Coast
Length: 56 minutes
Date: 2008
Cost: $19.99 (Educational DVD: $49.99)
http://www.madamsofthebarbarycoast.com/documentary.html
The Barbary Coast of San Francisco contained many brothels run by madams. Profiles include Belle Cora; the African American Mary Ellen Pleasant, who worked for civil rights; and Ah Toy, a Chinese woman suspected of being a slave trader. Segments include information on enslaved Chinese girls in Chinatown.

Prostitution: Behind the Veil
Length: 59 minutes
Date: 2005
Cost: $14.99
Source: Cosmo Film
http://www.dfi.dk/faktaomfilm/danishfilms/dffilm.aspx?id=16561
Two women, Minna and Fariba, make a living on the streets of an Iranian city and support each other as friends. Although prostitution is banned and adultery is punishable by the death sentence, men find a way to purchase sex. They practice "Sighe,"

a temporary marriage with Shia Islam legality that can last from hours to 99 years. The women are shown making decisions about whether or not to have their children accompany them as they seek a livelihood.

Prostitution: Beyond the Myths
Length: 28 minutes
Date: 2007
Cost: $24.99
Source: Volunteers of America–Minnesota
http://www.voamn.org/Learn-About-our-Services/
Corrections/WRC/BYM

Volunteers of America in Minnesota developed a video on the case histories of three women who experienced sexual victimization and violence before and after working as prostitutes. This video makes the connection between prior victimization of girls and women, drug addiction, homelessness, and criminal behavior. The women, members of the Minneapolis judiciary, law enforcement, and researchers are interviewed, and the work of the Volunteers of America Recovery Center is shown. This video received the Telly Award in the Documentary and Public Information categories.

Very Young Girls
Length: 84 minutes
Date: 2007
Source: The Fledgling Fund
Currently available through Netflix subscription
http://www.thefledglingfund.org/media/girls/very-young
-girls.html

While immigrant victims of sex trafficking can be assisted under the auspices of the VTPA Act, girls with citizenship who are found prostituting are treated as delinquents and criminals. This video provides the example of a 14-year-old girl enticed to leave her home and then beaten, raped, and enslaved to be sold for sex. It points out that if a male has sex with an underage girl, he can be charged with rape. If the girl receives money, then the man is treated as a "John" or customer and rarely given more than a fine. The girl is charged with prostitution and placed in detention. The video presents the view that underage prostitution is a form of commercialized sexual abuse and promotes advocacy for victims. The video illustrates how pimps use isolation, violence, and drugs to keep the girls under their control. GEMS, a recovery program for teen prostitutes found on the streets or in court, provides therapy for these girls who often originate from abusive homes, become mistreated by pimps, and fear that they will always be viewed as prostitutes.

Women for Sale
Length: 60 minutes
Date: 2009
Cost: $25.99
Source: Amazon Video-on-Demand

This Israeli documentary about immigrant women working in prostitution provides the message that the women do it for the money. In their home country, wages are low, but prostitution promises more. The film indicates that the women's dream of money is not matched by their actual income, and they are subject to ill treatment and not being paid by pimps. The video also presents a segment on a police raid of a brothel and explores the reasons why government and law enforcement are ill-prepared to protect these women.

Human/Sex Trafficking

A&E Investigative Reports: The Child Sex Trade
Length: 50 Minutes
Date: 1997
Source: Arts and Entertainment Network
http://shop.history.com/detail.php?p=66871&v=aetv

Thousands of children are trafficked for sex: bought and sold by sex rings that move their locations. Increasingly, children are being taken from middle-class suburbs. Kansas, Minnesota, and Las Vegas are among the pipelines.

Dying to Leave: The Dark Business of Human Trafficking
Length: 57 minutes
Cost: $149.95
Source: Films for the Humanities and Sciences
http://ffh.films.com/id/12833/Dying_to_Leave_The_Dark
_Business_of_Human_Trafficking.htm

Human traffickers are not choosy about how they transport people across borders, using sewage tunnels, shipping containers, ship holds, and even car chassis. Despite motivation to get ahead, many of those trafficked become sex workers and forced laborers. This Australian *Wide Angle* documentary feature looks at the social context of mass unauthorized migration, its connection to trafficking, and the situations endured by those who are enslaved.

Frontline: Sex Slaves
Length: 60 minutes
Cost: $59.95
Source: PBS Educational Media
http://www.pbs.org/wgbh/pages/frontline/slaves

This exploration of human trafficking uses hidden cameras to examine the activities of traffickers, pimps, and middle men who sell women. It uses the story of Katia, whose husband is searching for her, to illustrate the issue. It details the process of attracting women through offers of legitimate employment or smuggling services and how this can lead to entrapment involving rape, drugs, and confinement for prostitution.

Lives for Sale: Human Trafficking
Length: 60 minutes
Date: 2006
Cost: $169.95
Source: Films for the Humanities and Sciences
    http://ffh.films.com/id/15303/Lives_for_Sale_Human_
Trafficking.htm

Slavery has reemerged in the form of a black market in human beings for labor and the sex trade. Poverty leads migrants to seek employment abroad and, in the process, some become victims of exploitation at some point during their journey. This film features the Coalition to Abolish Slavery and Trafficking (CAST) and their work to free those trafficked. Interviews with U.S. Border Patrol agents and other law enforcement officers add information on the this human rights issue.

Modern Slavery
Length: 3 videos: 45 minutes each
Date: 2008

Cost: $509.85
Source: Films for the Humanities and Sciences
http://ffh.films.com/id/17183/Modern_Slavery.htm

Despite the prohibition of slavery and country-specific sanctions for not taking action against trafficking, slavery is expanding as a source of profit for others. This three-part series of videos is listed in sequence below.

Modern Slavery: Captive Servants and Child Prostitution
Length: 45 minutes
Date: 2008
Cost: $169.95
Source: Films for the Humanities and Sciences
http://ffh.films.com/id/17184/Modern_Slavery_Captive_
Servants_and_Child_Prostitution.htm

The first portion of this film illustrates enslavement of household servants through coercion occurs in Europe and the United States. This program interviews Rania, a Moroccan-born ex-house slave. Her father had been misled into sending her to Europe, where it was promised that she would receive an education. She was only eight years of age. The second part of the film covers child prostitution in the South Asian sex industry. Sino and La Thiya, child victims, are interviewed about deception and exploitation. The film stresses that they may come to transcend the situation and receive justice.

Modern Slavery: Debt Bondage and Child Soldiers
Length: 45 minutes
Date: 2008
Cost: $169.95
Source: Films for the Humanities and Sciences
http://ffh.films.com/id/17181/Modern_Slavery_Debt
_Bondage_and_Child_Soldiers.htm

In early America, indentured servitude of women and men was a basis for development of the colonies. Currently, debt bondage is prevalent in southern Asia, particularly in India. This film details the extreme amount of their personal debt formation and the constant labor to pay it off. The second part of the film explains the use and problems of child soldiers in African militias and armies.

Modern Slavery: Human Trafficking
Length: 45 minutes
Date: 2008
Cost: $169.95
Source: Films for the Humanities and Sciences
   http://ffh.films.com/id/17182/Modern_Slavery_Human_
Trafficking.htm

The process of promising jobs in order to induce young women to leave the homeland and of coercing them to work in prostitution is explained. Natasha and Galia Gutu were promised jobs in Turkey when they left their country of origin, Moldavia. They thought they would work as health aides, but were forced into prostitution. The film is unusual because it includes an interview with the mother-daughter pair who promised them legitimate work. It depicts the courtroom trial against their neighbors and asks the question of whether the experience will help them to heal.

Sold: Fighting the Modern Slave Trade
Length: 54 minutes
Date: 2009
Cost: $169.00
Source: Insight Media

The renewed knowledge of worldwide slavery has led to activism. This film interviews Symphorienne Kessouagni, Sunitha Krushnan, and Ansar Burney. Kessouagni provides protection for children in rural Togo. Krishnan runs schools for ex-brothel workers in Hyderabad, India, and Burney is a Krachi attorney who brings back Pakistani boys made to serve as camel jockeys against their will.

Juvenile Delinquency

Girlhood: Growing Up on the Inside
Length: 82 minutes
Date: 2004
Cost: $22.99
Source: Amazon.com

This documentary follows Shanae and Megan as they enter and exit the juvenile justice system over a period of three years. The film reveals pathways as it focuses on mother and daughter relationships, juvenile crime, and the adverse social circumstances of the girls. Twelve-year-old Shanae is involved in a fatal stabbing, while 16-year-old Megan is a runaway from the foster care system and charged with assault. This film won Best Documentary at the Atlanta Film Festival, the Audience Award at the Nantucket Film Festival, and the Audience Award at the South by Southwest Film Festival.

> *Street Life: Inside America's Gangs*
> Length: 43 minutes
> Date: 1999
> Cost: $169.00
> Source: Insight Media
> http://www.insight-media.com/IMShop.aspx?
> ShopID=14&ShopName=Criminal Justice

Gang membership has been increasing in the United States, and many females join. ABC News correspondent Cynthia McFadden interviews girls who have joined the Drifters and Tepa 13, Los Angeles gangs. The video includes unscripted footage shot by gang members and an interview with the head of New York City's Latin Kings.

Women in Prison: Offenders and Workers

> *Daughters Left Behind*
> Length: 52 minutes
> Date: 2007
> Cost: $19.95
> Source: National Geographic
> http://shop.nationalgeographic.com/ngs/product/dvds/
> culture%2C-history-and-religion/world-cultures/daughters-left
> -behind-dvd-exclusive

A majority of women incarcerated in the United States are mothers. These women are often single and sole caregivers. This investigative video seeks to explore the impact of the absence of a mother on children, a situation that may contribute to delinquency and criminal behavior. Children of women in prison are interviewed, and programs that break the cycle of incarceration from mother to child are showcased. Investigated and narrated by Lisa Ling (*Ultimate Explorer*).

Lockdown: Women behind Bars
Length: 52 minutes
Date: 2007
Cost: $19.95
Source: National Geographic
http://shop.nationalgeographic.com

Valley State Prison in Chowchilla, California, houses 3,900 violent women offenders. In 2009, its first inmate murder occurred, involving woman-on-woman violence. Drugs are related to violence among imprisoned women. The film includes a segment on administrative segregation, where women are given full-body searches and shackled, accompanied by two guards in stab-proof vests when outside their cell. Another segment details the prison's slow reaction in taking a pregnant woman to give birth. Her baby is taken away two days after birth. Interviews with prison officials and guards discuss how to stop the drug trade and control prison violence. The *Lockdown* Web site includes a video clip and photographs with brief commentary.

Sweethearts of the Prison Rodeo
Length: 90 minutes
Date: 2010
Cost: $24.99
Source: Amazon.com

A group of women prisoners are allowed, for the first time, to participate at the Oklahoma State Penitentiary rodeo. The film includes women who originate from broken homes, are substance abusers, or are alienated from their children,

War on the Family: Mothers in Prison and the Children They Leave Behind
Length: 48 minutes
Date: 2010
Cost: $25.99
Source: Amazon.com

Women prisoners describe their distress at leaving children and family behind. Advocates speak on behalf of providing access to children and sentencing reform. The negative impact of separation from mothers is connected to an intergenerational cycle of crime. This film was an Emmy Award nominee.

Women behind Bars: Rehabilitation or Retribution?
Length: 49 minutes
Date: 1999
Cost: $149.95
Source: Films for the Humanities and Sciences
http://ffh.films.com/id/848/Women_Behind_Bars_Rehabi
litation_or_Retribution.htm

This CBS production takes the position that women's prison experience has become structured around retribution, not rehabilitation. They indicate that it may be harder for women to survive in prison than on the street. The film covers the following issues related to prior victimization: family histories, sexual abuse, drug addiction, and breaking the cycle of crime and imprisonment. Interviews with women prisoners are used to illustrate major points.

Women's Victimization
Femicide
China's Lost Girls
Length: 43 minutes
Date: 2004
Cost: $9.95
Source: National Geographic
http://shop.nationalgeographic.com/ngs/product/dvds/
culture%2C-history-and-religion/world-cultures/china%27s
-lost-girls-dvd

China's one-child policy was implemented in a country that values boys over girls. Culture and socioeconomic conditions have led to sex-selective abortion, abandonment, and hidden girls. Tens of thousands of girls live in Chinese orphanages. In the United States, 25% of babies adopted are Chinese girls. Lisa Ling (*Ultimate Explorer*) examines families as they travel to China to adopt and provides information on the Chinese gender gap.

Dual Injustice: Femicide and Torture in Ciudad Juarez
Length: 17 minutes

Date: 2009
Cost: $29.95 (institutional, K–12); $19.95 (home)
Source: Witness.org [may be available online]
http://www.witness.org/index.php?option=com_
rightsalert&Itemid=178&task=view&alert_id=38

Witness.org, an international human rights organization, in partnership with Comision Mexicana de Defensa y Promocion de los Derechos Humanos (CMPDPDH), provides an overview of the violent deaths of women in Ciudad Juarez. Since 1993, more than 400 women have been tortured and murdered in this border city. This largely unprosecuted wave of femicide (violent deaths of women) is an international human rights issue.

Rape

The Age of Consent: Sex and the American Legal System
Length: 37 minutes
Date: 2007
Cost: $169.00
Source: Insight Media
http://insight-media.com/IMShop.aspx?
ShopID=14&ShopName=Criminal Justice

ABC's John Stossel examines issues regarding the age at which an individual is considered an adult and sexual behavior. Cases presented include an 18-year-old man convicted of having sex with a 14-year-old girl, a man facing sex offender charges who states he was framed, and a father whose sexual activity as a teen impacts his parental freedom. A segment considers Megan's Law, requiring registration of sex offenders.

Gai Shanxi and Her Sisters
Length: 80 minutes
Date: 2009
Cost: $295 (colleges, universities, institutions); $95 (K–12, public libraries, select groups); $195 digital download ($5 rental)
Source: dGenerate Film
http://dgeneratefilms.com/catalog/gai-shanxi-and-her
-sisters-gai-shan-xi-he-ta-de-jie-mei-men

This independent Chinese documentary details the use of comfort women by Japanese soldiers during World War II.

Chinese women were forcibly impounded and forced to sexually service the occupying Imperial Japanese army. Fifty years after sexual victimization occurred, she and other women tried to seek reparation, but died before seeking justice. Interviews with women who knew Gai Shanxi and former soldiers of the Japanese occupation are included.

Portraits in Human Sexuality: Nonconsensual Sexuality
Length: 40 minutes
Date: 2006
Cost: $149.95
Source: Films for the Humanities and Sciences
http://ffh.films.com/id/12724/Portraits_in_Human_Sexuality_Nonconsensual_Sexuality.htm

This film advocates that without consent, any sexual intercourse is rape. Interviews with a young woman raped by a stranger assailant in her home and an expelled young man who committed acquaintance rape provide insight into the issue of consent. A treatment center for sexual offenders is examined. This segment emphasizes treatment of deviant sexual arousal and psychological therapy to promote victim impact awareness, cognitive restructuring and empathy. The film contains mature themes and language.

Soldiers Raping Soldiers
Length: 22 minutes
Date: 2004
Cost: $99.95
Source: Films for the Humanities and Sciences
http://ffh.films.com/id/11476/Soldiers_Raping_Soldiers.htm

The problem of male-on-female sexual assault of women in the military is well known but not completely solved. This ABC News program examines the cases of two sexually assaulted women in the services and suggests that the military mismanages the way it handles rape. The director of a panel that produced a report on soldiers raping soldiers is interviewed.

Glossary

Addiction   A chronic, relapsing biological disease in which a substance user compulsively seeks and uses a drug with corresponding chemical and molecular changes in the brain.

Aggravated assault (UCR)   Unlawful actual or attempted or threatened inflicting of injury upon the person of another.

Altruistic suicide   The taking of life by an individual for benefit of a group or community.

Arrest   The act of taking a juvenile or adult into physical custody in order to charge them with a delinquent act, status offense, or criminal act through the authority of law.

Black Codes   Laws prohibiting African Americans but not white Americans from a range of behaviors associated with citizen rights such as voting. Enacted in southern states after the Civil War. Also known as Jim Crow laws.

Bootstrapping   A process in which juvenile girls on probation for a minor violation, often a status offense, are placed in secure detention for violation of a condition of probation, such as attending school.

Chattel slavery   A state in which an individual is considered to be legal property and exploited for labor and/or sexual activity by the owner.

Child abuse   Physical, sexual, or emotional abuse of a child

Controlled substance   A bioactive or psychoactive chemical substance specifically prohibited by law.

Co-occurring disorder   Diagnosis of an individual with both a mental disorder and substance dependency or abuse. Also known as dual diagnosis.

Criminal homicide   An act that causes the death of another person without excuse or legal justification.

Criminalization   The legal action by governing authorities to make a specified behavior illegal and subject to criminal penalties.

Dark figure of crime   Unreported crimes not known to law enforcement.

Date rape   Any type of unwanted sexual intercourse, oral or anal sex, and other sexual contact that occurs by use of force or threat of force between casual or intimate dating partners. This is not a legal term; "date rape" would be tried in a court as rape.

Decriminalization   Redefinition of activities considered a crime by making them legal.

Delinquency   Behavior in violation of criminal law or status offenses violating juvenile conduct rules.

Delinquent   A juvenile considered by the judicial officer of a juvenile court to have committed a delinquent action.

Delinquent Act   An act committed by a juvenile that is prosecuted in a juvenile court rather than in an adult court.

Determinate sentencing   A sentence to confinement to jail or prison for a specific length of time specified by law. An example would be mandatory minimum sentencing guidelines.

Deterrence   The idea that criminal acts can be prevented by the fear of punishment.

Domestic violence   A crime of assault in which the victim is a spouse or ex-spouse. Also applied in the case of children, a parent, and individuals in a dating relationship or engagement.

Dopamine   A chemical neurotransmitter found in the brain, which is associated with normal central nervous system function. It is associated with feelings of reward.

Drug abuse   Use of controlled substances that results in social, economic, psychological, or legal consequences for an individual.

Drug court   A specialized state, county, or municipal court that judicially mandates court-supervised treatment for first-time offenders as an alternative to jail or prison.

Drug trafficking   Trading or dealing in controlled substances. Cultivation, import or export, manufacture, storage, distribution, sale, or purchase are included under drug trafficking offenses.

Embezzlement   Misappropriation or unlawful disposal of legally entrusted property by the individual to which it was entrusted for the purpose of defrauding the legal owner or the intended beneficiary.

Emotional abuse   Verbal communication that has a negative impact on a target, often by calling them names, criticizing, playing mind games, humiliating, or otherwise putting them down.

Family violence   An act or threatened act of violence that results or threatens to result in physical injury committed against a person related by blood or marriage, co-residing or otherwise legally related.

Felony   A crime punishable by a sentence of one year or more in prison or death.

Filicide   The deliberate killing of a son or daughter by a parent.

Fraud   A criminal offense in which deceit or intentional misrepresentation of fact is used to unlawfully deprive a person of property or legal rights.

Home confinement   Individuals are confined to their homes under house arrest. They may be electronically monitored to make sure they do not leave. A person may be permitted to go to a place of employment.

Human smuggling   A process in which a citizen of another country is assisted to enter without legal documents.

Human trafficking   A process in which individuals are deceived or forced into unpaid labor. Both citizens and noncitizens may be trafficked.

Incapacitation   Criminal offenders are imprisoned to limit their ability to commit additional offenses.

Incorrigibility   Difficult to manage or control. A term applied to juveniles.

Indentured servant   An individual who works for another person until a debt is paid off.

Indeterminate sentencing   A prison term given for an indefinite period of time. The prisoner may be released for good behavior or due to factors such as overcrowding.

Infanticide   The act of killing a child in the year of its birth.

Institutionalized diversion   Also known as decarceration.

Intimate partner violence   Unlawful violence committed by a current or former spouse, opposite-sex or same-sex cohabiting partner, date, boyfriend, or girlfriend. These acts may include physical abuse and sexual violence and are often accompanied by emotional abuse. Also called domestic violence, spouse abuse, or battering.

Larceny   Theft of goods or money by another without permission.

Legalization   Removal of laws and associated criminal penalties. An example would be the possession of a specified controlled substance.

Mandatory arrest policy   The law gives police authority to make an arrest without a warrant, given probable cause that a domestic violence incident occurred and that the accused person committed the offense.

Medical model   The diagnosis and treatment procedures of medicine are applied to criminal offenders in corrections.

Misdemeanor   A criminal offense punishable by a sentence of less than one year in prison.

Neurotransmitter   A chemical that transmits nerve impulses across a synapse between neurons.

Out-of-home placement   A situation in which an individual under 18, classified as a child, is placed in foster care, a halfway house, or other nonfamilial circumstances.

Parentified child   An individual under 18 years of age who performs parenting duties in the care of younger siblings and can also care for their own parents and other family members.

Physical abuse   Any behavior that involves physically aggressing against a child or adult. Acts of physical aggression include punching, shoving, slapping, biting, kicking, using a weapon against a partner, throwing items, pulling hair, and physically restraining the partner.

Post-traumatic stress disorder   A psychological disorder precipitated by one or a series of very stressful incidents.

Preferred arrest policy   The law gives police authority to make an arrest without a warrant as a preferred, but not required, outcome in a domestic violence incident. If no arrest is made, an officer may need to file a written report explaining why no arrest was made. This is also known as pro-arrest policy.

Primary perpetrator   The individual considered most responsible for physical and sexual aggression in a domestic violence incident.

Probation   A legal status in which an individual is able to avoid juvenile detention, jail, or prison in return for meeting behavioral criteria such as attending treatment for substance abuse or providing community service.

Racialization   The process of attributing both biological and cultural difference to a social category, which demarcates a group. This process is associated with the development of prejudice and discrimination.

Racial profiling   A law enforcement practice in which officers use race, ethnicity, or national origin as a cue for criminal suspicion.

Secure detention   Placement of juveniles in a lock-down institutional setting.

Serotonin   A chemical neurotransmitter found in the brain, blood serum, and gastric mucous membranes, which is essential for normal central nervous system operation. Depletion of serotonin in the brain is associated with depression.

Sex trafficking   A process in which individuals are deceived or coerced into prostitution or other sex enterprises. Both citizens and noncitizens may be victims of sex trafficking.

Sexual abuse   Sexual behavior that is not mutually desired. Any sexual contact with a child below the age of consent (18 years).

Sexual violence   Unlawful acts of sexual aggression, including forcing a partner to perform sexual acts, including oral or anal sex, and rape.

Slavery An individual or societal practice that involves exploitation for labor, sexual activity, or reproduction.

Status Offense A noncriminal act committed by a juvenile that results in being placed on probation or secure detention.

Survival crime Sexual activity or property crime for pay or sustenance, especially in the case of juvenile girls after running away from parents.

Truancy Failure to attend school as established by a designated number of unexcused absences.

Vagrant A person who lacks a visible means of financial support and a place to live.

Index

321

About the Author

Judith A. Warner, PhD, is professor of sociology and criminal justice at Texas A&M International University, Laredo, Texas. Her published works include ABC-CLIO's *U.S. Border Security: A Reference Handbook* and the two-volume *Battleground: Immigration*.